B. Rotman.

DINNER AT MAGNY'S

By the same author:

THE LIFE OF J.-K. HUYSMANS
Oxford University Press

THE LIFE AND TIMES OF
FRÉDÉRICK LEMAÎTRE
Hamish Hamilton

THE GONCOURTS
Bowes & Bowes

THE FIRST BOHEMIAN:
THE LIFE OF HENRY MURGER
Hamish Hamilton

THE SIEGE OF PARIS
Batsford

THE DUEL: A HISTORY OF DUELLING
Chapman & Hall

THE MEMOIRS OF CHATEAUBRIAND
(*edited and translated*)
Hamish Hamilton

PAGES FROM THE GONCOURT JOURNAL
(*edited and translated*)
Oxford University Press

DINNER AT MAGNY'S

Robert Baldick

LONDON
VICTOR GOLLANCZ LTD
1971

ISBN 0 575 00678 1

Printed in Great Britain by
The Camelot Press Ltd, London and Southampton

For Jacqueline

CONTENTS

LIST OF ILLUSTRATIONS

Following page 128

The Rue Mazet in 1870, showing Magny's at the far end of the
  street

Edmond de Goncourt
Jules de Goncourt

Gustave Flaubert by Nadar
Ernest Renan

Claude Bernard
Théophile Gautier

Marcelin Berthelot
Guillaume Chevalier ("Gavarni")

Sainte-Beuve
George Sand by Nadar

Hippolyte Taine
Ivan Turgenev

Page from George Sand's diary (Bibliothèque Nationale)

FOREWORD

THIS BOOK WAS born, suitably enough, in Paris, one spring evening on the terrace of the Café des Deux Magots. I was talking to the most beautiful of all the women there, about the Paris I had known before we had met and married, and happened to mention a programme I had once written for the B.B.C. about the famous Magny Dinners which had been held in the eighteen-sixties in the nearby Rue Mazet. My wife suddenly asked me why I didn't develop what I had already written on the subject into a book about Magny's and the men who had made it immortal, and within a few days we were hard at work trying to discover what we could about the restaurant and its owner.

It was not an easy task. Hardly anything was known about Magny himself, who was always referred to simply by his surname, and the few writers who mentioned him gave different dates (all of them, as it happened, incorrect) for his death. As for his restaurant, although we found drawings and photographs in plenty of the ancient Auberge du Cheval-Blanc which stood next door, not a single picture of Magny's was listed in any of the public and private collections in Paris.

Eventually, however, our luck turned, and we discovered a photograph of the Rue Mazet which, for once, showed not only the Auberge du Cheval-Blanc, but also the Restaurant Magny beyond. We also discovered the basic particulars about the proprietor, Modeste Magny, found the few family papers which are still extant—including letters from George Sand to Magny's wife and a letter from his son describing one of the most famous dinners—and followed the traces of Magny's descendants. We learned that his son, Paul-Victor-Modeste Magny, became Senator of the Seine eleven years before he died in 1925, and that one of his grandsons, Charles-Paul Magny, was honorary Prefect of the Seine at the time of his death in 1945. We traced his only known surviving relative, his granddaughter-in-law Madame Charles Magny, called on her in Paris, and formed the impression that the widow of a Prefect of the Seine does not care to be associated with a mere cook, however eminent. This was borne in upon us even more strongly when we discovered where Modeste Magny was buried, and visited his grave in the Cimetière Montparnasse, for his tombstone bears the names of only Charles Magny and his brother Louis. There is in fact no visible indication that this grave (6th Division, 3rd line East, No. 3 North) is the last resting place of one of the greatest chefs and most famous hosts of modern times. The present book is in part an attempt to remedy this astonishing omission.

It is also an attempt to re-create some of the most fascinating conversations ever held across a dinner-table—conversations between Flaubert, Turgenev, George Sand, Sainte-Beuve, Gautier, Renan, Taine, the Goncourt brothers and other *habitués* of Magny's—against the background of the Second Empire and the Siege of Paris. Snatches of some of the talk at Magny's given in the Goncourt brothers' *Journal* have been combined with extracts from the diners' letters, diaries, notebooks, memoirs, and recorded conversations to make up six typical Magny dinners over the decade in which they were held. Thus, while the descriptions of the diners' behaviour, and the remarks made by Charles-Edmond, Claudin, Nefftzer, Robin, Saint-Victor and Veyne, are usually my own invention, every anecdote, opinion and aphorism attributed in this book to one of the principal members of the Magny fraternity was, to the best of my knowledge and belief, formulated in speech or writing by that person.

I must thank the British Broadcasting Corporation for permission to incorporate in this book fragments of the programme entitled *Dinner at Magny's* which I originally wrote for radio; the Directors, Librarians and staffs of the Bibliothèque Nationale in Paris, the Bibliothèque Historique de la Ville de Paris, the Musée Carnavalet, the Bodleian Library and the Taylorian Institute in Oxford for their valuable assistance; and the officials of the Archives de la Seine, of the Mairies of the Sixth, Eighth, Eleventh and Fifteenth Arrondissements in Paris, and of the Cimetière Montparnasse, for their immense patience and forbearance. I must also thank my dear friend Maurice Druon of the Académie française for some fascinating information on the history of the literary dinners of Paris; Monsieur Georges Lubin for generously communicating to me unpublished material from George Sand's correspondence; Monsieur Raymond Oliver, the proprietor of the Grand Véfour, for opening up to me his remarkable archives; Monsieur René Héron de Villefosse for talking to me about gastronomic Paris; Monsieur Robert Ricatte, the learned editor of the Goncourt *Journal*, for his friendly co-operation; and Monsieur Henry Lefai for supplying information on Modeste Magny's status and reputation as a restaurateur.

I owe a deep debt of gratitude, which can now never be paid, to three people who are no longer alive: my dear friend and colleague Enid Starkie, who often discussed this book with me and who died just after it was completed; Pierre Lambert, the scholar-bookseller of the Rue Jacob, who gave me the benefit of his vast learning for so many years; and Aurore Sand, George Sand's granddaughter, whose eyes, according to Flaubert, were "so like hers as to be a kind of resurrection", and who in 1958, three years before her death, movingly recalled for me her memories of her grandmother and the master of Croisset.

Finally I would like to record my thanks to my wife, Jacqueline Baldick, for the help and encouragement she gave throughout the preparation and writing of this book, which is dedicated to her in love and gratitude.

ROBERT BALDICK

Prologue

PROLOGUE

Dinner at Magny's . . .

THOSE THREE WORDS, mentioning a long-vanished little Left Bank restaurant in Paris, recur time and again in the letters and diaries of most of the leading novelists, critics, historians and scientists of nineteenth-century France. Sometimes they record a solitary meal, a lovers' *tête-à-tête*, a celebration or a family outing; but more often they refer to one of the fortnightly gatherings which in the eighteen-sixties brought together at the Restaurant Magny a group of remarkable Second Empire personalities. Contemporary writers who were not invited to these so-called Magny Dinners condemned them for their supposedly immoral and atheistic tone, and the fiery Catholic critic Barbey d'Aurevilly thundered against what he described as "the infamous dinners which are held at Magny's in defiance of God"; but in fact the only common factor among the vastly different men of letters and science who forgathered at the Restaurant Magny was a taste for entertaining company and completely uninhibited conversation.

The restaurant itself was opened in 1842, twenty years before the first Magny Dinner, in the Rue Contrescarpe-Dauphine, later renamed the Rue Mazet. This short, curving street which links the Rue Dauphine and the Rue Saint-André-des-Arts, following exactly the line of the old city wall, was dominated at that time by an old coaching inn which occupied half the right-hand side. Once part of the residence of the Archbishops of Lyons, it had been turned into a coaching establishment in the mid-seventeenth century, under the sign of the Carrosses d'Orléans, and had later taken the name of the Auberge du Cheval-Blanc. For two centuries the coaches and wagons for Orléans, Auvergne, Berry, Normandy and Bordeaux had started from the Rue Contrescarpe, and the vast courtyard with its picturesque dormer windows had echoed to the sound of tearful farewells, neighing horses, cracking

whips, and swearing postilions. It was not for nothing that
Massenet, when he was composing his opera *Manon*, came to the
Auberge du Cheval-Blanc for inspiration. But while the old inn
with its two time-worn, weather-beaten mounting-stones beside its
gate was a familiar landmark to travellers and a touching relic of
the past to romantic sentimentalists, nobody took any notice of
the seedy pot-house next door, at No. 3.

Nobody, that is, except a young man from the provinces with
very little money but a burning ambition to create a great
restaurant. Modeste Magny had been born at Montmort, in the
Marne, on 14 November 1812, and had come to Paris to seek his
fortune, taking the lowliest of all jobs in his chosen profession,
that of washer-up. But his employer was the great Philippe of the
Rue Montorgueil, a superlative chef and one of the most fashionable restaurateurs in Paris. Magny took every opportunity to
watch the cooks at work and was eventually allowed to help them,
with the result that within a few years he had become one of
Philippe's most trusted aides. Then, in 1842, he decided to set up
on his own account, and bought the pot-house at No. 3 Rue
Contrescarpe from the owner of the business, a man called Pariset,
for 48,000 francs. How he raised this sum is not known, but some
of the money may have been put up by two men, Jacques and
Baudon, registered as his partners, particularly as Baudon was the
son-in-law of the landlord of No. 3.

By all accounts the pot-house was a rough-and-ready establishment, and towards the end of the century a historian of the Left
Bank would recall that the only means of access to the first floor
was a ladder. But the almost rustic simplicity of the place was no
deterrent to the students who began patronising Magny's in large
numbers when he began serving cheap meals as well as wine. The
Rue Contrescarpe was in fact an excellent site for a restaurant
catering for a student clientele, for the Boulevard Saint-Michel
had not yet been opened up, and the centre of student life was the
gay, noisy Rue de l'Ancienne-Comédie, only a hundred yards
away. Magny could not have foreseen that within the next thirty
years Paris would be completely transformed, and that premises
which seemed positively spacious and ideally placed in 1842

would appear cramped and out-of-the-way to the next generation.

During the next few years Magny set about transforming the sometime pot-house into a comfortable and attractive restaurant taking up two floors of the building, with two main rooms, one large and one of medium size, and seven private dining-rooms leading off a central corridor. The floor above the restaurant he furnished as his living quarters, and it was there that he brought his bride in December 1846, when he married Ernestine-Laure Brébant, the sister of a fellow restaurateur. It was there too that both he and his wife would die.

Fired by his ambition to create a first-class restaurant, and determined not to be outclassed by his brother-in-law, he improved the decoration and furnishings of his establishment and began serving more elaborate and expensive dishes. The business prospered as the students were replaced by a more monied clientele, and Magny was soon able to buy his partners' shares in the restaurant, becoming sole proprietor. But the golden age of the Restaurant Magny began only in the eighteen-fifties, with the establishment of the Second Empire. After the violence of the 1848 Revolution and the political turbulence of the short-lived Second Republic, the French people welcomed the strong government of the man whom Victor Hugo, living in exile in the Channel Islands, castigated in virulent prose and verse as "the little Napoleon", and saw no reason to regret the approval they had given his régime by plebiscite. They approved his marriage to the beautiful Eugénie de Montijo, cheered the news of the birth of a Prince Imperial, crowded the great Paris Exhibition of 1855, applauded the French victories in the Crimean War, and swelled with pride to see the statesmen of Europe choose Paris as the setting for the peace conference of 1856. Above all they rejoiced in the unexampled prosperity and social security which the Second Empire had brought to France, and which was nowhere more evident than in Paris. For this was the age of the *ville lumière,* a dazzling gaslit capital of broad boulevards created by Baron Haussmann to delight the eye with splendid perspectives—and, incidentally, to provide a clear field for guns to mow down any popular insurrection. Prosperity gave rise to an unprecedented desire for enjoyment, a desire satisfied by a host of theatres, dance-halls, café-concerts, taverns and restaurants. Pleasure was the order of the day, and the purveyors of pleasure—sexual, artistic, alcoholic or gastronomic—thrived mightily.

Magny was not slow to take advantage of the public's new prosperity. In 1855, the year of the Paris Exhibition, he raised all his prices, but he also improved the range and quality of his cuisine. Distinguished Parisians took to dining in the Rue Contrescarpe, led by the composer Rossini, who invented the *tournedos Rossini* there in collaboration with Magny; the novelist George Sand, who transferred her allegiance to Magny's from the Restaurant Pinson in the Rue de l'Ancienne-Comédie, and became a firm friend of the restaurateur and his wife; and the critic Sainte-Beuve, who dined there every Saturday night in a private room with a woman friend.

Their host welcomed them with an affable assurance born of well-deserved success. "Distinguished to a suitable degree," wrote Théodore de Banville, "with a lively, intelligent face, very polite without being either arrogant or familiar, and a little lame, like Lord Byron and La Vallière, he was adored by his clientele, which was uniquely composed of those perceptive Parisians who can discover good restaurants as unerringly as pigs discover truffles. When one of those princes of money or the mind entertained some friends in his establishment, Magny never failed to come along several times during the meal to make sure that all was well. He accepted praise modestly, but as his due, and at dessert he would not refuse an invitation to have a drink with the diners, who were really not customers but guests, for when a man gives you good food and drink in Paris, can the debt you owe him ever be paid in money?"

The only blemish on Magny's contentment in this halcyon period was caused by a new establishment next door to his restaurant. The Auberge du Cheval-Blanc had ceased to be a coaching-inn, and for some time had been used by the carriers who owned it simply to house their wagons. But then the proprietors leased the large one-storey building adjoining No. 3 to a certain Aublin, who turned it into a *boui-boui*, or music-hall.

Aublin named it *Les Folies Dauphine,* but everybody else called it
Le Beuglant, or "The Bellower", on account of the noise made by
the singers and their audience. The din could occasionally be
heard in the Restaurant Magny, especially in the summer when
the windows were open, but the diners never let it spoil their
appetites, and eventually even Magny himself became inured to it.

The reputation of the Restaurant Magny obtained final con-
secration in the authoritative *Guide Joanne* compiled in 1862. In this
work Adolphe Joanne conscientiously divided all the catering
establishments in Paris into categories, from the first-class restaurants, "where one goes in search of great wines, early vegetables,
prime game and delicate fish, without regard to expense", through
the *tables d'hôte,* the *pensions bourgeoises,* the *bouillons,* the *crémeries*
and the cafés, to the four thousand pot-houses in the capital,
which he contemptuously dismissed as "frequented only by workmen and coachmen". Magny must have smiled to see that his own
restaurant, which only twenty years before had been one of the
despised pot-houses, was now listed with Philippe's in the first
class. "Magny's cuisine," stated Joanne, "is reputed to be one of
the best in Paris, and behind its rather humble exterior, his
establishment occupies one of the highest ranks in the hierarchy
of Parisian restaurants."

Among the dishes which had won Magny this accolade were
several he had created himself, including the *purée Magny,* the
tournedos Rossini, and above all the *châteaubriand.* His customers also
went into ecstasies over his *bécasses à la Charles,* named after his
head waiter Charles Labrau, who had been with him since the
beginning and would remain with him till he died; his *pieds de
mouton à la poulette,* which were generally agreed to be unsurpassed
anywhere in Paris; and his *écrevisses à la Bordelaise,* of which one
customer wrote that "once you had begun eating them, there was
no reason to stop, and you didn't stop either, unless there was a
revolution or an earthquake".

One of the Restaurant Magny's most devoted *habitués* was
Sainte-Beuve's friend and physician, Doctor Veyne, who for some
years had cherished the idea of introducing the great critic to
another friend of his, the caricaturist and illustrator Gavarni. In

1862 the visit to Paris of a fellow southerner called Charpenne provided him with the pretext he required, and he held a small dinner-party at Magny's in Charpenne's honour, to which he invited both men. To his delight they took a liking to each other, and in a subsequent article Sainte-Beuve quoted approvingly a critical remark about Balzac which Gavarni had made to him. Later that year, Gavarni fell into one of his frequent fits of depression, and Veyne suggested to Sainte-Beuve that they should try to raise his spirits by founding an informal dining-club which would meet fortnightly at Magny's. Sainte-Beuve leapt at the idea, according to his secretary, who later recalled that "this had always been a dream of his, for he considered that such gatherings helped to break down prejudices and to foster mutual understanding and esteem".

On Saturday, 22 November 1862, Sainte-Beuve's dream came true, when he dined at Magny's with Veyne, Gavarni, and the latter's ardent admirers, the novelists Edmond and Jules de Goncourt. "We had an exquisite meal, perfect in every respect," the Goncourts wrote in their *Journal* that night, "a meal such as we had thought impossible to obtain in a Paris restaurant. This dinner was the inauguration of a dining-club which is to meet twice a month and which is to be enlarged to include other guests. . . ."

The Magny Dinners had begun.

Dinner at Magny's

CHAPTER ONE

6 December 1862

SHORTLY BEFORE SIX o'clock in the evening of Saturday, 6 December, two men climbed the stairs to the first floor of the Restaurant Magny, to be greeted by the proprietor and shown by Charles into the private dining-room where the second Magny Dinner was about to be held. At first sight they seemed very different in appearance and attitude—the one a pale, slim, youngish man with fair hair and a golden moustache, darting into the room and pointing excitedly out of the window, and the other older, darker, more ponderous, pausing deliberately in the door-way and listening calmly to his companion's remarks. Closer study, however, would have revealed an affectionate, boyish, almost teasing deference in the younger man, and a tender solici-tude in the older, suggesting that they were linked by a bond of unusual closeness. This was in fact the case, for these two men were the Goncourt brothers, who constituted one of the most remarkable literary partnerships of their own or any other age.

Before their mother had died in 1848, Edmond de Goncourt had solemnly undertaken to look after and watch over his younger brother Jules, and although they were now forty and thirty-one respectively, the relationship between them was still that of the serious-minded guardian and the mischievous ward. But if the brothers differed in age and temperament, they were one in ideas, taste and sensibility. They rarely disagreed about people or things; in company each found himself involuntarily nodding or smiling at the same time as his brother; and in conversation they de-veloped each other's arguments or anecdotes in a two-part monologue which alternately delighted and irritated their listeners. Not unnaturally this collaboration was extended to the books they wrote together, and their writing was so closely integrated that it was impossible to attribute any passage with certainty to one or other of the two brothers. Their first efforts at writing—a couple of amateurish plays and a jejune novel—had been unsuccessful, while an incursion into journalism had resulted in a prosecution for obscenity, with the result that for the greater part of the eighteen-fifties they had confined themselves to producing historical monographs on the eighteenth century. In the last two years, however, they had published two more novels—about journalism in Paris and hospital life—which were to be the first of a series of similar studies of contemporary society. They had also continued work on their monumental *Journal*, drawing on Jules's phenomenal memory and the notes Edmond took on his cuff to record their day-by-day impressions and conversations. Fortunately for the peace of mind of Magny's *habitués*, they knew nothing of the *Journal*, and it would be another twenty-five years before the surviving diners would learn of its existence from Edmond's publication of carefully edited extracts.

One of their principal victims, a diarist himself who was to die without ever suspecting that the Goncourts were outdoing him in malicious portraiture, was the next diner to arrive. Charles-Augustin Sainte-Beuve was now almost sixty years old, a tubby little man with a long nose, prominent cheek-bones, and a bald head always surmounted by a small black skull-cap. People meeting him for the first time were struck by his remarkable ugliness, but he had a ready smile and a friendly, rather avuncular manner; and indeed, Gautier usually called him "Uncle Beuve". A perceptive contemporary wrote that judging by his appearance "one might take him for an intelligent provincial coming out of a cloister of books under which there was a cellar of rich burgundy"; and Sainte-Beuve was in fact both fond of sensual pleasure and utterly dedicated to literature. During the past thirty years the Romantic poet and sometime lover of Victor Hugo's wife had given place entirely to the literary critic, who every week since 1849 had produced one of his famous *lundis*, the long critical articles published every Monday, first in the *Constitutionnel,* then in the *Moniteur,* and in 1869 in the *Temps.* His life had become a weary treadmill, with him writing an article from Tuesday until Friday, correcting the proofs on Saturday and Sunday, and taking

Monday off, before starting all over again on Tuesday. "He works from eight in the morning till five in the afternoon," the Goncourts observed, "and then takes a stroll from five till six to *deserve* an appetite. On Tuesday he takes his secretary Troubat and a *little lady* out to dinner. On Saturday he takes another *little lady* to dinner at a restaurant where he has ordered dinner in advance. He prefers the exhaustion of work to boredom or emptiness, but admits that he is overworked because of lack of money." Because he wrote for a Government paper, had never shown any opposition to the Empire, and frequented Princess Mathilde's *salon*, his enemies sneered at him as a mealy-mouthed vassal of the imperial régime. But once he was appointed a Senator, in 1865, and became financially independent, he would express in public the liberal opinions which he privately shared with most of Magny's other *habitués*.

Hard on Sainte-Beuve's heels came his doctor, François Veyne, a handsome, dark-eyed man in his late forties, whose youthful features contrasted sharply with the long white hair which framed his face. Veyne had been an intern at the Salpêtrière hospital with Claude Bernard, and had later been both friend and physician to a whole generation of writers and artists, including Champfleury, Gavarni, Courbet, Nadar and Murger. As one contemporary put it, "he had nursed them through the pox, delivered their children, and sent their mistresses to hospital to die of consumption", and had thereby earned the affectionate title of "the Doctor of Bohemia".

A native of Gigondas in Provence, Veyne bore a striking resemblance to the first Napoleon, and this had helped him in the courting of the girl who had become his wife. Her father, a veteran of the Napoleonic Wars, had found a portrait of young François Veyne concealed in his daughter's room and had asked her for an explanation, only to be silenced by the retort: "What? Don't you recognise your god?" But despite this reason for gratitude to the Bonapartes, Veyne had been a staunch republican all his life, plotting against the monarchy under Louis-Philippe and refusing to accept any of the official posts which Sainte-Beuve tried to obtain for him under the Second Empire. To wealth and position he had preferred the life of an ordinary physician with extraordinary patients, and Sainte-Beuve's secretary described him as the critic's doctor, friend, adviser, and Minister of the Interior. With his radiant smile and his lilting Provençal accent he was one of the best beloved of all Magny's *habitués*, thoroughly deserving the tribute once paid to him by a little maidservant: "Monsieur Veyne lights up the whole table."

With Veyne came his friend Gavarni—Guillaume Chevalier by his real name—for whose benefit the Magny Dinners had been devised. A bowed figure with a heavily lined face and threads of grey in his golden beard and hair, he was now only a shadow of the handsome young man who had been the arbiter of Parisian elegance in the eighteen-thirties. During that decade he had turned out hundreds of lively, elegant illustrations for *La Mode* which had completely outdated the stiff fashion-plates of old, and had gone on to produce amusing lithographs of Parisian life for *Le Charivari*. After a stay in London in 1847, however, his personality and art had become increasingly misanthropic, and with the death of his son Jean he had become a bad-tempered, eccentric recluse, digging up his garden over and over again, and designing elaborate bedrooms for his dogs. The Goncourts had originally intended to call the fortnightly reunions at Magny's the Gavarni Dinners, but the artist was usually so morose and contributed so little to the conversation that after a few dinners they reluctantly gave up the idea.

The next person to appear, or rather to burst into the room, was a burly, powerfully built man with protuberant blue eyes under puffy lids, a heavy, drooping moustache, and a mottled red complexion. This was forty-year-old Gustave Flaubert, eleven years after he had returned from his tour of the Middle East, bald, stout and syphilitic, and five years after the publication of *Madame Bovary* which had brought him fame, recognition . . . and a sensational prosecution for obscenity. He spent the greater part of every year at his home at Croisset, near Rouen, where he toiled ten hours a day at his books and occasionally received male or female friends on brief visits, but from which he had brutally evicted his mistress Louise Colet eight years before, when she had rashly tried to invade his almost anchoretic privacy. The remaining months of the year he spent in Paris, reading in the Bibliothèque Impériale, dining with Madame Sabatier, the notorious *Présidente,* seeing friends such as Gautier, and, for the next few years, attending the Magny Dinners. At the moment he was in Paris for the publication of his exotic historical novel of life in ancient Carthage, *Salammbô,* and the previous day, the Goncourts had taken a cruel pleasure in repeating to him the slighting comments Sainte-Beuve had made to them about the book. As a result, he had no sooner entered the room than he drew Sainte-Beuve into a corner, where the two brothers observed him "trying, with the aid of expressive gestures, to convince him of the excellence of his work".

In the meantime two more men had come in: one the dramatic critic Paul de Saint-Victor, and the other the philologist and historian Ernest Renan. They formed a curious contrast. Saint-Victor was a handsome, distinguished figure, with an elegantly waxed moustache, fiery eyes, and a disdainful expression which concealed a violent, passionate temperament. Renan, on the other hand, was almost as ugly as Sainte-Beuve; and the Goncourts described him as "short and podgy, badly built, with a calf's head covered with the callosities of a monkey's rump, a huge drooping nose, and his whole face streaked and speckled with red blotches". He sometimes remarked jokingly in his thin, squeaky voice that his unfashionable black stockings were all that remained about him of the priesthood, which after years of seminary education he had decided not to enter in 1845; but in fact many of his gestures had a certain ecclesiastical urbanity. His religious education made him seem much more dangerous to the clergy than any sceptical layman; and when, in January 1862, in his first lecture at the Collège de France, he had called Christ "an incomparable man", they had secured the suspension of his course. But they could do nothing to prevent the publication, in 1863, of his *Life of Jesus,* which was to prove one of the most widely-read and influential books of the century.

Another curiously assorted pair arrived immediately afterwards. First came the journalist Gustave Claudin, a dapper, exquisitely dressed little man whose conservative opinions and naïve ideas were a constant source of amusement to his sophisticated, liberal-minded friends. In his wake lumbered a giant of a man, with sky-blue eyes and white hair and beard, whom the Goncourts likened variously to a gentle forest or mountain genie, a Druid, and the kindly old monk in *Romeo and Juliet*. "With the kindliness of his gaze," they wrote later, "goes the soft caress of the Russian accent, something like the singing of a child or a Negro." For this gentle colossus was the novelist Ivan Turgenev, already famous in France for his *Sportsman's Sketches* and *Scenes of Russian Life*. For some years now he had lived chiefly in Baden-Baden and Paris, where he was widely cherished and admired, largely for his personal charm, liberal ideas and literary talents, but partly too for the touch of Slav exoticism he brought to the Parisian scene.

While he was walking slowly round the room, being introduced to those guests who, like the Goncourts, had never met him before, Flaubert suddenly realised who he was and hurried across to clasp his hand in a fervent grip.

"My dear colleague," he growled, "I've long regarded you as a master, and I can't say how happy I am to shake your hand. I'm spellbound by your talent, and lost in admiration for your sympathy, which makes even your landscapes speak and set us dreaming. How can I put it? . . . Whenever I read *Don Quixote* I long to ride a horse down a dusty white road and eat olives and raw onions in the shade of a rock—and whenever I read your stories of Russian life I want to be jolted across snow-covered fields in a telega, with wolves howling in the distance. And I love the bitter-sweet perfume that your books give off . . . a delicious sadness that reaches to the depths of my soul."

While he was speaking, a slow flush had spread across the Russian's face, and he lowered his eyes in confusion.

"Praise from you, my dear Flaubert," he said at last, "is worth its weight in gold, and I only wish that I deserved it. I admire and love the artist in you, and now I have met you I feel as if I could talk to you for weeks on end: after all, we are two moles burrowing in the same direction. . . ."

"Where's Gautier?" the elder Goncourt broke in, anxious to

interrupt this conversation from which he and the others were being pointedly excluded. "Magny's waiting to serve dinner, and there's no sign of our great Romantic."

"Théo's nearly always late," murmured Sainte-Beuve. "I suggest we start our meal without him, and he'll soon turn up."

"Did you see, gentlemen," Saint-Victor asked as everybody was sitting down, "that the Duc de Gramont-Caderousse has been acquitted of killing our poor colleague Dillon?"

"I don't know either of those names," said Turgenev. "Who is the duke you mention, and why was he accused of killing this Monsieur Dillon?"

Saint-Victor smiled indulgently at him.

"The Duc de Gramont-Caderousse," he explained, "is one of the most celebrated dandies of the Jockey Club and the Boulevard des Italiens, a young man of extravagant tastes probably inherited, like his immense wealth, from his illustrious father, a gentleman who spent fifty thousand francs on walking-sticks and twenty thousand on hats. He is also a fanatical and extremely capable duellist, as he showed recently by dispatching the unfortunate Dillon, a humble journalist on the staff of a periodical called *Le Sport*."

"Poor Dillon!" murmured Claudin. "Did you know he earned only four hundred francs a month? Not much of a salary for a writer who has to defend his opinions with sword and pistol, correcting proofs with one hand and penning challenges with the other. . . ."

"To be fair to Gramont-Caderousse," Saint-Victor pointed out, "I should add that he's a man with a highly developed sense of chivalry. I'm told he once fought a duel on behalf of the Blessed Virgin, not because he's particularly religious, but because he couldn't permit anything to be said against a lady."

"He has always been like that," said Veyne. "There was a time when he was having an affair with the Duchesse de Persigny, and he was present when Persigny happened to utter some mild complaint about his conjugal unhappiness. 'I cannot allow your Grace,' protested Caderousse, 'to say things against my mistress!'"

"You didn't attend his latest victim in a professional capacity, did you?" asked Gavarni.

Veyne's eyes creased with amusement.

"No," he replied. "The last deathbed of any distinction which I've visited was poor Murger's, last year."

"The Doctor of Bohemia seeing off the Great Bohemian, eh?"

"I suppose you might say that, though I only went to see him as a friend—Marquet and Ricord were treating him. I must say he had a terrible end, what with the pain and the smell, and hallucinations of a savage trying to pull his leg off."

"What exactly did he die of?" somebody asked.

"Ricord's diagnosis was arteritis in the left leg—and then of course gangrene set in."

"I heard that he simply rotted alive," said Claudin. "A friend of mine told me that when they tried to trim his moustache the day before he died, the lip came away with the hairs."

"I must say," the elder Goncourt observed, with malicious satisfaction, "that that death by decomposition struck me as a judgement on Bohemia, combining everything in Murger's life and the world he described—the orgies of work at night, the periods of poverty followed by periods of junketing, the neglected cases of pox, the ups and downs of a homeless existence, the suppers instead of dinners, and the glasses of absinthe bringing consolation after a visit to the pawnshop. . . ."

"A life," his brother added, "opposed to all the principles of physical and spiritual hygiene; a life which results in a man literally disintegrating at the age of forty-two, complaining of only one thing, the smell of rotten meat in his room—the smell of his own body. . . ."

Saint-Victor shuddered delicately and turned to Veyne beside him.

"No wonder his last words were 'No more of Bohemia'," he said. "But you've seen pleasanter deaths than that, Veyne, and heard wittier last words as well. What was that anecdote I heard you telling Sainte-Beuve the other day for his article on Royer-Collard?"

"Oh—just that in his last illness, when his valet was trying to get him to urinate, I heard him mutter: 'The little beast won't do it any more.'"

"But that isn't witty, or even funny!" protested Edmond de Goncourt. "It isn't a patch on what that comic actor—Grassot, wasn't it?—said to his penis in the same circumstances. You remember the exact words, Jules. . . ."

"'Don't be silly,'" quoted his brother. "'Come on out: it's just to piss.'"

There was a roar of laughter from the other diners.

"It's unjust," the elder Goncourt continued in a petulant tone, "that insipid remarks by politicans should be remembered, while witticisms by lesser folk are forgotten."

"Or even stolen from them," said Claudin, "and attributed to the famous. Perhaps they should be made the exclusive property of the man who coins them, like a work of literature."

"No, no!" protested Sainte-Beuve. "People who quote us are paying us in fame and reputation. Anybody who writes or talks should beg people to use what he says."

"Nonsense!" bellowed Flaubert. "If I'd invented the railways, I wouldn't let anybody so much as get on to a train without my permission."

Sainte-Beuve shook his head stubbornly.

"No," he said, "there shouldn't be any property, in words or trains or anything else. Everything ought to be continually renewed and replenished, and nobody should be allowed to cling to anything. . . . But while I'm opposed to exclusive ownership of anecdotes and witticisms, I'm all in favour of preserving them. Because it's heartbreaking how many remarks and conversations which give the flavour of a period or a personality are lost for ever! Did you know, for instance, that when Louis XVIII decided to make Madame du Cayla his mistress, he told his ministers: 'Gentlemen, there will be no meeting of the Council on Tuesday: the King will be taking his pleasure'? And everybody was so sure that the experience would kill him that the whole Court gathered in the anteroom to eavesdrop afterwards, and heard Baron Portal saying as he took the royal pulse: 'Slow, very slow.'"

There was a pause as he searched for another example.

B

"It's quite possible," he went on, "to record a jewel of a saying without even realising its value. Take Roederer, for instance. He wasn't a very intelligent man, but while he was with King Joseph in Spain he met General Lasalle at Burgos, and wrote down what the general said to him in a letter to his wife. He asked Lassalle whether he was going to pass through Paris on his way to join Napoleon, and the general replied: 'Yes, it's the shortest way: I'll arrive at five in the morning, order myself a pair of boots, father a child on my wife, and be on my way again.' Now there isn't a document in existence that gives a better idea of that period than that report of a brief conversation dashed off in a letter from a husband to his wife. . . . Oh, there's so much that gets lost!"

At that moment the door opened and a pathetic figure appeared on the threshold: a middle-aged man with shoulder-length hair which was dripping water on to the floor.

Flaubert stood up and walked over to the apparition, full of concern.

"Théo, my dear fellow," he boomed, "what's happened to you? You look like a drowned rat."

"A Merovingian rat," Claudin chimed in.

"The heavens have just opened up outside," replied Gautier, "and the wretched cab-driver let me off at the wrong end of the street."

"You should carry an umbrella, Théo," Sainte-Beuve purred reprovingly.

"An umbrella?" The poet looked comically indignant. "Never, do you hear, never shall Théophile Gautier be seen carrying that philistine instrument! Not that I would criticise anyone else for using one, least of all you, Uncle Beuve. After all, you once fought a duel carrying one, unless I'm mistaken."

"That's perfectly correct," said the critic. "As I said at the time, I don't mind dying, but I'm damned if I'll get wet."

"Sit down, Théo," said Flaubert, "and I'll ring for your soup. Why the devil are you late?"

"I've only just got back from Nohant," explained Gautier. "The first time I've been to one of George Sand's house-parties, and the last time too if I've any say in the matter."

"Why, Théo," asked Gavarni, "isn't the good lady of Nohant feminine enough for you?"

"She's feminine enough. Positively matronly. And too moral for words."

"What, no orgies?" said Claudin. "No fun?"

"Orgies? Fun? It's about as much fun as a Moravian monastery! You breakfast at ten. On the last stroke everybody sits down and tucks in. Then Madame Sand arrives looking like a sleep-walker, and stays asleep all the way through the meal. After breakfast you go out into the garden and play bowls, and after a while your hostess wakes up and starts talking."

"What about?" somebody asked.

"You'd never guess," grinned Gautier. "Pronunciation. How to pronounce *ailleurs* and *meilleur* and that sort of thing. But the principal conversational pleasure at Nohant is the scatological joke."

"Get along with you!" said Gavarni.

"It's true! All their fun comes from breaking wind. But never a word about relations between the sexes. I do believe they'd throw you out of the house if you made the slightest reference to the subject. And there's no shop-talk either. In fact, on the second day I said that if there wasn't going to be any talk about literature I was going to leave. That shook them and no mistake."

"Does the old lady still work as hard as ever?" asked Claudin.

"Work? She never stops. And I must say the place is beautifully organised for turning out copy. She can't sit down in a room without pens appearing in front of her, as well as ink, cigarette paper, Turkish tobacco, and striped note-paper. And it just pours out of her! From three o'clock to six, and then again from midnight to four in the morning. You know what happened to her once? Something really monstrous. One day she finished a novel at one in the morning. 'Good gracious,' she said, 'I've finished!' And she promptly started work on another."

"Who else was there, Gautier?" asked Flaubert.

"The painter Marchal, of course, as devoted as ever. And Dumas *fils*. And Madame Calamatta."

"And how is Dumas *fils*? Still ill?"

"Oh, terribly down in the mouth. You know what he does these days? He sits down in front of a sheet of paper for hours and hours, and finally writes three lines. He goes off to have a cold bath and do some exercises, because he's full of ideas on hygiene. Then he comes back and decides that his three lines are stupid."

"Well, that at least shows sense," Saint-Victor remarked.

"So he crosses out everything except three words," Gautier continued, ignoring the interruption. "Then along comes his father and says: 'Get me a chop and I'll finish your play for you.' The old man writes the scenario, brings in a tart, borrows some money and goes away again. Dumas *fils* reads the scenario, likes it, goes and has a bath, reads the scenario again, decides that it's stupid, and spends a year rewriting it. And when his father comes back, he finds the same three words from the same three lines as the year before!"

"Sounds as finicky as you, Flaubert," remarked Gavarni.

"And just as futile," snorted the novelist. "Because can you imagine anything more futile than struggling to find the right word, or trying to eliminate a repetition? Who for, in heaven's name? And then, if your book or play succeeds, the success is never the sort you wanted. Look at *Madame Bovary*. It was the theatrical bits in the book that made it a success. As for your style, how many readers appreciate it? Not one in a thousand. And remember that style is what makes us suspect in the eyes of the law, because our precious judges are all for the classics."

"Which they probably haven't even read," the elder Goncourt remarked drily.

"Precisely, Goncourt. And not just the judges either. Why, with all respect, I don't think there are eight men of letters in France who have read Voltaire—I mean *really* read him. And there aren't five who could tell you the titles of Thomas Corneille's plays. Oh no, what's the use of writing for a public like that?"

"You remember," said Gautier, pushing away his soup-plate, "that incredible review of *Madame Bovary* by Lamayrac or Limayrac? About its ignoble style?"

"Limayrac," snapped Flaubert. "I'll never forget it."

"What did it say, Flaubert?" asked Claudin.

"The gist of it was in one splendid sentence which ran something like this: 'How can anybody allow himself to write in such an ignoble style when the throne is occupied by the greatest master of the French language, the Emperor Napoleon III?'"

There was a roar of laughter around the table, and as the next course was being served, Saint-Victor could be heard indignantly complaining of the Emperor's lack of hospitality towards his fellow writers.

"I do declare," he said, "that literature and the arts have never been treated with such contempt as by Napoleon the Little. He hauls us up before the courts, but he never thinks of inviting us to court."

"Oh, come, Saint-Victor," said Jules de Goncourt, "we mustn't be too hard on him. Every now and then a writer or artist of some sort is included at the very end of the guest-list at Compiègne. And sometimes His Majesty even deigns to speak to him. That happened to Berlioz only the other day."

"He had a conversation with the Emperor?" someone asked incredulously.

"I suppose you might put it that way. The Emperor was complaining to some of his courtiers that his sight was failing. 'The queer thing,' he told them, 'is that I can't tell the difference between black and blue any more. Now who is that standing over there?' 'Sire,' said some flunkey, 'that's Monsieur Berlioz.' The Emperor raised his voice. 'Monsieur Berlioz,' he asked, 'is your tail-coat black or blue?' 'Sire,' said Berlioz, 'I would never take the liberty of appearing before Your Majesty in a blue tail-coat; it is black.' 'Good,' said the Emperor. And that was all he said to Berlioz in four days."

"Oh, I wouldn't mind his despising us," said Gautier, "if only he'd leave us alone. But the trouble is that you never know where you are with him. I used to get on very well with the Orléans régime when Louis-Philippe was on the throne. Then '48 came along and the Republic put me on the shelf for a while. But then I got on to the *Moniteur,* only to be saddled with an Emperor who wobbles from left to right, so that you never know which way he's going. You daren't say what you think or write what you want.

What can you do when they won't let you describe a little ordinary love-making in a novel? I ask you . . ."

"Oh, get along with you," said Claudin. "You may not be able
to write what you like in a novel. But as a leading critic on the
Government paper, you're in a powerful position."

"But that's just the point: I can't say what I think as a critic
either. Let me tell you a little story. One day Monsieur Walewski
told me that I must stop being indulgent, and that as from the
following day I could say exactly what I thought about the plays
I reviewed. 'But this week,' I pointed out, 'there's a play by your
friend and colleague Doucet.' 'Ah!' said Walewski. 'In that case,
suppose you wait till next week.' Well, I'm still waiting for next
week to arrive!"

"Yes," said Jules de Goncourt, "we're all of us gagged by our
beloved Emperor and his minions. But what really sickens me is
the deification of the wretched little man. Did you hear what that
fool Chapuys-Montlaville did in the course of the Emperor's tour
of the South of France? After His Imperial Majesty had taken a
bath at the local prefecture, Chapuys-Montlaville had the bath-
water drawn off and bottled, as if it came from the Jordan or the
Ganges."

"And then we have the impudence," said Edmond, "to laugh
at a nation which worships a Grand Lama's excrement!"

"Yes, but you must be fair," objected Claudin. "An idiot like
Chapuys-Montlaville may behave like that, but it doesn't follow
that the Emperor approves of that sort of thing."

"Oh, doesn't he just!" exclaimed Veyne. "Why, the fellow even
lays down liturgical rules for his sexual relations! I was talking to
a medical colleague the other day who told me how the Emperor's
amorous adventures are organised. It appears that every new
woman is brought to the Tuileries in a cab, undressed in an ante-
room, and taken naked into the room where the Emperor is
waiting for her. And just before the Chamberlain hands her over,
he hisses into her ear: 'You may kiss His Majesty anywhere except
on his face.' Now, in the whole history of deification, have you
ever met another instance of a man's face being made a holy of
holies that would be sullied by a kiss?"

"I presume that your medical colleague examines the ladies in question, Veyne?" said Saint-Victor. "Otherwise the Republicans could use the same method against the Emperor that the Duc Decazes used to overthrow his uncle."

"Are you suggesting that the Duc Decazes overthrew Napoleon?" asked Renan.

"I'm simply repeating a story I heard from Dumas *fils*, who had it from King Jérôme in person. It seems that after the return from Elba, when Decazes was fleeing from Paris with Louis XVIII, he left this final instruction: 'If Napoleon asks for a woman, give him one with a disease.' So they sent one to meet him, he had her at Lyons, and by the time he got to Waterloo he could scarcely mount his horse. You can draw your own conclusions."

"The power that women wield," said Claudin, "even unconsciously, is utterly horrifying."

"Nonsense!" protested Sainte-Beuve, pushing his skull-cap back on his head. "I won't listen to such blasphemy against the fair sex. There's nothing real in life except a woman."

"Just one woman, Sainte-Beuve?" Veyne asked maliciously.

"Heaven forbid, my dear fellow! Two, three, four, five . . . the more the merrier. Frenchwomen of course: they're so graceful, so delicious. And when you consider that about quarter-day, when the rent is due, you can have any number of the sweet creatures for next to nothing! Because women's wages, you know, are unbelievably low. . . . That's something the Government hasn't thought of remedying yet, I'm happy to say. . . ."

"Uncle Beuve, you horrify me," said Gautier. "I always thought you were so chaste and respectable."

"Oh, come now, Théo, after all the stories I've heard you tell, you aren't going to pretend that you think of bed as simply somewhere to sleep!"

"No," replied Gautier, "I won't go as far as that. But I've never had any passionate enthusiasm for that sort of intimate acrobatics. . . ."

There was a general exclamation of disbelief.

"No, that's the truth. It isn't that I'm not as well made as anybody else. I'm a man, I've made seventeen children . . ."

"Bravo!" said a voice.

". . . all of them quite good-looking too—I can show you samples. I've even worked to order. I was offered ten thousand francs once to father a child. But I can assure you that one fuck a year is quite enough for me. And it always leaves me absolutely cold—I could do mental arithmetic at the same time. . . . There's another thing too—I consider it humiliating to let a trollop think you need to jump on her. Take Alice Ozy, for instance. When I slept with her she was eighteen and worth the trouble, I can tell you that. I'd seen a show that night from her box, and when I got home, at two in the morning, I found a note from her asking me to go straight away to her apartment. When I got there, she told me that she wanted to see whether I was spending the night at home or sleeping with one of the chorus-girls. I said that she could see that I hadn't been sleeping out, but that at two o'clock in the morning I couldn't decently go off and wake both the porters all over again. So she gave me a sofa to sleep on, and then, half an hour later, got worried that I might catch cold and offered me a place in her bed, saying: 'Dear me, I don't know you very well. . . .' Well, it annoyed me, her thinking that I was going to jump on her, that I wanted her so badly . . . so I turned my back on her and went to sleep. At six o'clock the next morning she tapped me on the shoulder and said: 'Don't you think we've pretended long enough, the two of us?' 'You're right,' I said, and set to. But she'd learnt her lesson."

"I agree with you entirely, Gautier," said the younger Goncourt. "Edmond and I find that one week of love disgusts us for three months, and we come out of it spiritually sick and physically tired."

"One week?" Sainte-Beuve exclaimed. "But that's what women of the world consider the ideal length of an affair. I'm surprised at you, Goncourt. I've always considered a week either too much or too little. My motto is a quarter of an hour or forever."

Both brothers coloured slightly at the old critic's reproof.

"If you're talking of love as a sentiment, Sainte-Beuve," said Edmond, "then one of us has been in love for a week with a woman of easy virtue, and the other for three days with a ten-franc whore: that makes eleven days of love between the two of us. But if you mean love as a physical contact, then we give it five hours a week at the very most—from six o'clock to eleven, without a single thought before or after."

"Apart from a certain revulsion," added Jules. "I remember a night rather like Gautier's with Alice Ozy. I was staying at Sainte-Adresse at the time, with a stockbroker called Turcas. A friend of his on the Stock-Exchange had asked him to look after his mistress while he was away—Fanny Dubuisson of the Folies-Dramatiques. Well, one night when I was on my way home—it was eleven o'clock and her hotel was shut—she appeared on her balcony in a white dressing-gown. I was with Asseline, who had been paying strenuous court to her, and the two of us started climbing the trellis up to her window. Asseline gave up before long, because it wasn't very safe. But once I'd started, I went up very seriously while the woman stood there laughing and pretending to scold me. This went on for a few seconds, and during those few seconds something inside me loved that woman, wanted her, hankered after her as you might hanker after a star in the sky. Finally I reached the top and jumped on to the balcony. I got my reward, of course, but I wasn't in love with the woman any more. What I mean is that in the whole of that night, I was in love for a distance of fifteen feet, and that was all."

"But what did you feel for her while you were with her?" asked Sainte-Beuve.

"Nothing but a sort of macabre curiosity. You see, after every thrust her heart went *tick-tock* like a clock in a village inn—an eerie sound, the sound of pleasure tolling the death-knell. And she knew it, too. 'If I lived a fast life for six months,' she told me, 'it would be the death of me. With a chest like mine I'm sure to die young, and if I started going out to supper every night it wouldn't take long. . . .' I remember she said I looked like a little boy staring at a jam sandwich, but really I was as cold as ice. You see, apart from sobering up during the climb, I was afraid that she might ask me next morning for a little marmoset I had bought during the day at Le Havre. I had a feeling that she was bound to like monkeys."

Turgenev shook his head in bewilderment.

"I don't understand," he said. "I just don't understand."

"What don't you understand?" asked Flaubert.

"The things I have just heard from Gautier and Goncourt. I have always regarded love as something very important, and it amazes me to hear anyone speak of it with so little respect. Surely it is a wonderful experience, the first time at least, even if it is spoiled later?"

"Was *your* first time wonderful?" Jules asked him.

"Oh, yes!" the Russian answered in surprise. "I was very young at the time—only fifteen—with all the longings a boy has at fifteen. At my mother's house there was a pretty chambermaid with a stupid face—but as you know, there are some faces to which stupidity adds a certain grandeur. It was a dull, rainy day, and dusk had begun to fall. I was walking round the garden when suddenly that girl came straight up to me and took hold of me— and remember that I was her master and she was just a serf—took hold of me by the hair at the back of my neck and said: 'Come!' What followed was similar to what we have all experienced so often. But that gentle gripping of my hair with that single word sometimes comes back to me; and just remembering it makes me happy."

"I know exactly what you mean," said Flaubert. "My first time was something like that."

"Tell us, Flaubert," said Gautier.

"If I can have some more wine first. . . . Thank you, Théo. . . . Well, I was on my way to Corsica, and I'd taken a room in a little hotel in Marseilles. There were some women from Lima there who had arrived with their furniture—wonderful sixteenth-century ebony inlaid with mother-of-pearl. There were three of them, with silk dressing-gowns falling in a straight line from the neck to the heels, and they had a little Negro servant dressed in a nankeen suit and Turkish slippers. You can imagine that for a young Norman whose travelling had been from Normandy to Champagne and Champagne to Normandy, this was all very tempting and exotic. Then one day, when I came back from a bathe in the Mediter- ranean, one of the women, a magnificent creature of thirty-five, invited me into her bedroom. I gave her a passionate kiss, one of those kisses into which you put your whole heart and soul. She came to my room that night and started sucking me straight away. There were some wonderful days after that, then a tearful farewell, then a few letters, then silence."

"You never went back to Marseilles?" asked Turgenev.

"Oh, yes, several times. But nobody could ever tell me what had become of those women. The last time I went through, on my way to Tunis to collect material for *Salammbô*, I went to have a look at the hotel as usual, but I couldn't find it. I hunted all over for it, and finally noticed that it had been turned into a toyshop with a barber's on the first floor. I went upstairs and asked for a shave . . . the wallpaper in the barber's saloon was the wallpaper of my old bedroom."

"You were lucky, Flaubert," said Edmond. "I hesitate to tell you about *my* initiation. It wasn't very pretty."

"Go on, Goncourt," said Gautier.

"I had been looking forward to it for months," Edmond began. "You see, I often spent my school holidays at Bar-le-Duc, staying with my cousin Fanny and her husband. They were a young, newly-married couple, and never stood on ceremony with me, letting me go into their rooms whenever I liked. One morning I wanted the husband to help me with a fishing line and I went into their bedroom without knocking. Fanny was lying on her back with her knees up, her legs apart and her bottom on a pillow, on the point of being impaled by her husband. They pulled the sheets up so quickly that I might have thought I had had an hallucination. But I had seen enough to be haunted every night by a vision of a pink bottom on a pillow with a scalloped border."

"But what about your initiation?" Turgenev asked impatiently.

"That should have happened at Bar-le-Duc too," Goncourt continued. "There was a sweet little solicitor's wife there who contrived to be late whenever there was an outing to the woods, and kept me behind so that I might accompany her. She complained of suffering from a heart ailment; and as there was a steep slope up to the woods, she used to get me to put my hand on her uncorseted heart, to show me how fast it was beating. . . ."

"With the inevitable result," Gautier broke in.

"With the result that I swore to myself I was going to seduce her on our next outing to the woods. But her sister-in-law, who happened to be my cousin, read our thoughts—or my thoughts at least—and stayed with us all day. The next morning I left the town to go back to school in Paris, and a fortnight later, determined to lose my virginity, I lost it in the arms of a prostitute called Madame Charles. She was an enormous woman with a rhomboidal torso fitted with two little arms and two little legs; and in bed she looked like a crab on its back." He made a grimace of disgust. "I've never forgotten her."

"Sounds a horrible experience," Saint-Victor said drily. "But after all, Goncourt, even when the woman isn't as rebarbative as your Madame Charles, the man always feels a certain sadness after the act. You know—*post coitum omne animal triste.* . . ."

"*Praeter asinum et sacerdotem,*" Renan added suavely.

"What did he say?" Jules whispered to his brother.

"Except for donkeys and priests," came the answer.

"Dammit, Renan," Flaubert snorted, "that just isn't true. And I'd have you know I'm neither a donkey nor a priest. When *I've* finished making love with a woman, I do a little dance in front of the mirror."

A great bellow of laughter came from Turgenev.

"By God, Flaubert," he shouted, "that's a sight I'd like to see!"

"So should we all," said Gautier mischievously. "But how do *you* feel afterwards, Turgenev?"

"Ah," replied the Russian, "with me something very peculiar happens. After it is all over I enter into communication again with the things around me. Objects take on again a reality they had lacked a moment before. I feel myself once more, and the table in the room becomes a table again. . . . Yes, what happens is that relations are restored between myself and Nature."

"Once again," said the elder Goncourt, "all I can say is that I envy you and Flaubert. Jules and I come away from our mistresses' beds as if they were so many museums of anatomical specimens."

"And heaven knows," said Jules, "what ghastly surgical memories we keep of those lovely bodies!"

"Have you ever wondered," Saint-Victor asked cuttingly, "what memories your mistresses keep of *you*? Or whether indeed you pleasure them at all?"

The brothers were so taken aback by this unexpected attack that they sat for a moment open-mouthed.

"That isn't a fair question to ask the Goncourts," growled Flaubert, "They were at my apartment the other day when Suzanne Lagier was expounding her ideas on the subject, and according to her, a woman can only come with a man who's inferior to her. With a superior she's troubled by a vestige of modesty or a desire to pleasure her partner."

"Or she may pretend to come," interposed Veyne, "to please the man, just as Eastern women on the contrary make it a point of honour to give no sign of any pleasure they experience."

"We have observed the phenomenon," Edmond said stiffly. "We have noticed that in thin women pleasure produces a nervous spasm, in fat women a sort of convulsion. The 'little death' makes the former ecstatic and the latter apopleptic."

"It makes them all unbearably garrulous," Gavarni remarked. "They can't understand the beauty of it all and go on chattering away when a man simply wants to go to sleep."

"And they're selfish into the bargain," said Jules. "Let me give you a sample of their conversation."

Gautier and Flaubert looked up from their plates with interest, knowing from past experience that the younger Goncourt was about to treat them to a display of his remarkable talent for mimicry.

"*Bibi*," cooed a shrill, quavering voice, "*push hard . . . . Oh, oh, oh! . . . Oh, Bibi, you're going too far. . . . I can feel your heart beating down there. . . . Bibi, I can't stand it any more. . . . I'm going to come. . . . Ooooh. . . .* And then, when she has had her pleasure and the man hasn't: *Oh, dear, my leg's hurting. . . . That's right, never mind me, you brute. . . . Oh, I'm all wet. . . .*"

There were a few chuckles, and a loud guffaw from Flaubert.

"The trouble with you two," said Saint-Victor, "is that you just don't like women."

"Why *should* we like them?" asked Edmond. "Unless she is

educated and civilised to a high degree, a woman is a stupid, evil animal, incapable of dreaming, thinking or loving. Only the woman of the world is a woman; the rest are females."

"You only have to look at a woman," said Jules, "to see the inferiority of the feminine mind. All her beauty and strength and development is concentrated in the central and lower parts of her body: her pelvis, her buttocks, her thighs; while a man's beauty is in the upper, nobler parts of the body: the pectoral muscles, the broad shoulders, the high forehead. Venus has a narrow forehead, and Dürer's *Three Graces* have flat heads at the back and narrow shoulders; only their hips are big and beautiful!"

"Woman," Edmond concluded, "is an admirable machine for lovemaking and childbearing, but nothing more."

"But if you don't want children," said Claudin, "and regard women—to quote your own words—as nothing but lovemaking machines, you might just as well replace them with manikins."

The elder Goncourt's eyes lit up with a triumphant gleam.

"Precisely, my dear Claudin," he said, "and an enlightened manufacturer has already begun doing just that. A friend of ours has seen one of the artificial women he produces, and says they are complete in every detail, with all the uses and attractions of real women. They have flesh which feels like the real thing, hair you would swear was genuine, eyes which roll, a tongue which darts in and out for five minutes, and moistness and warmth where you would expect to find them. Apparently the manufacturer makes them for religious communities and rich sailors, and they cost a great deal, but there are others to suit all pockets, down to imitation genitals at only 300 francs."

"And you approve of these . . . things?" asked Saint-Victor.

"Of course we do," snapped Jules. "The person who makes them is a philanthropist, an artist, a public benefactor, trying to spare men a host of evils, not least among them that insufferable period of a woman's existence we call the change of life. . . . I need scarcely add that he was prosecuted recently and sent to prison, presumably on a charge of immorality."

"Oh dear, oh, dear," murmured Turgenev. "What you have just been saying makes me very sad. Because for me a woman is so much more than—what did you say?—an animal, a machine. But then, my life has always been saturated with femininity. There isn't a book or anything else in the world which can take the place of a woman for me. How can I explain that to you?"

He bowed his head for a moment, searching his memory, and when he looked up again his face was radiant.

"Listen," he said, "when I was a young man I had a mistress, a miller's daughter, who lived near St. Petersburg and whom I used to see when I went hunting. She would never accept anything from me, but one day she asked me for some soap. I brought her a tablet. She took it, disappeared, came back covered with blushes, and held out her scented hands to me, saying: 'Now kiss my hands as you kiss the hands of the ladies in the drawing-rooms of St. Petersburg!' And I fell on my knees before her. . . . Well, there isn't another moment in my life to equal that one!"

He looked enquiringly at his listeners, and, seeing only blank or amused expressions, made another attempt to explain himself.

"I believe," he declared, "that love—the love between man and woman—produces a flowering of the whole personality which nothing else can achieve."

"But that's exactly what we object to in modern love," exclaimed Edmond. "It isn't the calm, tranquil, almost hygienic love of ancient times. Woman isn't regarded as a pleasure-giving machine any more. We've turned her into the object of all sorts of aspirations, the focus of all kinds of painful, delirious, exotic feelings. We try to find satisfaction, in her and through her, of all the passionate, insatiable longings inside us. . . ."

"We've forgotten," Jules concluded, "the secret of simply and crudely going to bed with a woman."

Flaubert thumped the table hard, and the glasses and china jumped into the air.

"I agree with you there," he roared. "I've always believed that one of the causes of the moral degeneration of the century has been the exaggerated 'poetisation' of women."

"Oh, I think you're going too far," said Claudin. "A fellow can't have any exotic or poetic feelings when he's faced with a little Parisienne in a nightcap."

"In a what?" asked Sainte-Beuve.

"In a nightcap. . . . Dammit, Sainte-Beuve, you know what I'm talking about. Every lady wears one in bed at night."

"Then I've never slept with a lady," sighed the great critic. "My women don't wear nightcaps. I've never seen anything more than a hairnet. But perhaps they put them on after I've gone. Because I've never in my life spent a whole night with a woman . . . on account of my work."

"Men like ourselves shouldn't sleep with ladies," said Edmond, "let alone live with them. We need a woman of little breeding and education who is nothing but gaiety and natural wit, a woman who can amuse and charm us like a pet animal."

"You mean like my panther woman?" Gautier asked mischievously. "She was certainly one of the best mistresses I ever had. She worked in a sideshow and had a skin as spotted as her name suggested. A lovely skin it was, too. . . ."

"But if a mistress," Edmond continued, ignoring Gautier's interruption, "acquires a veneer of breeding and tries to talk on an equal footing about art and literature, then she becomes as unbearable as a pianoforte out of tune."

"The ideal, in fact," Jules concluded, "is an educated man of the upper classes and an unsophisticated woman of the people."

"As a matter of interest," Claudin asked, "do you practise what you preach?"

With one voice the brothers answered unhesitatingly:

"We do."

"We have a unique mistress," said Edmond, "who admits to being forty but doesn't look it, who is plump and pretty, with the body of a Rubens matron and a silky white skin; a mistress to whom we give a meal once a week, and never more often than that, who arrives at half-past six and leaves on the stroke of ten; a mistress who has a job and lives on what she earns, whom we don't shave for and never take home, who never writes to us and would never dream of coming to bother us between visits. . . ."

"A mistress," continued Jules, "who can scarcely read and doesn't even know the titles of the books we write; a mistress with whom we've suppressed all the speechmaking and letter-writing of love, and even Chamfort's 'exchange of two fancies', leaving just the 'contact of two skins'. . . ."

"You say: 'we'," observed Claudin. "Do you mean you share her?"

"She's like the public," said Edmond.

"She accepts our collaboration," said Jules.

A murmur of admiration went round the table, and Turgenev leaned forward to take a closer look at the remarkable pair.

"I must say," remarked Sainte-Beuve, "that I approve of the Goncourts' attitude. I certainly can't think of anything worse than having an affair with a *femme de lettres*. Because all the time you'd have the feeling that she was giving the whole world what she ought to be keeping for you alone."

"You mean an awful blue-stocking like Louise Colet?" said Claudin.

There was a deathly silence as everybody glanced automatically at Flaubert and the enormity of his gaffe dawned on the unfortunate journalist.

"My dear fellow," said Flaubert, "you mustn't be embarrassed. That's all ancient history. My affair with Widow Colet has left no wound in me—just the memory of a long irritation."

Everybody heaved a sigh of relief.

"I'm afraid that she doesn't feel quite the same way about it as you," said Saint-Victor. "The last time I saw her she was complaining bitterly that while you'd never given her the smallest present, she'd given you a jewel she'd inherited from her mother, set in a cigar-case engraved with the motto: *Amor nel cor*. 'Imagine my indignation,' she said, 'you who have an upright character, when I read *Madame Bovary* and found a passage in which Rodolphe receives a seal bearing the motto: *Amor nel cor*. . . .'"

Flaubert lay back in his chair and howled with laughter.

"What a woman!" he groaned. "Always in a transport of passion or indignation, love or hate! And once she nearly drove me too far. I was sitting by her fireside one evening and she was screaming at me because I'd arrived a little late. She kept saying that I'd been with a whore and that I preferred that sort of woman to her. Well, after a while I'd had more than I could take. I'd noticed a log lying in the fireplace and I started measuring the distance between the log and her head. Then, all of a sudden, I saw myself in the Assize Court and heard the bench in the dock creaking under me. I got up and walked out, and never went back."

"The good lady is still as ardent and irascible as ever," said Veyne. "I heard the other day that she'd put the fear of God into the friend of some medical student she'd taken as her lover. 'What's become of that friend of yours?' she screamed at him. 'I haven't seen him for three weeks now. And at my age, with my temperament, that simply isn't healthy!'"

"She's incorrigible," laughed Flaubert, "and so easy to take in. I remember fooling her the very first time by playing the desperate melancholic on the verge of suicide—all this while I was taking her home in a cab. And I thought it was so funny that I had to keep putting my head out of the window to be able to have a good laugh."

"You were lucky that she didn't knife you like poor Karr," observed Saint-Victor.

Turgenev's shaggy white eyebrows rose a good inch.

"Do you mean to say," he asked, "that this lady has actually knifed somebody?"

"Yes—Alphonse Karr," replied Veyne. "It happened years ago, when she was pregnant by Victor Cousin, who was Minister of Education at the time. Karr wrote a venomous article in his paper congratulating the 'interesting poetess' on being about to give birth to something other than an Alexandrine, and expressing the hope that the 'venerable Minister of Education' wouldn't refuse to act as Godfather to the child. Madame Colet went straight round to his house, armed with a kitchen knife, lay in wait for him in the street, and stabbed him from behind while he was letting himself in."

"And did she kill him?"

"No. Fortunately for him, women have a very poor understanding of human anatomy. He survived, and hung the knife on the wall of his study, with an inscription reading: *Presented by Madame Colet . . . in the back.*"

"Sounds like something out of Hugo's latest novel," remarked Claudin, who was anxious to change the subject, "What do you think of the book, Flaubert—or haven't you had time to read it yet?"

"*Les Misérables?*" Flaubert's face clouded over. "Yes, I've read it, and I must say that it infuriates me: our god is going downhill. Nobody can criticise it in public without being taken for a police spy, but here at Magny's I can say what I think—that it possesses neither truth nor greatness. Where on earth will you find a prostitute like Fantine, a convict like Valjean, a bishop who asks a revolutionary for his blessing? And all those digressions, all those sermons about universal suffrage and education for the masses! No, there are some good bits in it, but on the whole it's decidedly childish."

"Yes, the book's a terrible disappointment," agreed the elder Goncourt. "The title is unjustified, the style is pompous and the plot is improbable. . . ."

"As for the characters," added Jules, "they're made of bronze or alabaster—anything but flesh and blood. All the novel does is diminish Hugo's reputation and make Balzac seem greater than ever."

"Ah, that wonderful man!" exclaimed Gautier.

"You knew him, didn't you?" asked Claudin.

"More than that—I collaborated with him! What an amazing fellow he was! I'll always remember the first time I met him, when he was about thirty-six. My heart was pounding madly, because I've never approached a great master without trembling, and all the speeches I'd prepared on the way stuck in my throat, so that all I brought out was a commonplace remark about the weather. But Balzac soon put me at my ease, and lunch with him was a feast of Rabelaisian fun and monkish joy."

"Is it true that he used to dress as a monk at home?"

Gautier nodded.

"Yes, he wore a sort of white flannel dressing-gown with a cord round the waist. Why he chose that costume I don't know—possibly as a symbol of the monastic life to which his work condemned him. In any case it suited him admirably. He was very proud, too, of the fact that he had never soiled its purity with a single inkstain, and I remember him showing me the immaculate sleeves and saying that a writer should be clean in his work."

"But he wasn't very clean in other respects," Gavarni broke in. "I once spent a few days with him at Bourg, and I was always having to spruce him up and tie his cravats. I told him one day that what he needed was a friend to wash him, dress him, and keep him clean; and he said: 'If I had a friend like that, I'd pass him on to posterity.'

"And he was so impatient, so eager to be doing something. On that journey to Bourg he kept trying to make the postilions drive faster by telling them: 'Hurry up, hurry up! This gentleman earns fifty francs a day, and I earn a hundred, so you can see that every minute counts.' And the figure went up at every posting-house. . . ."

"He could be impatient about the business of writing too," remarked Gautier, "at least when it came to writing plays. I'll never forget the time he invited me round to a room he had in the Rue de Richelieu, together with Belloy, Ourliac and Laurent-Jan. I arrived late, as usual, and he delivered a mild reproof, reminding me that I should have been there an hour before, and explaining that he had to read a five-act play the next day to Harel, the manager of the Porte-Saint-Martin.

"'So you want our opinion?' I said, settling back in my armchair in preparation for a long reading session.

"'No,' he said, 'because it isn't written.'

"'Then you'll just have to postpone the reading for six weeks,' I told him.

"'Not a bit of it,' he said. 'I've got a lot of bills falling due pretty soon, so we've got to knock off this *dramorama* to raise the wind.'

"I pointed out that we couldn't possibly write a five-act play by the following day—that there wouldn't even be time to copy it out—but he was undeterred.

"'Let me explain how it's going to be done,' he told me. 'You'll write one act, Ourliac another, Laurent-Jan the third, Belloy the fourth, I'll take care of the fifth, and at midday tomorrow I'll read

the whole play as arranged. An act doesn't contain more than four
or five hundred lines, and anybody can turn out five hundred
lines of dialogue in a day and a night.'

"'Well,' I said, rather taken aback, 'if you'll tell me what it's
about, let me have some idea how the plot develops, and sketch
out the characters for me, I'll set to work.'

"I've never seen anything like the look of astonishment and
scorn he gave me.

"'Good Lord,' he cried, 'if I've got to tell you what it's all
about, we'll never get it done!'"

In the midst of the laughter that followed, Veyne asked whether
the play had ever been written.

"Yes," replied Gautier, "but not that night, needless to say. It
was *Vautrin*, and you may remember that it was banned after a
single performance because Frédérick Lemaître wore a wig that
made him look almost as pear-shaped as Louis-Philippe."

"And did Balzac write any of the play himself?" asked Renan.
Gautier grinned.

"That I can't say," he replied. "I know that the only one of us
who really worked hard on *Vautrin* was Laurent-Jan, and he
complained later that Balzac began by calling it 'your play', then
'our play', and finally 'my play'."

"That's typical of the man," Gavarni remarked with unusual
vehemence. "He had the vanity of a commercial traveller, but he
was ignorant and credulous and stuffed full of clichés. He was a
hard man too: when Dutacq of the *Siècle* sent a poor devil who
was dying of consumption to collect Balzac's copy from Les
Jardies, he kept him waiting outside in the pouring rain for six
hours."

"All I can say is that he was always very kind to me," replied
Gautier. "He even gave me a list of recommendations for a
healthy and hygienic working life. I had to shut myself up for two
or three years, drink nothing but water, go to bed at six o'clock in
the evening, get up at midnight, work until the morning, spend
the day revising what I'd written, correcting proofs and taking
notes, and above all practise absolute chastity. When I raised a
few timid objections to that last point, recalling that the greatest

geniuses had not deprived themselves of love or pleasure, Balzac replied: 'They would have achieved much more without women.'"

"Yes," said the elder Goncourt, "he was always adamant on that subject. Lacroix told me the other day that he was quite happy playing the love game up to the point of ejaculation, but not any further. It seems that he regarded sperm as an emission of cerebral matter and a waste of creative power; and after one incident in which he forgot his theories he arrived at a friend's house complaining: 'I lost a book this morning.'"

Flaubert let out a great guffaw, but Turgenev shook his head sadly.

"I know," he said, "that some of you admire Balzac greatly, but I must confess that I have never been able to read ten pages of him at a time, I find him so repugnant and alien to me. He seems to me to be an astonishing example of a great talent existing in one and the same man side by side with a total incomprehension of artistic truth."

"I know how you feel," said Flaubert, suddenly turning serious. "I myself admire him much less than I did, because I've grown hungry for perfection, but perhaps I'm the one who's wrong. He was neither a poet nor an artist, but that didn't prevent him from being a very great man. And after all, an artist wouldn't have done so much, wouldn't have had his enormous scope."

He paused to take a gulp of wine.

"Besides," he went on, "those great men have no need to be stylists. They are strong in spite of all their faults, and because of them. I would even put forward a proposition I would hesitate to express anywhere else: namely that very great writers often write badly, and so much the better for them. We mustn't look to them for formal perfection, but to writers of the second rank."

"I don't see you rushing to Balzac's defence, Uncle Beuve," Gautier observed maliciously.

"My dear nephew," Sainte-Beuve replied, "you must remember that every critic has his favourite victim, whom he pounces on and tears to pieces in preference to every other. Mine is Balzac. . . . But perhaps I have been unfair to him. . . . Although he was intoxicated with his work and apparently so full of himself, he did know how to listen and absorb. True, what he didn't take in at a first glance, he usually missed altogether, and later reflection failed to reveal it to him, but he did absorb a great deal at that first glance. And there's no denying that he knew the corruption of his time better than any other novelist—and was just the man to add to it. What was it that Ampère said about his descriptions? 'When I've read such things, I always feel I have to wash my hands or brush my clothes.' But then, even in his best novels, Balzac has always kept something of his lowly, one might even say his sordid, beginnings. . . ."

"Sainte-Beuve," the younger Goncourt broke in angrily, "nothing you can say will alter the fact that Balzac was a genius."

The critic shrugged his shoulders disdainfully.

"All right, he was a genius if you like, but a monster."

"We are all monsters, Uncle Beuve!" said Gautier.

"And who painted the age we live in? Where can you find a picture of our society if not in Balzac?"

"But it's all imagination and invention!" Sainte-Beuve protested. "I knew that Rue Langlade he describes in one of his novels, and it wasn't a bit like that!"

"Then what novels do you read," asked Edmond, "to find reality? Madame Sand's?"

"I must say," remarked Renan, "that I find Madame Sand more realistic than Balzac."

"You can't mean that!" said Edmond de Goncourt.

"Yes, I do. The passions she depicts are universal."

"But passions are always universal!"

"And then there's Balzac's style!" said Sainte-Beuve, encouraged by Renan's support. "It's all twisted; it's a *corded* style."

"Three hundred years from now," Renan continued, "people will still be reading Madame Sand."

"As much as Madame Genlis. She won't last any more than Madame Genlis."

"Balzac was nothing but a painter of interiors," declared Claudin. "He knew more about furniture than the human heart."

"He's already rather old-fashioned," added Saint-Victor. "And what is more, he's too complicated."

"But look at Hulot! *There's* a wonderful human character for you."

"Beauty is always simple," Saint-Victor went on. "There is nothing more beautiful in all literature than the feelings of Homer's characters. They are still as fresh and youthful as the day they were created. And you must admit that Andromache is more interesting than Madame Marneffe."

"Not to me!" the Goncourt brothers exclaimed in unison.

"You can't be serious! Homer. . . ."

"Homer," Gautier interrupted, "is just a poem by Bitaubé for most Frenchmen."

"Bitaubé?" said Turgenev. "Who is Bitaubé, if you please?"

"Was, my dear Turgenev, was," corrected Gautier. "Bitaubé was an old boy who translated Homer in the last century and made him *acceptable* to the French reader. But Homer isn't anything like Bitaubé. You've only to read him in the Greek to see that. He's really terribly barbaric, all about people who *paint* themselves!"

"Besides," said the elder Goncourt, "Homer depicts nothing but physical suffering. Showing moral suffering is a different matter. I'd go so far as to say that any little psychological novel moves me more than Homer!"

"What's that you say?" Saint-Victor exclaimed incredulously.

"Yes. *Adolphe*, for instance, moves me more than Homer."

Saint-Victor flushed scarlet, and his eyes looked as if they were going to start out of his head.

"It's enough to make a man throw himself out of the window," he said, "to hear things like that. Why . . ."

"But Homer's style, Goncourt," Renan intervened in a persuasive voice. "Expressions like *the long-tailed birds*. . . ."

"Or *the unharvestable sea*," piped Sainte-Beuve. "A sea where there are no grapes! Now what could be more beautiful than that?"

"An *unharvestable sea* doesn't make sense," said Renan. "But there's a German society which has found another meaning for the phrase."

"And what's that?"

"I can't remember—but it's wonderful."

"Of course it's wonderful," shouted Saint-Victor. "All Homer's wonderful. It's one of the eternal beauties of world literature."

"But there *aren't* any eternal beauties of literature," retorted the elder Goncourt. "Schoolmasters may pretend there are, but then antiquity is their bread and butter. Why, if Homer wrote his *Iliad* today, no publisher would print it. . . ."

"And if Molière," said Jules, "offered his *Misanthrope* to the Comédie française now, they wouldn't even consider it."

"The same is true of present-day writers," Edmond went on. "Even Balzac will seem a trifle dusty in a hundred years. But now he's still fresh and exciting, and I'd rather read him than Homer any day."

"But that's blasphemy!" shrieked Saint-Victor. "Without Homer, Balzac wouldn't exist! There's no arguing about the Greeks."

"Nonsense!" retorted Edmond. "At Magny's everybody's free to argue about anything under the sun, and we refuse to be shouted down just because ours is a minority opinion."

"It's not an opinion! It's an insult to the religion of all intelligent people! Why, Homer's an article of faith for me!"

"It must be pleasant having a literary faith," said Edmond acidly. "It dispenses one from having any taste."

"Gentlemen, gentlemen!" cried Sainte-Beuve, pushing his skull-cap to the back of his head in consternation. "Let's not quarrel over the greatest of all poets! Perhaps we could reconcile all our differences by founding a Homer Club to examine the beauties of the *Odyssey* and the *Iliad*?"

He looked around the table hopefully, but the Goncourts were sitting with folded arms, gazing grimly ahead, while Saint-Victor was still fuming with rage. Clearly some other palliative would have to be discovered.

"Or better still," Sainte-Beuve continued, "let me treat you all to a little liqueur of which I think Homer himself would have approved. Charles, could you bring me that tray over there?"

The head waiter placed a tray in front of the critic, holding two bottles, a dozen or so glasses, and a decanter, and the company watched with mingled amusement and fascination while Sainte-Beuve filled the decanter from first one bottle and then the other,

tasting the resultant mixture now and then in a glass. At last he
appeared to find the golden liquid satisfactory, the glasses were
carefully filled and circulated, and the diners prepared to sample
Sainte-Beuve's offering.

"Capital!" Gautier said at last. "A subtle, almost oriental
flavour . . . oranges, I think. But what is it, Uncle Beuve?"

The old critic smiled benignly.

"I call it the *mélange About*," he replied.

"Abu Hassan?" Gautier asked mischievously.

"No, Théo, it isn't as oriental as all that. *About,* after Monsieur
Edmond About, who invented the drink. Basically it's simply a
mixture of rum and curaçao, but the secret lies in the proportions."

"Which you aren't going to divulge to us. Well, so be it. But I
think you deserve a little entertainment, Uncle Beuve, as a mark
of our appreciation. Flaubert, why don't you do your *Drawing-
Room Idiot* for Beuve while I perform the *Creditor's Dance*?"

Without waiting to be asked a second time, Flaubert promptly
turned up the collar of his jacket, rumpled what remained of his
hair, contorted his face into an expression of fatuous imbecility,
and started lumbering around the room, uttering loud grunts. In
the meantime Gautier had taken off his jacket and flung himself
into a wild dance, his long hair flying about him and sweat
pouring down his face, while the others cheered him on, and
Sainte-Beuve clapped his podgy hands in glee.

After that, anything else would have been an anticlimax, and the
company reluctantly broke up. The last to leave, as they had been
the first to arrive, were the Goncourt brothers, who had no sooner
climbed into their cab and given the driver his instructions than
they began conducting a post-mortem on the dinner.

"That was a fascinating evening," said Jules, "though a stormy
evening too. You know, Edmond, I sometimes feel that every
political argument boils down to saying: 'I have more sense than
you', every literary argument to saying: 'I have more taste than
you', and every argument about religion to saying: 'I'm a better
man than you.'"

"Yes, and have you noticed how, in every discussion, we are
always on our own and never make any converts?"

"We certainly didn't make any converts to our views on Homer! It's odd, isn't it? One may argue about the Pope, deny God, question anything, attack Heaven, the Church, the Holy Sacrament—anything except Homer! Literary religions are peculiar things."

"Especially when they have priests like Saint-Victor. The longer I know that man, the more I despise him. In spite of all his talent, he's got no opinions of his own and always toadies to consecrated opinion on every subject under the sun."

"Yes, I've considerable admiration for his work, and moments of sympathy with his personality, but I can't stand his boorish intolerance."

"Talking of boorishness, what did you think of Flaubert this evening?"

"Pathetic, quite pathetic," murmured Jules. "You know, he once told me that one of his grandfathers had married a native woman in Canada, and watching him this evening, I could well believe it. You can see something of the redskin in his appearance, his behaviour, his very tastes—a certain violence and vulgarity."

"And how provincial he is! If you take away the ox in him, the hard-working animal, the manufacturer of books at the rate of a word an hour, you find yourself left with a creature of very ordinary talent, of very little originality. Heaven knows he does his best to disguise the bourgeois resemblance of his mind to everybody else's with his loud voice and his truculent paradoxes, but it just doesn't work. The poor fellow makes himself out to be the most passionate, complicated lover in the world. . . ."

"Witness those stories he told us this evening about his affair with Colet."

"Exactly. And in fact we all know that woman plays a very minor role in his life. Again, he makes himself out to be the most extravagant of men when it comes to spending money; but in fact he hasn't any tastes to indulge, never buys a thing, and has never been known to allow a sudden whim to make a hole in his pocket. No, our good Flaubert has exactly the same ideas and tastes, habits and prejudices as the majority of men."

"'The same is true of Sainte-Beuve," said Jules. "But at least he has the honesty to admit it. He told me the other day that he was all for the ordinary, commonplace ideas—that it's better to be young than old, rich than poor, handsome than ugly. The fact is, of course, that his life has been a long regret at not having what he calls a physique, at not being irresistible to women. There's a sad, disappointed satyr at the bottom of that little old man, and he's morbidly conscious of his ugliness, his repulsiveness, and above all his age.

"He may be honest about his ideas on youth and age, but he would probably claim to be original and independent in his ideas on literature. And in fact the only writers he has ever praised are those consecrated by time, tradition or authority. Remember that so-called witticism of Royer-Collard he admired so much this evening. . . ."

"And behind all his kow-towing to the powers-that-be, there's hate and envy. Did you see his face when he was fulminating against the idea of property? He looked and spoke like one of the revolutionaries of 1792, full of a fierce destructive urge, a secret hatred for the men of power and wealth he has rubbed shoulders with for years, a terrible envy which extends even to men like Claudin who've slept with ladies—ladies in nightcaps—without having to pay."

"But I must say," remarked Edmond, "that my heart went out to him when he talked about all the conversations that were lost to history. He must have been thinking of all that he himself was going to save of his own times, of the indiscretions and anecdotes he was going to pass on to us from beyond the grave."

"And you were thinking . . ."

"Yes, I was thinking of all that *we* were going to record for the future, including what he was saying to us then and probably thought was being lost for ever."

In the gloom of the cab's interior, two pale faces turned to smile at each other, and two hands were clasped in a conspiratorial squeeze.

CHAPTER TWO

12 February 1866

DURING THE NEXT three years the Magny Dinners became an established institution, with the regular members of the club dining in the Rue Contrescarpe-Dauphine whenever they were in Paris and free of other commitments. Some of them were often away for long periods—Renan, for example, was in the Middle East for several months in 1865, doing research for his book on St. Paul—but even so, there were sometimes more would-be diners than could be accommodated in the private room at Magny's, especially as membership was extended to a few more people every year. At one point Doctor Veyne, one of the founders of the club, actually suggested transferring its meetings to the larger Restaurant Brébant, owned by Magny's brother-in-law, but Sainte-Beuve gently squashed the idea.

"I have been thinking," he wrote, "about what you said to me on the subject of the Magny Dinners. I appreciate and admit the force of your arguments. I have only one desire—to see these agreeable dinners maintained in their original circumstances; and the first location is not a matter of indifference. The spirit of a thing changes every time it is moved: witness Rome and Byzantium. . . ."

It was accordingly decided to continue dining at Magny's, at least for the time being, but one change in the original arrangements was made at an early stage. Instead of Saturday, Monday was chosen as the day on which the dinners were held, largely to suite the convenience of the three major critics—Sainte-Beuve, Gautier and Saint-Victor—who were regular diners. Since their reviews appeared at the beginning of the week, Monday was their day of rest, and Gautier would often collapse happily on to his chair at Magny's, sighing: "Well, I've earned enough to keep me alive for another week—or to bury me decently tomorrow!"

By 1866 the situation of the imperial régime in France, which
had seemed so impregnable at the beginning of the decade, was
rapidly deteriorating. Political unrest had grown enormously
during the last few years, a coalition of the régime's opponents
had polled two million votes in the 1863 elections, and the three
largest cities in France had voted solidly against the Empire.
Unfortunately for Napoleon III, his half-brother the Duc de
Morny, the architect of the *coup d'état* and the President of the
Legislative Assembly, had died in 1865, and by himself the ageing
Emperor, vacillating by nature and suffering increasingly from ill-
health, was a poor match for his opponents at home or abroad.
Just as he had underestimated the difficulties of his ill-conceived
attempt to foist a puppet emperor on Mexico, so that he now
found himself obliged to abandon the unfortunate Archduke
Maximilian to his fate, he had underestimated Prussia's strength
and mistaken her intentions, promising Bismarck French neutral-
ity in the imminent conflict between Prussia and Austria, with
what were to prove disastrous consequences.

Nothing of all this interested the *habitués* of the Restaurant
Magny, who regarded the Empire as a despicable but probably
long-lasting institution, and who had continued their work with a
sublime disregard for the political events of the day. Thus Flaubert
had begun writing his masterly study of an ineffectual anti-hero
and his times, *Sentimental Education*; the Goncourts had published
a sensitive if rather melodramatic novel, *Renée Mauperin*, about
two new social types, the emancipated young woman and the
calculating young bourgeois; and Renan had followed the
sensational success of his *Life of Jesus* with a less controversial but
no less remarkable volume on the Apostles.

At the dinner of 12 February 1866 there were two fairly recent
newcomers to Magny's, neither of whom showed as yet any more
interest in contemporary politics than the older *habitués*. One was
Hippolyte Taine, whose *History of English Literature,* expounding
his theory of *la race, le milieu et le moment,* had caused a considerable stir three years before. The Goncourts, who would later
attack him viciously in their *Journal*, ridiculing his "Protestant"
views and suggesting that he had married for money, were greatly

impressed by him at first, and praised "his kindly gaze behind his spectacles, his almost affectionate attention, his rather sickly but distinguished air, his facile, voluble, vivid conversation, full of scientific and historical notions, and the impression he gives of a young, intelligent, even witty professor, obsessed by the fear of appearing pedantic".

The other diner of recent standing was Marcelin Berthelot, a thirty-eight-year-old scientist so brilliant that the government had just created a chair in organic chemistry for him at the Collège de France, at the request of the professors of the college and the chemists of the Académie de Médecine. At this and other dinners he remained so silent that Gautier felt obliged to remind him that at Magny's everybody was supposed to compromise himself, in fairness to his fellow-members.

The diner who received the most attention, however, on this February evening, was not one of the regular members of the club, but a woman, the only member of her sex ever to be invited to attend the Magny Dinners: George Sand. The dark-eyed, top-hatted beauty of Delacroix's portrait, the tempestuous mistress of Musset and Chopin, was now a rather plump, sedate old lady of sixty-one. Her last lover, the engraver Alexandre Manceau, who had been her devoted companion for fifteen years, had died the year before, leaving her with nothing to fill her life but the sentimental novels she continued to write with unfailing facility, the elaborate puppet theatre at her country house at Nohant, and her new-born granddaughter Aurore. When she arrived at Magny's, wearing an elegant but simple dress with lace cuffs almost completely hiding her delicate little hands, she clung shyly to Flaubert's arm while he performed the necessary introductions, and at one point whispered in his ear: "You are the only person here who doesn't frighten me." But then Magny came into the room, and her eyes lit up at the sight of another familiar face.

"Monsieur Magny," she said, "you don't know how pleased I am to see you! How are you, and how is your dear wife? Please remember me kindly to her, will you, and could you ask her to send me some more of those lovely pink cigarettes she gets for me?"

Just then, Gautier, whose lips had been moving noiselessly while he looked round the room, uttered a cry of horror.

"Thirteen!" he exclaimed. "There are thirteen of us here! I can't possibly dine here this evening if we're thirteen at table!"

"Théo, my dear fellow," purred Sainte-Beuve, "you don't really mean to tell me that you believe in that superstitious nonsense?"

"Of course I do. In ghosts too, and the evil eye. I'm certainly not going to take the risk of staying here."

"Then we must do something to remove that risk. Magny, if my memory serves me aright, you have a young schoolboy son, haven't you?"

"Yes, Monsieur Sainte-Beuve; my boy Paul."

"Well then, I suggest that we allay Monsieur Gautier's fears of the figure thirteen by inviting your boy Paul to join us for dinner —that is, if you have no objections."

"None whatever, Monsieur. The boy will be honoured by the invitation."

Paul Magny was duly summoned to the dining-room, introduced to the company, and seated with Sainte-Beuve at a small side-table which was brought in specially.

"Gautier," said Veyne, "I never realised that you were so superstitious."

"Come now," cried Saint-Victor. "If you think that Gautier's superstitious, you should have seen his fellow-Romantic, old Papa Hugo, twelve years ago on Jersey."

"That was his table-turning period, wasn't it?"

Saint-Victor nodded and made a grimace.

"It was amazing how completely he fell for it," he said. "It all started with Delphine de Girardin coming to his house there and calling up the shade of his daughter Léopoldine. After that there was no holding him. He conjured up hundreds of spirits during the next year or so, including Shakespeare and Dante, Jesus and Mahomet, Marat and Charlotte Corday, not to mention the local ghost, a certain White Lady, and a few abstractions like the Novel and the Drama. Oddly enough, all the spirits, even Shakespeare and Dante, spoke to him in French, and the poets rattled off first-

rate Hugolian verse by the hour, but he never had the slightest
suspicion that he was doing it all himself. He even convinced
himself that he'd made contact with the Almighty, and Vacquerie
showed me an astonishing photograph of the old boy on which
he'd written: '*Victor Hugo listening to God*' . . ."

"I wonder whether he really does believe that," Sainte-Beuve
murmured thoughtfully. "I suspect it's all just another pose, like
his whole attitude in exile. We love the theatre in France, we love
tragedy and tragic poses, even if we don't write tragedies any
more. And posing is all that Hugo has been doing since 1851.
Instead of taking advantage of the amnesty, or not taking advantage of it but keeping quiet and leaving other exiles free to
act, he took up that tragic pose of his, draping himself in his toga
like a Cornelian hero. And that point of honour of his prevented
a lot of poor devils from taking advantage of something which
wasn't a grace but simply the restoration of a right, the right to
live in one's own country."

"But surely it's natural for him to refuse to return from exile,"
said Claudin. "After all, he's always been a liberal. . . ."

"Oh no he hasn't," objected Gautier. "Hugo wasn't a liberal
in 1830, any more than I was. That's why I always insist that it
wasn't a red waistcoat I wore on the opening night of *Hernani*, but
a pink doublet."

There were chuckles on every side, and he went on with mock
indignation:

"But it's a very important point. A red waistcoat would have
had a political meaning, signifying that I was a republican, when
in point of fact politics didn't come into it. We were simply
medievalists, every one of us, including Hugo. We were the
portcullis party, that's all. And later on, when I sang the praises
of antiquity in the Preface to *Mademoiselle Maupin*, the party broke
up. But till then it was portcullises all the way. Oh, I admit that
Uncle Beuve here has always been a liberal. But in those days Hugo
was for Louis XVII."

"Oh, come now!" Saint-Victor protested.

"Yes, Louis XVII. Nobody can tell me that Hugo cared two
hoots about all that liberal nonsense in 1828. It was in July 1830

c

that he started changing sides. But at bottom the man is still absolutely medieval. His house at Jersey was littered with his coats of arms, and he was always the Vicomte Hugo."

"Théo," said Sainte-Beuve, "do you know how Hugo and I spent the day of that first performance of *Hernani*? At two in the afternoon we went to the Théâtre-Français, climbed up into a lantern-turret, and looked down at the queue of people going into the theatre, all Hugo's troops."

"Then you must have seen me, Uncle Beuve!" said Gautier.

"We couldn't miss you, my dear fellow, in that . . ."

". . . pink doublet!" everybody chorused.

"I remember Hugo took fright for a moment," Sainte-Beuve continued. "That was when he spotted Lassailly going in, because he hadn't given him a ticket. But I told him I could vouch for Lassailly, and that calmed him down. And then we went and had dinner at Véfour's before the battle began."

"But why did you go into the theatre as early as two o'clock?" asked Claudin.

"Ah, that was the perfidious cunning of the Classicists. The official claque was usually let into the theatre an hour before the performance, and that would have been early enough for us. But we were told to arrive at two o'clock and then were locked in the theatre with eight hours to wait till the curtain went up. The Classicists probably hoped that we'd cause a disturbance and give the police an excuse to intervene."

"But you didn't, did you?"

"No, we were very patient. We played round games, we talked about the play, we sang songs and we made animal noises— anything to pass the time. Some of us had brought food and wine, and we picnicked in the pit on chocolate and bread and sausages. The Philistines said later that there was garlic in the sausages and we made the theatre stink, but I don't think that was true—after all, garlic's a classical herb. Then, after a few hours, the lights came on, and the chandelier descended and lit up. The audience started arriving, and gradually the theatre filled up. I remember that we clapped and cheered all the pretty young women, which didn't seem to please the ugly old ones. And finally the three knocks sounded, the curtain went up, showing an old duenna in a sixteenth-century bedroom, that first famous couplet was spoken with its scandalous *enjambement,* and all hell broke loose in the auditorium. . . ."

He closed his eyes for a moment, as if reliving the scene.

"Do you know," he went on, "that ten years later, when I was travelling in Spain, I came to a little town, half in ruins, with coats of arms carved above the doorways and locks on all the windows. I asked my *zagal* the name of the town, and he answered: '*Ernani.*' Those three syllables had a magical effect on me. I seemed to hear a note of Hernani's horn in the distance, and I suddenly saw before me the proud bandit himself in his leather cuirass, his green sleeves and his red breeches, Don Carlos in his golden armour, Dona Sol all pale and dressed in white, and Ruy Gomez standing in front of his ancestors' portraits. It even seemed to me that I could hear again the din of that stormy first night. . . ."

"What a night it must have been!" said Flaubert. "For me, of course, the Battle of *Hernani* was just a legend, and so indeed was Hugo himself for quite a time. You told us once, Gautier, how you felt about meeting Balzac for the first time. Well, I'll never forget the first time I saw Hugo, back in '43 at Pradier's. You see, I found to my surprise that he was a man like any other, with a rather ugly face and a fairly common appearance. He had splendid teeth and a superb forehead, but no eyelashes or eyebrows, and he was rather stiff and formal. And yet I gazed at him in awe and admiration, as if he were a casket full of gold and royal diamonds, thinking of everything that had come out of him and staring at that right hand of his that had written so many fine things. Because, after all, he was the man who had done more to make my heart throb than any other in the whole of my life, and the man whom I loved best, perhaps, of all those I didn't know. . . . And even now, I think I'd rather be Victor Hugo than anybody esle."

"Oh, you mustn't say that!" Sainte-Beuve exclaimed in a tone of shocked reproof. "In literature, you should never wish to be anybody but yourself. . . . All the same, I'd be the last to deny that Hugo has a marvellous gift for initiation. It was he who taught

me how to write poetry. And one day, at the Louvre, he taught
me about painting too, though I've forgotten it all since.

"Physically too, the man's a marvel. His barber told me once
that his beard was three times as stiff as anybody else's, and that it
nicked all his razors. He used to have the teeth of a shark, and he
could crack peach-stones with them. And his eyes! You know,
when he was writing his *Feuilles d'automne* we went up to the top of
the towers of Notre-Dame nearly every evening to watch the
sunset—not that I found that terribly amusing. Well, from up
there, he could tell the colour of the dress Marie Nodier was
wearing on the balcony of the Arsenal. . . ."

"He's still appallingly healthy," reported Saint-Victor. "The
only time he's ever been ill was eight years ago, when he had a
carbuncle on his back which kept him in bed for ten days or so.
But Vacquerie told me that he just went on writing poetry lying
on his belly, and he says that ever since the doctors cauterised his
back he's been impervious to heat or cold. The old monster
actually thinks he's invulnerable."

"And I suppose," Jules de Goncourt said sharply, "that you
and Sainte-Beuve think his genius springs from that constitution
of his?"

"I imagine it has a great deal to do with it," replied Sainte-
Beuve. "His work has an enormous vitality, the robust force of
health and temperament. Speaking for myself, of course, I prefer
intellectual power to physical strength, and Monsieur de Turenne
with thirty thousand men to Genghis Khan with all the hordes of
Asia. And Hugo's powerful talent has grown coarser and cruder
with every year that passes."

"Precisely," agreed Jules. "And my point is that while a healthy
constitution may be the strength of a man's genius, it has a
complementary defect of coarseness. The coarse vulgarity of
his health enters into his genius, and produces coarse, vulgar
writing. . . ."

"Whereas," his brother went on, "if a writer is to produce
delicate works of exquisite melancholy, and play delicious variations on the vibrant cord of the heart and soul, then he must have
a sickly side to his nature."

"Oh, come now," protested Saint-Victor, "you two have been tucking in with plenty of appetite. What do *you* think, Gautier? Surely *you* don't believe a fellow's got to be sickly to write well?"

"It depends what the Goncourts mean by being sickly. I'm all for sickliness if it means a taste for the exotic."

"You mean the inscrutable Orient, green gods and yellow women and all that sort of thing?"

"Yes," said Gautier, "the exotic in space. Or even more subtle, the exotic in time. Flaubert, for instance, would love to go to bed with a princess in Ancient Carthage; the Goncourts probably dream of copulating with an eighteenth-century courtesan, and as for me, I'd like nothing better than to make love to an Egyptian mummy. . . . Is that what you're getting at, Goncourt?"

"Not exactly," replied Edmond, "though I don't deny what you say about the eighteenth-century courtesan. No, what Jules and I feel is that gross and healthy writers—an Aristophanes or a Molière—were the ideal representatives of the gross and healthy societies they lived in, but that our tired, decadent, complicated civilisation calls for sensitive, subtle, neurotic writers. . . ."

"We feel," said Jules, "that in order to render the complexities of modern life, a writer needs to be neurotic to the point of illness, such a martyr to his nerves that he's as sensitive as a photographic plate. He should be like Heine, somewhat crucified physically."

"Oh, Heine!" snorted Sainte-Beuve. "I knew the man: he was an absolute scoundrel, an utter rogue."

There were cries of protest, and the critic covered his face with both hands.

"Did you ever hear the remark Heine made on his deathbed?" asked Saint-Victor. "His wife was praying at his bedside that God might forgive him. 'Have no fear, dear,' he said. 'He'll forgive me all right: that's his job.'"

Everybody laughed, including Sainte-Beuve, but Veyne's interest as a medical man had been aroused by the earlier argument.

"Now I come to think of it," he said, "there may be something in the Goncourts' point. I know that Michelet agrees with them.

Do you know what he said about *you* the other day, Flaubert? He said he hoped you weren't going to try to get rid of your boils, because if you did, you'd lose your talent at the same time."

"Nonsense!" said Gautier. "No, if that's what the Goncourts mean, then I beg to differ. I remember the time when sickness was all the rage among the Romantics, and every self-respecting poet had to look pale and consumptive. Well, one fine day I decided I'd had enough of that. I was a bit of a weakling, so I sent for Lecour, the athlete, and said to him: 'I'd like to have magnificent biceps, and chest-muscles like you see in bas-reliefs.' He felt my arms a bit and said: 'Yes, I think I can do that.' Every day after that, I ate five pounds of underdone mutton, drank three bottles of claret, and exercised with Lecour for two hours at a go. At that time I had a mistress who was dying of consumption. I chucked her out and got myself a big strapping wench, and put her on the same diet as me: legs of mutton, claret and dumbbells. After a while she was so tough that when I beat her up, the chair-legs broke in two on her back. As for me, I registered 520 on a try-your-strength machine once—and a new one at that! Remember that Aussandon, who crushed a bear in his arms at the Barrière du Combat when it attacked his dog, never scored more than 480!"

"I still believe," said Edmond, "that a certain sickliness is necessary in a writer in order to portray the sickly times we live in. A new style too, a new language, to replace the crude instrument handed down to us by our seventeenth-century predecessors, an instrument from which they expected only clarity, logic, approximate definition. . . ."

"We need new words," continued Jules, "to describe the indescribable new sensations which our healthy ancestors never experienced, just as we need new technical terms to identify the new facilities which their simple civilisations never knew."

"I've heard you advance that argument before," sighed Gautier. "New words for new things—that's it, isn't it? Well, you know my opinion on the subject: there just aren't any new things. What people call an invention or a discovery is simply the bringing back to light of some neglected commonplace. I imagine that Aristotle knew as much as Voltaire, and Plato as much as Monsieur Cousin. Archimedes undoubtedly discovered the secret of steam locomotion long before Salomon de Caus and Robert Fulton. If the Greeks disdained to use it, they must have had their reasons. They probably decided that people were travelling fast enough already. No, I don't feel any overwhelming need for new words, however old-fashioned and reactionary that makes me appear. Besides, your neologisms are nasty, horrid things— mixtures of Greek and slang, infusions of English and Latin, a Tower of Babel jargon coined by apothecaries and herbalists. If you *must* have new words, I'd like to see them thoroughly vetted like a candidate for the Jockey Club before they're admitted to the dictionary. I'd like the Academy to do its job properly, so that a Frenchman wouldn't have to go all the way to Russia for the pleasure of hearing his language spoken. . . ."

"Surely," said Taine, "if language and style differ from one age to another, as the Goncourts argue, they must also differ from one writer to another. I would have thought that a man's style is a very individual thing, which shows us that man feeling and acting with all the peculiar characteristics of his nature, the complexity of his emotions, the interplay of his ideas, the changing nuances of his joys and sorrows, his hopes and fears, his greatness and his weakness."

"And inimitable," interposed Sainte-Beuve. "A great writer's style should be like a great captain's horse: nobody should dare to mount it after him."

"What do *you* think, Flaubert?" asked Saint-Victor. "After all, nobody here is more dedicated to style than you."

The novelist sat hunched over the table as he weighed his words. At last he raised his head and spoke.

"I don't believe," he said, "that there should be a series of styles, each peculiar to its author, each an individual mould into which one author pours his thoughts. I believe in *style* in the singular, in other words a unique way of expressing a thing in all its colour and intensity. For me, the form of the work is the work itself: in the same way as, in human beings, the blood feeds the flesh and determines its very shape and appearance, so, for me, the inner meaning and essence of the work inevitably imposes the only correct expression of it, the measure, the rhythm, the whole finish of the form."

"You mean there's only one style for any book, whoever writes it?"

"Exactly. Whatever the thing you want to express, there's only one noun to express it, only one verb to animate it, only one adjective to qualify it. The writer has to look for them until he finds them—that noun, that adjective, that verb—and never be satisfied with approximations."

"But that could mean days of work for a single sentence!" said Claudin.

"And why not?" asked Sainte-Beuve. "I've always felt the greatest admiration for Olivier Patru for taking four years to perfect a solitary line in his translation of Cicero."

"Good for you, Sainte-Beuve!" cried Flaubert. "I'd rather see the United States perish than a principle, and I'd die like a dog rather than hasten by a single second a sentence that isn't ripe."

"Dear Flaubert," said George Sand, "I've never ceased to wonder at the way you torment yourself over your writing. When I see the agonies you go through in order to produce a novel, I feel depressed at the thought of my own facility. I tell myself that the stuff I turn out is just slipshod. . . ."

"And I for my part," said Turgenev, "confess that I don't understand some of your scruples. The care you take, for instance, to avoid using *qui* and *que*, those tiny little words which are so useful for joining phrases together. If you realised the enormous length of our Russian equivalents, you'd thank heaven for your conjunctions instead of trying to get rid of them!"

"I'm with you there, Turgenev!" cried Gautier. "I can't say that I write as easily as Dumas *père*—you know he once said that if he were put in a room with five women and a play to write, he'd write the five acts and fuck the five women within an hour—but I don't worry about my writing like Flaubert. . . . Oh, back in 1830, when I lived in the Rue du Doyenné with Houssaye and Nerval, I believed in the mission of the writer, the sacred vocation of the poet, the divinity of art. But now I know that a writer sells copy as a draper sells handkerchiefs: the only difference is that calico fetches a higher price. . . . Shall I give you an account of my working day? What wakes me up in the morning is feeling hungry and dreaming of tables groaning with food. I get up at half-past seven, have my breakfast, and enjoy a smoke, and all that takes me to eleven. Then I drag up an armchair and put paper, pen and ink on my table. In fact, I have three inks—red, green and black—to relieve the monotony of writing, because it's always bored me. I don't go fast, but I keep going at a steady pace, and I write as it comes. It's like a child: either you've made it or you haven't. I don't worry about it, because I'm not aiming at perfection, and besides, I've got my syntax tidily arranged in my head. I throw my sentences into the air like so many cats, and I know they'll fall on their feet. It's all very simple: all you need is a good grasp of syntax. I could guarantee to teach anybody to write in twenty-five lessons. . . ."

"I envy you, Théo," Flaubert said feelingly. "At times I don't know why my arms don't drop off my body with fatigue, and why my head doesn't turn into pulp. I lead a grim existence, empty of all external pleasure, an existence in which I've got nothing to sustain me but a sort of permanent rage, which never abates for a single second. I love my work with a frenzied and perverted love, as an ascetic loves the hairshirt that scratches his belly. Sometimes, when I find myself completely empty, when the words refuse to come, when, after scribbling endless pages, I find I haven't written a single sentence, I collapse on my divan and lie there dazed, sunk in a swamp of boredom. And sometimes I've shouted so loud for hours on end that I've felt something hot rising in my throat and I've been afraid of spitting blood."

"Shouted?" repeated Claudin. "Why do you have to shout?"

"Because I have to test every sentence in my *gueuloir*, by reading it at the top of my voice. You should try that yourself, Claudin. Read a page of Chateaubriand's *Martyrs* aloud and listen to the rhythm: it's like a duet for flute and violin. You can be sure that all the great works of history have survived for the same reason— the rhythm in the writing. If your prose doesn't follow the rhythm of the human lungs, then it isn't worth a damn."

"I disagree," murmured Sainte-Beuve. "You should write as

you talk—as well as you can talk, of course—otherwise you'll find yourself writing like Bossuet."

"Besides," Gautier broke in, "a book isn't meant to be read aloud. *You* hear it, Flaubert, when you try it out in your *gueuloir*, but your reader misses the spoken rhythm unless he does the same. I think perhaps the visual rhythm may be more important— making sure, for instance, that a sentence that begins slowly doesn't finish abruptly. But then, I've sometimes produced a rhythmical phrase myself without going to all the trouble you take!"

"All I can say," George Sand remarked quietly, "is that I've never worried overmuch about questions of style. The wind bloweth as it listeth through my old harp; my style has its ups and downs, its harmonies and failures. And in my heart of hearts I don't *mind*, as long as the emotions come through and my opinions are expressed."

Flaubert seized his neighbour's hand in horror.

"*Chère maître*," he moaned, "you mustn't say that! The novelist hasn't the right to express his opinion about anything at all. Has God ever stated his opinion on anything? That's why, although there are a great many things sticking in my gullet which I'd like to spit out, I swallow them down. Because what's the point of saying them? Anybody under the sun is more interesting than Monsieur Gustave Flaubert, because he's more *general* and conse- quently more typical."

"I don't see what you mean," she replied. "Are you saying that you shouldn't put any part of yourself in your books? But it seems to me that you can't put anything else. Not putting myself heart and soul and mind in my work seems to me as impossible as weeping with something other than my eyes or thinking with something other than my brain."

"Perhaps I expressed myself badly," said Flaubert. "What I meant was simply that the novelist shouldn't *express* his personal opinion on the things of this world. He can *communicate* it, but that's a different matter. He certainly mustn't point a moral. If the reader doesn't draw from a book the moral it contains, then either the reader's a fool, or the book isn't true to life. Because, as long as a thing is true, it's good. That's why obscene books aren't even immoral—they lack truth; life *simply isn't like that*!"

"If the novelist can't express his opinions or point a moral," said Claudin, "shouldn't he at least choose a subject that's beautiful and uplifting?"

Flaubert snorted impatiently.

"No, Claudin, there aren't any beautiful or uplifting subjects in literature. The artist must lift everything up himself. He's like a pump with a big tube which reaches right down into the heart of things, a tube which makes what was hidden underground burst into the sunlight. So Yvetot is as good as Constantinople, and the novelist can write about anything or nothing. In fact, what I would dearly love to write one day is precisely that—a book about nothing, a book with no external connections, which would stand up by the inner force of its style, a book which had no subject, or at least a subject which was almost invisible. . . ."

George Sand was still pondering over what he had been saying to her earlier.

"It's all right for me to *feel* with my characters, isn't it?" she asked plaintively. "Because I do get so involved in their emotions and experiences. I even dreamt of them a few years ago when I was ill, and I remember scolding them for jumping off a tower I was describing in my novel. I kept telling them it was very inconsiderate of them all to commit suicide, because I shouldn't be able to finish my book."

Flaubert smiled benignly at her under his great moustache.

"Of course it's all right for you to feel with them, my dear. I know that my own imaginary characters affect me and pursue me, or rather I live inside them. When I was describing the poisoning of Emma Bovary, I had such a taste of arsenic in my mouth, and I was so thoroughly poisoned myself, that I had two attacks of indigestion one after the other and threw up my entire dinner. . . ."

"The novelist really is a martyr to his art," the elder Goncourt observed sententiously. "When I think of all that we suffer, Flaubert, and remember how I once imagined that a novelist's life was all travel and champagne. . . . You critics"—he turned towards Gautier and Sainte-Beuve—"don't know how fortunate you are."

"So you think a critic's life is a bed of roses, do you?" Gautier said with unusual truculence. "Well, let me assure you it isn't. It calls for the constitution of an athlete and a tireless mind that's always on the alert. It means being witty on order, without ever taking account of sadness, illness or fatigue, and being witty about everything and nothing, however inane or non-existent the subject might be. It means transforming an inept play into an amusing notice while keeping all its character, and taking care not to wound the *amour-propre* of the actor—an *amour-propre* even touchier and pricklier than that of the poet. It means keeping nothing of your life or time or leisure for yourself, and combining the activity of a man of the world with the labour of a man of learning, and throwing to the wind pages of prose which would do honour to any book. But you and the public regard all that as just a frivolous amusement, a game we play to pass the time!"

"But, Théo," said Jules de Goncourt, "you can't possibly defend the critic's profession. It's like the profession of a priest or a judge: it puts an ordinary human being on a level above the rest of humanity, and it demands perfection from a man who isn't perfect."

"Not a bit of it!" protested Renan. "The critic is the humblest of men, searching diligently for the truth, doubting his luck when he finds a particle of it, and refusing to impose his findings on others as the last word on the subject."

Sainte-Beuve nodded vigorously and clapped his hands together.

"Exactly!" he piped. "A critic is really just a man who knows how to read and teaches others how to read."

"You're too modest, Sainte-Beuve," said George Sand. "I truly believe that you are probably the last of the great critics."

"Oh, criticism isn't disappearing, *chère maître*," said Flaubert. "On the contrary, its dawn has barely begun. It's simply that its nature has changed. In the time of La Harpe critics were grammarians; now they are historians. But when will they be artists, nothing but artists, real artists? When has there been a piece of criticism concerned, intensely concerned, with the work itself? The environment in which a work was produced is closely

analysed, but is the poetic impulse from which it sprang? Its
composition? Its style? The author's point of view? Never!"

"We do our best, we do our best," Sainte-Beuve murmured
soothingly. "I myself have tried to introduce into criticism a
certain charm and at the same time a greater reality—in other
words a little poetry and a little physiology. And whenever I
consider a writer, I try to blend into him, even borrowing his style
and adopting his diction. For me, criticism is a metamorphosis."

"I still think," said Edmond de Goncourt, "that criticism is the
enemy of genius, just as the newspaper is the enemy of the
book. . . ."

"Critics," said his brother, "must have been created on the
seventh day. Because if God had created them on the first day,
what on earth would they have done? Criticise *His* creation,
perhaps, before damning the creations of their fellow men?"

A slow flush spread across Sainte-Beuve's bald head.

"Criticism," he retorted softly, "as I understand it and would
like to practise it, is itself a creation, a perpetual invention. And
the critic who, in a period when public taste is undergoing a
revolution, is able to discern with precision and certainty what is
good and what is likely to survive, and whether the originality of
a new work outweighs its faults, is a genius himself."

"But without exactly damning the works of other writers,"
said Veyne, "aren't you sometimes rather severe in your judg-
ments?"

"Never," Sainte-Beuve assured him. "For me, criticism is"—he
searched for another definition—"criticism is the pleasure of
getting to know minds, not of correcting them; it is an eyeglass,
not a cane."

"What about what you wrote on Vigny?" asked Claudin. "You
were pretty hard on *him*."

"I, hard on the late lamented Alfred de Vigny?" repeated
Sainte-Beuve, opening his eyes wide in innocent amazement.
"Nonsense, my dear Claudin. I merely told the truth about him,
and people don't like the truth, writers least of all. Satire, yes, but
not the truth—the totality of qualities and defects, virtues and
vices, which make up a human personality. They want their man,

their hero, all of a piece, angel or devil, and they don't like you to
show them the dead man's face, warts and all, in a faithful mirror."

"And you showed them Vigny's warts?" said Saint-Victor. It
was more a statement of fact than a question.

Sainte-Beuve took a sip of wine, dabbed his lips with his napkin, and settled himself comfortably in his chair.

"I formulated a few reservations about Monsieur de Vigny," he
said, "based on notes taken from life at various times. Take for
example the incident which occurred one day at the Imperial
Library. It was a Friday, the day when readers are not allowed to
take books away, so that the staff may bring their records up to
date. Monsieur de Vigny presented himself at the desk all the
same and asked for a number of books. The librarian replied that
it was Friday, and no books could be issued. 'Do you know who I
am?' asked Vigny—and you should have seen the curl of his lip.
'No,' said the librarian. 'I am the Comte Alfred de Vigny.' 'What
of it?' said the librarian, and that was the end of the matter.
Though I should add that with any man of merit who had
approached him with less arrogance, the librarian would have
behaved very differently."

He paused to take another sip of wine.

"Now consider that title of his, which he was always flaunting
at people. The fact is, nobody can be sure that he was a nobleman
at all, because nobody has ever seen his family. He was a member
of the 1814 nobility, and in those days people didn't look too
closely into those matters. In Garrick's correspondence there's a
letter from a person called Vigny asking him for money, but
doing it very *nobly*, and explaining that he was doing the actor an
honour by picking him. It sounds just like one of our Vigny's
ancestors, doesn't it? And remember that whenever he used to
talk about the fortune his family had lost during the Revolution,
his mother would interrupt him to say: 'Alfred, you're forgetting
that we had nothing before the Revolution.'

"He was an angel in some ways, of course, for whom the
physical world didn't exist. Nobody, for instance, ever saw a beef-
steak in his house. When you left him at seven o'clock to go and
have dinner, he would say: 'What, are you going already?' And

he was so naïve! After he had delivered his speech to the Academy, a friend of his told him that it had struck him as rather long. 'But I'm not in the least tired!' said Vigny."

"Oh, come now!" protested Saint-Victor. "Just because the man behaved rather stupidly now and then. . . ."

"My dear Saint-Victor," the critic retorted, "you clearly feel with Horace Walpole that stupidity is like smallpox: everybody has to have it once in his lifetime. And I quite agree. But a man shouldn't suffer from it all the time, as a permanent condition, which was the case with Vigny. Look what happened every time he recommended anybody for one of our prizes at the Academy. He would bring along extracts from the book he was championing and read them aloud, putting everybody out of patience. Take your book on Livy, Taine. We had all agreed to give it the prize. Then Vigny came along, said that it was excellent, and asked the Academy's permission to read out a few passages. The first passages he quoted were an unfortunate choice, and Saint-Marc-Girardin said: 'If it's no better than that, I'm not giving it the prize.' With the result that he put that prize back a whole year.

"Mind you, I'm not denigrating the quality of his work—though he did idolise his own poetry, and, as somebody once remarked, he'd probably have called every sonnet he wrote an epic, if only he had dared. But while we praise his talent, let's see the man clearly for what he was."

"Sainte-Beuve," Jules de Goncourt said feelingly when the older man stopped speaking, "when I die, God forbid that I should be mourned by you!"

"You wouldn't know anything about it, my dear fellow," the critic replied with a bland smile. "Unless, of course, you believe in an after-life."

"An after-life!" exclaimed Gautier. "You're joking, Uncle Beuve!"

"Oh, I don't know," said Jules. "I'm never quite certain what I believe about that. I think it depends on the weather we're having, the food I'm eating and the mood I'm in. The prospect of an impersonal after-life, with all of us mixed up together, doesn't interest me, but when I think of Edmond here and our mother, the idea of personal immortality rather appeals to me."

"Except," said Edmond, "on days when we're exhausted by writing, thinking, talking and proof-correcting. Then we sometimes wonder anxiously whether we'll have to work just as hard in the next world as this."

George Sand spoke up suddenly in her clear, quiet voice.

"A friend of mine," she said, "was discussing the after-life with me shortly before he died. He complained that the first to go couldn't let those they left behind know whether they were happy and whether they could remember their friends. I said: 'Who can tell?' and we swore that whichever of us died first would appear to the other, or at least try to talk to the survivor. . . . He never came, never spoke to me. He had a tender heart and a strong will, and he always kept his word—so he must have been prevented. Perhaps it isn't allowed, or perhaps I didn't hear or understand. . . . But I'm convinced that the dead are all right, that they take a rest perhaps before coming back to life, and that they come out of the melting-pot with all the good qualities they had before, and something more besides."

"Metempsychosis, eh?" growled Flaubert. "Why not, indeed? I sometimes have a feeling that I've always existed, and I have memories that go back to the times of the Pharaohs. I can see myself very clearly at different periods of history, pursuing different occupations and enjoying varying fortunes. My present personality is the result of my past existences. I've been a boatman on the Nile, a *leno* in Rome at the time of the Punic Wars, then a Greek rhetor in the Suburra, where I was eaten up with lice. I died in the Crusades from eating too many grapes on the Syrian beaches. I've been a pirate and a monk, a tumbler and a coachman —perhaps even an Oriental emperor. . . ."

His neighbour laughed in delight.

"How lucky you are," she said, "to have such clear memories of other existences! I suspect they come from a great deal of imagination and erudition, but if *I* can't remember anything precise, I do have a feeling that I've been here before. My brother often used to say: 'When I was a dog . . .' and he thought that he'd only recently become a human being. Speaking for myself, I think I must have been a vegetable or a stone. Sometimes I don't feel sure that I exist completely, and at other times I feel an accumulated fatigue from having existed too much."

"Surely the idea of metempsychosis is an insult to God?" Veyne remarked. "It suggests that he has no more souls than the producer of a military drama has soldiers, and has to keep bringing on the same actors in different uniforms."

"For my part," murmured Sainte-Beuve, "I wouldn't want to live my life over again. There are so many doubtful, uncertain things in a man's existence, and so many difficult decisions to make, that if you come through it all without being completely destroyed, you should rest content with that."

"I entirely agree," said Taine. "My only consolation for living is the thought that it's a game that lasts only fifty or sixty years at the most, and that at the end of it there's an eternity of sleep."

"But what have you all got against the Christian doctrine of the after-life?" asked Claudin.

"It's just unthinkable!" said Gautier. "Can you imagine my soul remaining conscious of my ego after death, remembering that I wrote for the *Moniteur* at No. 13, Quai Voltaire, and that the owners of the paper were called Turgan and Dalloz?"

"Or can you imagine," asked Saint-Victor, "Monsieur Prud-homme's soul appearing in front of God wearing gold-rimmed spectacles and launching into a speech beginning: 'Architect of the Universe'?"

"We all accept the idea of unconsciousness before life," Gautier continued. "Why not after death? The old fable of the cup of water from the river Lethe—that's what it must be like. All I'm afraid of is the actual transition, the moment when my ego will enter into darkness and I shall lose the awareness of having lived."

"But in that case," complained Claudin, "what are we here for? I don't understand. . . ."

"Look, Claudin, there are bugs for which a ray of sunshine is an aurora borealis."

"No, you can't convince me. . . . I believe that there exists a great Clockmaker. . . ."

"Oh, if we're going to start on clockmaking!" groaned Gautier.

"Remember what Heine said," Saint-Victor broke in: "'We ask what the stars are, what God is, what life is. Our mouths are stopped with a lump of clay, but is that an answer?'"

"Then none of you believes in God?"

"Oh, I wouldn't say that," replied Renan. "Not in a personal God perhaps, but in some sort of divine principle."

"And how would you define this principle of yours?" asked Gautier.

"It's rather difficult to explain. How can I put it? A sort of vast, vague diffusion in which the planets are just so many globules or crab-lice. . . . Or an oyster. . . . Yes, a gigantic oyster."

"No, Renan," Edmond protested, "not an oyster! I'm not at all certain that God exists, but if he does, then he's definitely not an oyster. For one thing, an oyster isn't cruel, and God, if he exists, is cruelty itself."

"Yes," said Jules; "sometimes he strikes us as a terrifying torturer and executioner, a sort of superhuman Marquis de Sade, and sometimes as a fiendish practical joker, the sort who puts horse-hair in your bed. . . ."

"Except," continued his brother, "that his kind of joke is to make the loveliest places on earth uninhabitable, by poisoning them with fever and disease, reptiles and insects."

"But nobody can believe in God," Claudin objected, "and not believe in his goodness."

A groan went round the table.

"Oh, Claudin," said the elder Goncourt, "how can you possibly believe in a good God? Why, if he exists, he must be far more wicked, far more cruel than man! What has man invented that is bad or wicked or cruel? War and justice, that's all."

"Whereas look at your God's achievements," said Jules. "Apart from death, which is bad enough in itself, he's responsible for all the sickness, suffering, grief and torment in life. And you, Claudin, admire an omnipotent deity who uses his power to do that!"

"God gives us suffering to test our faith," Claudin asserted stoutly.

This was too much for Flaubert.

"Surely," he said, "a God who amused himself by tempting men to see how much suffering they could bear would be as cruel and stupid as a boy who knew that a may-bug was going to die, but first of all pulled its wings off, then its legs, and then its head?"

"With the difference," said Edmond, "that Claudin's God is far more ingenious in his cruelty than the nastiest little boy who ever lived. Do you remember that letter from a hunchback that you showed me at Croisset, Flaubert?"

Flaubert nodded.

"It's a letter," Goncourt explained to the others, "written by a poor devil who had grown a hump in front and behind at the age of three, had contracted an agonising skin disease, had been burnt with nitric acid and cantharides by a succession of quacks, and had finally written this horrifying description of his martyrdom. . . ."

"Which was all the more horrifying," added his brother, "in that it didn't contain a single word of complaint."

"You ought to read that letter, Claudin," Edmond went on. "It's the greatest objection I've ever encountered to the idea of Providence and a benevolent Deity. Read that letter, and you'll lose your faith straight away."

"I doubt it," retorted Claudin.

"I doubt it too," said Renan. "Claudin isn't the man to lose his faith as easily as my Englishman."

"What Englishman?" asked Taine.

"A complete stranger who came to see me the other day, and asked me in abominable French if I knew whether the Bible said that the hare was a ruminant. I said I didn't, but I got out a Hebrew Bible and finally I found the text he was asking about: 'Thou shall not eat the hare, because it ruminates.'

"'Yes,' I said, 'it's perfectly true, the Bible does say it's a ruminant.'

"'I'm delighted to hear it,' he said. 'I am not an astronomer, I am not a geologist. The things I don't know are none of my business. But I *am* a naturalist. Now since the Bible says that the hare is a ruminant, and since that isn't true, the Bible is not a book of revelation. I'm delighted, absolutely delighted!'

"And off he went, relieved at one fell swoop of his religiosity. And a happy man."

"A *happy* man?" Claudin repeated incredulously. "You think it makes a man happy to lose his faith?"

"Good heavens, yes, Claudin!" said Edmond. "A gentle scepticism is the height of human happiness and wisdom. You shouldn't believe in anything, not even your doubts. Every conviction is as stupid . . . as stupid as a Pope!"

"I simply can't agree," muttered Claudin, "that scepticism can bring a man happiness."

"Oh, Claudin," groaned Gautier, "you make me tired! Look at me! I'm a sceptic and perfectly happy. You know, the immortality of the soul, free will and all that—it's very amusing to talk about up to the age of twenty-two, but not after that. At *your* age, you ought to be giving your mind to enjoying yourself without catching the pox, arranging your life as comfortably as possible, having a few decent drawings on the wall, and above all writing well. That's the important thing: well-made sentences . . . and then a few metaphors. Yes, a few metaphors. They embellish a man's existence. . . ."

"What about *you*, Renan?" Claudin asked in desperation. "You don't think that religious belief is ridiculous, do you?"

"Claudin," said Renan, "the aim of human life is and always will be sacred. While it's true to say that intellectual culture, even at its humblest level, will one day exclude belief in the supernatural, it's also true to say that the most highly developed culture will never destroy religion in the loftiest sense of the word. Man doesn't depend on a capricious master who makes him live, die, prosper and suffer. But he does depend on the universe as a whole, which has an aim on which everything converges. Man is a subordinate being: whatever he does is an act of adoration and service. Virtue consists in contributing joyfully and eagerly to the supreme good. Evil consists in giving grudging service, like the bad soldier who curses his leader while going into battle with the rest. But the worst of men contributes more to the designs of providence by his unconscious activity than he thwarts them by his rebellious deeds."

"I don't think Claudin's any the wiser," said Saint-Victor.

"What he really wants to know is whether you believe in the divinity of Christ."

"Christ?" murmured Renan. "A good man, Claudin. A great man. Indeed, the greatest man who ever lived. But nothing more."

"Renan," Gautier exploded, "you're a coward."

"I beg your pardon?"

"I said you're a coward. I thought so when I read your *Life of Jesus*, and now you've confirmed my opinion. You're just sitting on the fence. You know the sort of book I'd have written in your place? I'd have shown Jesus as a thoroughly bad lot, leaving his parents, roaming about with a bunch of whores and petty criminals, and plotting against the government—a fellow who *deserved* to be crucified. I'd have shown him as an out-and-out socialist, attacking property and the family, fulminating against the rich; telling people to abandon their children or rather not to have any; bringing into the world the horrors of the Inquisition, persecution, the wars of religion; and killing art and stifling thought, so that the arrival of a few manuscripts from Constantinople and the discovery of a few broken statues in Italy at the time of the Renaissance was like the return of daylight and sunshine. . . . There you'd have had a book worth reading. It might be all wrong, but at least it would make sense. . . . Or else you could write a book putting the opposite point of view, the sort of book Claudin would write. But what I can't understand is a book like your *Life of Jesus*, half-way between this and that."

"Gautier, my dear fellow," said Renan, "you're much too violent in your opinions; a reader isn't convinced by violence. Besides, what would you have me say? That I believe in the divinity of Christ? But I don't. And why should I? After all, you can call yourself a disciple of Plato or of Descartes without worshipping them; so why shouldn't you call yourself a disciple of Jesus, without worshipping him, but simply regarding him as the greatest of men and the supreme moralist?"

"But Christ founded a religion, not just a philosophy."

"He did more than that, Claudin. He founded the absolute religion, a religion which excludes nothing and knows no bounds. Its symbols aren't rigid dogmas, but images susceptible of infinite variations, and whatever changes may take place in dogmas, Jesus will remain the undisputed creator of the religion of pure sentiments: the Sermon on the Mount will never be outstripped or outdated. And nothing can ever prevent us from belonging in religion to the great intellectual and moral family which bears his name. In *that* sense we are all Christians, even if some of us reject existing Christian tradition on nearly every point."

"The Sermon on the Mount!" snorted Sainte-Beuve. "A lot of nonsense! 'Blessed are the meek, for they shall inherit the earth!' It just isn't true!"

"If you reject Christianity—or Christian tradition as you put it," Saint-Victor asked, "what about deism?"

Renan pondered for a moment.

"I recognise the good sides of deism," he said at last, "and I'd give it a high place in the history of the human mind, but I can't accept it as the final formula in which all religions must meet and merge. Its very clarity will always prevent it from being a religion. You see, only something which allows a free personal choice can create a bond between one man and another. The more obvious a truth is, the less likely it is to be adopted, because proof excludes individual choice, and consequently men prefer mystery to obscurity."

"Which they've certainly got in Catholicism," remarked Edmond de Goncourt. "But you're right about people's unwillingness to accept the facts. That's why I'm convinced that science will never destroy religion. You can analyse a host and publish the results, but people will still believe they're eating the body of Christ. . . ."

"Because they want to believe it," said Jules. "They want a faith to give them comfort and consolation when things go wrong. The great strength of Catholicism is that it's a religion of sadness and misfortune, grief and sickness, while the religions of antiquity were religions of joy and celebration. As the world grew older and sadder, the ancient faiths lost ground, and the crown of roses gave place to the pocket handkerchief. Yes, that's what Catholicism is—a pocket handkerchief: it comes in useful when you cry."

"I suppose that's one reason why women love it so much," said Saint-Victor. "The faith they put in it is certainly quite extraordinary. Do you know, Prince Napoleon's chaplain told me once that on Plon-Plon's wedding night in '59, that pious child bride of his asked the Abbé for some holy water. He sent her a carafe, but a little later she asked for another, and then another. It turned out that Princess Clotilde was indefatigably sprinkling her bedroom and the other rooms of her apartment to cleanse them of the abominations she suspected her rake of a husband of having perpetrated in them."

"How touching!" purred Sainte-Beuve.

"But that isn't all. The third carafe, full of holy liquid for the following day's aspersions, was placed on the mantlepiece in the Princess's bedroom, and that night the Prince felt thirsty and poured himself a glass of water. 'This water tastes horrible,' he said, but the Princess kept mum, rejoicing in the blessed purification of her wicked bridegroom. And it must be admitted that that holy water had a miraculous effect: it purged Prince Napoleon better than any potion prescribed by his pharmacist!"

"My dear Saint-Victor," boomed Flaubert, "you shouldn't be surprised at the piety of the fair sex. With all respect to our *chère maître* here, are they not, in Proudhon's words, 'the desolation of the righteous'? Have they ever been able to do without chimeras? After love comes piety: that's only natural. When a flirt no longer has any men in her life, she turns to God. . . . In any case, there are few human beings who have no need of the supernatural. Philosophy will always be the prerogative of the aristocrats of life. Fatten the human cattle, bed them with straw up to their bellies, and even gild their stable—it will all be in vain: they'll remain brutish in spite of everything. The only progress you can hope for is to make the beasts a little less vicious. But as for elevating the ideas of the masses and giving them a broader concept of God—which means a less human concept—I'm very dubious, very dubious indeed."

"Christianity," said Sainte-Beuve in a silky voice, "is a mercury which cured the world of the pox of paganism. But the world has taken too much of it, and now it needs to be cured of the remedy. . . ."

He paused, and his eyes narrowed to thin slits.

"Do you know," he asked, "what I hate the Church for most of all—and especially Bishop Dupanloup? It's for setting up homes for pretty little girls who'd be quite happy earning a living on the streets, and making them die virgins without ever having given pleasure to a man. Oh, I'll never forgive that scoundrel Dupanloup!"

"Sainte-Beuve, you shock me," said George Sand. "I didn't think you were that sort of man."

"Oh, come now, *chère maître*," protested Flaubert, "why be so hard on old Beuve for wandering in the Cyprian groves? After all, he isn't a Jesuit or a schoolgirl. Men will always regard sexual pleasure as the most serious thing in life. Because woman, for all the members of my sex, is a Gothic archway opening on to the infinite. That may not be a very high-minded attitude, but it's fundamental to the male."

"No, I can't accept that," retorted Sand. "I'm not a Catholic, but I draw the line at monstrosities. I maintain that old men who buy young girls' bodies aren't making love, and that what they do has nothing in common with Cyprian groves, Gothic arches, the infinite, or males or females. It's something utterly unnatural, because it isn't desire that's pushing the young girl into the old man's arms, and an act in which there's neither liberty nor reciprocity is an offence against the sanctity of Nature. . . ."

There was an embarrassed silence, and a slight flush tinged the cheeks of the *bonne dame de Nohant* as she realised that she had gone too far.

"Forgive me, gentlemen," she said, getting up from her chair. "I was carried away by my feelings. I've enjoyed this evening more than I can say, but I see that it's high time I left you to your masculine discussions."

Flaubert lumbered to his feet.

"Allow me to take you home, *chère maître*," he murmured. "And don't take what you've heard here too seriously. We exaggerate everything—luckily for literature, and luckily for our individual happiness."

The others all stood up and came forward to take leave of their

guest, some—such as Renan—with affectionate admiration, and
others with impassive politeness.

After she and Flaubert had left, Magny came back into the room
with rum and curaçao for Sainte-Beuve's liqueur, and Renan
asked him if he was right in thinking that the mistress of Nohant
was an old customer of his.

"Yes, Monsieur Renan," replied the restaurateur, "I have had
the honour of knowing Madame Sand for many years, since the
time when I used to work at Philippe's."

"Was that the time when she used to dress as a man?" asked
Claudin.

Magny nodded.

"Yes, Monsieur. But she did not always wear male attire, of
course, and I remember one of my colleagues saying: 'It's funny,
Magny, but when she's dressed as a man I call her Madame, and
when she's dressed as a woman I always call her Monsieur!'"

"I only saw her wearing men's clothes once," said Sainte-
Beuve, as Magny and Charles left the room "I was asked to go to
the rooms where Buloz was living, and as I went in, a young man
jumped up from the divan to greet me. 'Hullo, friend,' he said,
'Musset knows everything. Will you take me to see the Abbé de
Lamennais?' It was Madame Sand in the throes of breaking with
Musset on her return from Venice. Just think of it—Lamennais
was still a priest at that time. But he was in Brittany just then, so I
took her to see Musset instead, after urging him to make it up
with her. . . .

"I didn't see what happened at that meeting," he added, with a
pathetically disappointed expression. "At the door of Musset's
apartment, when I asked her whether I should stay, she drew the
sword from her swordstick and said: 'No, thank you.' And I
bowed and left her."

"What a commonplace creature she is," said the younger
Goncourt. "That mechanical, monotonous voice, and that
elephantine gravity and dignity! She reminds me of those cold,
calm women in Miervelt's portraits, or perhaps the mother
superior of a Magdalen hospital. And not a gleam of light in the
sound of her voice or the colour of her speech!"

His brother shifted uneasily: Jules had been too severe for his liking.

"We ought to remember," he said, "the difficulties she has had with her children. Albéric Second was telling me the other day that when he started the *Comédie Parisienne* ten years ago, Madame Sand took out a subscription. He told Fiorentino about it when he came to see him one evening, and the Italian said: 'What, that old whore? Well, at least she'll have done one good deed before she kicks the bucket!' There was an awkward silence among Second's guests, because one of them was Madame Sand's son Maurice, whom Fiorentino didn't know. But they needn't have worried: Maurice didn't bat an eyelid."

"Her daughter's no better," said Saint-Victor, "not to mention her son-in-law Clésinger."

"The sculptor?" asked Veyne.

"The monumental mason," sneered Claudin.

"There was that splendid exchange," Jules de Goncourt recalled, "between Madame Sand and her son-in-law, when she shouted: 'I'll put you in one of my books, and everybody'll recognise you,' and he retorted: 'Then I'll do a sculpture of your backside, and everybody'll recognise that!'"

"What has always astonished me," said Edmond in the midst of his companions' laughter, "is the basic coldness which allowed her to write about her lovers when she was practically in bed with them. When Mérimée got out of her bed one day and picked up a sheet of paper lying on the table, she snatched it out of his hand; but he had time to see that it was a pen portrait she had done of him."

"But she didn't just *write* pen-portraits of her lovers," Sainte-Beuve pointed out; "she *published* them. Madame d'Agoult delivered her sometime lover Liszt to the public in *Nélida*, and Madame Sand did the same thing for Chopin in *Lucrézia*. Those good ladies aren't content with destroying their lovers and desiccating them: they have to dissect them into the bargain. As Pyat remarked of Madame Sand, she eats up her lovers like the *Tour de Nesle,* but instead of throwing them into the river afterwards, she puts them into her novels. . . ."

"Madame Sand," Renan interrupted indignantly, "is the greatest artist of our times, and the truest talent."

"Madame Sand," retorted Sainte-Beuve, "has a great soul and a perfectly enormous bottom. . . . Oh, Renan," he pleaded, as the other stood up to leave, "there's no depth in the woman, only a facile talent. She's an echo which amplifies the voice, but hasn't a voice of its own—and the voice is that of Latouche, or Musset, or Michel de Bourges, or Lamennais. For a long time I was close to the author of *Lélia*, and it was like being close to an abyss whose edge was covered with a rich and splendid vegetation. I lay there in the long grass, gazing at it in admiration. But one day I finally leaned over and looked down. *O quanta Charybdis!*"

He broke off, for he had lost his audience. The others had got up from the table and were already collecting their coats and sending out for cabs. Soon only little Paul Magny was left, with two old men, one erect and bald, the other a hunched figure with long, flowing hair.

"Uncle Beuve," Gautier murmured to his old friend, "that was unkind of you. You couldn't be just a little jealous, could you, of Sand's life of passion?"

The old critic's features quivered slightly before he regained control of himself.

"Théo," he replied sadly, "of all men I am perhaps the one who has most often been repulsed by love, and who has most often rejected friendship. In love, I had only one real and substantial success, my affair with Adèle Hugo. I am like those generals who suffer defeat after defeat, reverse after reverse, and live on the memory of a single victory, won by luck rather than merit. . . . I have never had a springtime or an autumn—just a dry, burning, sad and cruel summer, which has consumed me utterly. And you have no idea, Théo, what it means to a man to know that he will never be loved—not just because I'm old now, but because it would be ridiculous since I'm so ugly."

He slowly got to his feet, and Gautier followed suit. While the waiters went to fetch their coats, and Magny hovered in the background in readiness to escort them to their cabs, they ceremoniously took their leave of the drowsy little boy who had spent the last few hours listening in bewilderment to their conversation.

When Magny went back upstairs, he found his son sitting with his head in his arms, slumped over the little table he had been occupying with Sainte-Beuve. He was fast asleep.

"Dear Mama," the boy wrote to his mother the next day, "I am writing to say that I am happy to be able to tell you that I had six *accessits* at school and that I am going to work hard next year to win some prizes. I must also tell you that last night I had dinner with thirteen authors. I made the fourteenth because they did not want to be thirteen. I drank some white wine and some Champagne. I was a little tipsy, but I was not sick! Hugs and kisses. Your little son, Paul Magny."

CHAPTER THREE

8 October 1867

NEVER HAD PARIS been gayer, more beautiful or more brilliant than it was in the summer of 1867, when eleven million people flocked to see the Universal Exhibition which was to be the splendid swan-song of the Second Empire.

In the vast chocolate-and-gold palace built for the Exhibition on the Champ de Mars, with its six concentric galleries covering forty acres of ground, the visitors could admire such wonders of European civilisation as Millet's pictures or the new metal called aluminium, marvel at such engineering innovations as compressed-air machines and coal-extractors, and savour the delights of foreign travel by dropping into the "typical" national homes, from the Chinese pagoda and the Tyrolean hut to the Swedish log-house and the English cottage.

Most of the visitors to Paris, however, whether they came from the provinces or abroad, were less interested in the instructional displays in the Exhibition Palace than in the entertainments of various sorts provided by the *ville lumière*. When the new wedding-cake Opera designed by Charles Garnier was opened by the Emperor in August 1867, *Le Temps* thoughtfully observed that the monumental and moral centre of the city had moved from Notre-Dame in the Middle Ages to the Louvre in the Grand Siècle, and to the Hôtel de Ville under the Revolution, and now appeared to be an opera house. "Must our future glory," it asked, "consist above all else in perfecting our public entertainments? Are we no longer anything more than the capital of elegance and pleasure?" There could be no doubt about the answer the foreign visitors to Paris would have given, or that of the brothel-keepers, restaurateurs and theatre managers of the French capital.

Certainly the greatest attraction in Paris that summer after the Exhibition itself—and there were many who would have put it

first—was the Offenbach-Halévy production of *The Grand
Duchess of Gerolstein* at the Variétés, with the lovely Hortense
Schneider in the title role. Of the fifty-seven monarchs and royal
princes who visited the Exhibition, only one—the Emperor Franz
Joseph of Austria—is recorded as having failed to visit the
Variétés, and one of Schneider's less charitable rivals wittily
nicknamed her the *Passage des Princes*. The Prince of Wales—the
future King Edward VII—applied directly to Schneider for a box
as soon as he arrived in Paris, and later displayed such a close
acquaintance with the theatre's repertoire that Halévy wrote in his
diary: "*There's* a prince who will obviously govern England
well." The Tsar of Russia was even more impatient, sending a
telegram to his Ambassador from Cologne ordering a box at the
Variétés, and other eminent visitors to the theatre included
Bismarck and von Moltke. While the Prussian Chief of Staff
smiled grimly at Schneider's hit song, *Ah, que j'aime les militaires!*,
Bismarck seemed to be more interested in the operetta's satire on
petty courts such as those of the minor German states—or of
France itself—and he kept turning to von Moltke to say: "That's
it . . . that's it to a *t*!"

The Prussian party—led by King William but dominated by
the enormous Bismarck in his white Landwehr uniform—caused
a feeling of disquiet wherever they went, for it was less than a year
since Prussia had crushed the Austrian army at Sadowa, and
many Parisians had an uneasy suspicion that France had been
chosen as the next victim of the new Great Power. Prussia's chief
contribution to the Exhibition, the biggest cannon from the
Rhine fortifications, did nothing to dispel this disquiet, and
Charivari published an ominous cartoon showing an Exhibition
attendant vainly reminding an armed and helmeted Prussia that
"Weapons are to be left in the cloakroom". Another sinister
omen, which cast a chill over Paris at the beginning of July, was the
news that France's *protégé* in Mexico, the Emperor Maximilian, had
been shot on the orders of Benito Juarez. Small wonder that Prosper
Mérimée noted that "everyone is afraid, without really knowing
why", or that another observer compared the Universal Exhibition
to a dazzling meteor in a sky about to be torn by a thunderstorm.

Meanwhile, the distinguished company of writers and savants who made up the Magny dining club continued to meet at the little restaurant every other Monday. Three of their number had received honours from the imperial Government in the last two years, thanks to the support of that well-meaning if somewhat overbearing patroness of letters, Princess Mathilde: Flaubert had been made a Chevalier of the Legion of Honour, as had also the elder Goncourt—the Government, unlike the midwife Maria, apparently refused to regard the two brothers as one—while Sainte-Beuve had at last achieved his ambition to become a Senator. In his first contribution to the Senate's debates, in March 1867, and again in his maiden speech in June, he had stoutly defended a fellow *habitué* of Magny's, Ernest Renan, against the clerical party, describing Renan as "a man of principle whose friendship I honour", and declaring that there were "certain respectable philosophic views which I defend in the name of freedom of thought and which I shall never allow to be attacked without protesting". After that, all Paris was ready to accept Arsène Houssaye's description of the Magny gatherings as "the Atheists' Dinners".

The man for whom the Magny Dinners had been initiated, Gavarni, had died in November 1866, but two new members had been elected to the club: Doctor Charles Robin, the Professor of Histology at the University of Paris, and Charles-Edmond—by his real name Charles-Edmond Chojecki—a charming playwright and journalist whose friendship with Prince Napoleon had led to his appointment as Librarian of the Senate. During the summer the more eminent *habitués* had been absent at various times, and it was not until 8 October that nearly all of them gathered together once more in the Rue Contrescarpe-Dauphine, now renamed the Rue Mazet after a French doctor who had died in 1821.

The conversation when they sat down to dinner was all about the Exhibition, which was due to close in another three weeks. Gautier in particular was enthusiastic about the Exhibition Palace, which more critical observers had likened to an enormous gasometer.

"I went right up to the ceiling in a hydraulic lift one day," he told the company, "and imagined that I'd been transplanted to an ancient arena. Looking down, I visualised gladiators doing battle below, and chariots thundering over the floor."

"I hated it," said Jules de Goncourt. "To me it represented the final stage in the Americanisation of Paris, the victory of Industry over Art, the triumph of the steam-driven thresher over the painting—in a word, the Federation of Matter."

"The only thing we really liked," said his brother, "was the unwrapping of that Egyptian mummy we watched with you, Robin. Why don't you tell the others about it?"

"No, *you* tell them, Goncourt. You're much better at that sort of thing."

The elder Goncourt breathed a little sigh of pleasure and settled back happily in his chair.

"It was quite fantastic, gentlemen," he began. "We were in a big room above the Egyptian *okel*, with the sunlight falling through the lacework windows and forming arabesques on the sarcophagi lying all around us. There was quite a crowd of us there, gathered round the table on which there was the mummy Mariette was going to unwrap, a mummy two thousand four hundred years old.

"Mariette's assistants started unwinding the rolls of linen, a task which seemed to go on for hours. At one point, to hurry things up, they stood the mummy on her feet, which struck the floor with a sharp noise as if they were made of wood, and spun her around in a hideous dance. Then they put her back on the table and went on removing the last of the yellow wrappings. The first thing they found was a sweet-smelling flower in one of the armpits, then a green scarab, and then a gold plaque with an inscription which Mariette said was a prayer for her heart and entrails to be reunited with her body at the end of time. . . ."

"But what did the body look like when they unwrapped it?" Saint-Victor asked impatiently.

"The flesh was black—absolutely black. That was quite a shock to us, or at least to me, because I somehow expected the body to be as fresh as the wrappings around it. Little by little the pincers and knives stripped the flat, sexless chest and belly and exposed the hands with their gilded finger nails modestly folded over the pubis. . . ."

"Dumas *fils* was there," Jules broke in, "representing the spirit of modern times, and at that point you could see him searching for some witty remark. But he couldn't think of anything to say, and went out in a huff just as the last coverings were being taken off the mummy's face."

"The eyes were made of enamel," Edmond continued, "and looked quite startling in that black face, and there was a gold leaf smile on the lips. But the most touching thing was the hair—little strands of it stuck to the forehead as if it were still wet with the sweat of the death-agony. And there she lay, a poor, naked little corpse exposed to the daylight and our profane eyes, while we stood around laughing and smoking and chatting. I don't know about Robin and Berthelot, but the two of us felt sad and a little ashamed."

"I suppose *you* didn't find time to see the Exhibition, Flaubert?" said Saint-Victor.

The master of Croisset looked up from his plate and nodded his head.

"Yes, I did. I saw it twice in the spring, and was utterly overwhelmed. There are a lot of splendid things there, but a man would have to know all the arts and sciences to take an interest in everything there is to see on the Champs de Mars. And then, the whole thing is so colossal. Everything in Paris is growing out of all proportion. I sometimes think we're moving towards a new Babylon."

"It has always seemed unfair to me," said Taine, "that Paris should dominate France so completely, in a way that London doesn't dominate England, nor Berlin Germany. It absorbs everything, attracts everything, does everything in this country, and I sometimes think that France is doomed to die of a cerebral haemorrhage. Paris makes me think of Alexandria in its hey-day: admittedly Alexandria had the valley of the Nile dangling below it, but it was a dead valley."

"There I take issue with you," murmured Renan. "I yield to no one in my love and admiration for this extraordinary centre of

D

life and thought which bears the name of Paris. Paris is the *raison d'être* of France, a prodigious permanent exhibition of all that is most excellent in this country."

"You call it a centre of life and thought? *Now*, in 1867? A centre of frivolity and immorality would be nearer to the truth."

"Oh, our age isn't any more frivolous than others. And the superior man who wishes his fellows well has always had to lend himself to the weaknesses of the mob. If you want to serve mankind you have to lower yourself to its level, speak its language, adopt its prejudices, go with it into the workshop and the tavern. As for the immorality of our times, better an immoral people than a fanatical people, because the masses do no harm when they are immoral, but when they are fanatical they reduce the world to stupidity and bestiality."

"But you can't possibly admire this crazy, frivolous society with its tin-pot Emperor and its comic-opera Court. Why, even Turgenev here finds it more than he can stomach."

"That's true," agreed the Russian. "The last official ceremony I attended here was simply ludicrous. The red, yellow and gold headgear of the lawyers and judges had such a comical pseudo-Oriental look that I could have died laughing. And all the ribbons, medals, gold braid, helmets and plumes! To think that all that flummery impresses people! What am I saying? Why, it rules the world!"

"It's scarcely surprising," said Saint-Victor, "that we should have a comic-opera Court when you remember that it was all designed by Morny, the power behind both Napoleon and Offenbach. Did you know that when he was presiding over the Chamber and had just reproved some opposition speaker—Jules Favre, for instance—he would signal to Halévy to come round to his office. There he'd say to him: 'What if we changed the third scene and had the comic come in through the cupboard instead of the door?' 'Why, Monsieur le Duc,' Halévy would say, 'what a splendid idea!' And there you had the man—a writer for the Bouffes-Parisiens dressed up as a statesman!"

"You're right," said Edmond de Goncourt. "I was talking to that young fellow Daudet who brought out those charming

Provençal stories last year, and he told me of an incident like that
which happened when he was Morny's secretary. He'd arrived one
morning with a comic Negro song that Morny had asked him to
write, and in the excitement of the first hearing, the duke's official
visitors were completely forgotten. So that while Daudet, the
composer L'Épine and Morny himself were all three jumping
about on stools and singing: '*Zim boom, zim badaboom*' at the
tops of their voices, the Ministers of the Interior and Police sat
twiddling their thumbs outside."

"Oh, just because Morny took an interest in the theatre," said
Robin, "you shouldn't sneer at him. You can gauge a man's
intelligence by the weight of his brain—a good brain weighs anything between 1·350 grammes and 1·400, while a brain that weighs
only 1·100 grammes nearly always belonged to an idiot. Well,
when we removed Morny's brain, we found that it weighed
1·600 grammes!"

"Besides," said Claudin, "I don't understand what you've all
got against operettas. Anybody who's heard Schneider sing or
laughed at that wonderful comic Bache . . ."

"Bache?" said Saint-Victor, looking up sharply. "Don't
mention that name in my hearing! Haven't I told you the story of
the trick he played on the Mayor of Hauvrincourt—and in this
very restaurant, as Magny here will confirm?"

Magny nodded gravely, and the others clamoured for the story.

"I heard about it last summer," began Saint-Victor, "when I
was on holiday at Hauvrincourt. I happened to make the acquaintance of the local mayor, found that he did a little writing in his
spare time, and rashly asked him why he hadn't tried to follow a
literary career in Paris. He explained to me that he had, but
without success, and poured out the whole sorry tale.

"It turned out that on a visit to Paris he had met an old
school friend of his from Hauvrincourt who was employed in
comic roles at a little theatre where he had obtained a certain
notoriety. . . ."

"Bache!" chorused the others.

"Exactly. Bache the skeletal Styx of *Orpheus in the Underworld*,
Bache the eccentric who takes his own knife to dinner-parties,

Bache the greatest practical joker in town. The poor Mayor, of
course, didn't know the reputation he enjoyed in Paris—he only
remembered the little schoolboy he had known at home—and so
he told Bache about his literary ambitions and the five-act drama
in verse that he was writing. Bache asked to see the part he had
already written, went into ecstasies over it, and declared that it
must be presented to the public at all costs. And when the Mayor
asked how this might be arranged, the actor suggested inviting the
leading playwrights and critics of Paris to a dinner at Magny's,
where he could read extracts from his play to them and thus
convince them of its quality."

A groan went round the table.

"I see that you've guessed the nature of the deception perpetrated on the unfortunate Mayor," said Saint-Victor. "But you
have yet to learn the identity of the eminent personalities whom
Bache proposed to invite.

"'First,' he said, 'we'll have Sainte-Beuve. . . . He never goes to
the theatre, but he'll give you some very good advice. . . . And
Jules Janin? Why not? Admittedly he usually goes to sleep over
dessert, but we'll put Paul de Saint-Victor next to him to keep him
awake. Then we'll invite Dennery, the king of the boulevard
theatre, and Théophile Gautier. . . . He can't refuse me anything,
because he's got me to thank for the success of his *Pierrot posthume*
at the Vaudeville. . . .'"

An unintelligible expletive came from Gautier's direction.

"'Then let's have Sardou—he's my prize personality, and I
don't lay him on very often, but this is a special occasion. . . . And
Edmond About, Voltaire's grandson. . . . And how about a
Dumas? . . . Why not both?—You mustn't be greedy, old chap,
you can only have one at a time. . . . And finally, to make everything absolutely certain, the master of masters, the incomparable
Scribe. . . .'

"Well, the Mayor agreed to all Bache's suggestions—who
wouldn't, in his position?—and Bache for his part produced all
the promised playwrights and critics on the appointed day."

"*All* of them?" asked Gautier in a strangled voice.

"All of them. All the princes of the press and monarchs of the stage. And do you know who sat next to the Mayor of Hauvrin-court? Scribe on his right hand and Théophile Gautier on his left! Admittedly when he questioned the great dramatist about his working methods, all that Scribe said was that he couldn't write a line until he'd played two or three games of piquet. And when he asked the great critic what had happened to his Merovingian locks, Gautier laughed at his provincial simplicity and admitted that his abundant hair was really just a wig."

A low moaning sound came from further down the table.

"Worse still, when the budding dramatist started reading his play after dinner, half the eminent guests fell asleep, and the others quietly slipped out of the room. Finally, in desperation, the Mayor went out into the corridor and started questioning the waiters. Where was Monsieur Scribe?—Monsieur Scribe hadn't dined at Magny's that evening. . . . But he had been sitting next to Monsieur Jules Janin!—Monsieur Jules Janin was dining with friends in Room Number Five. . . . Then had anybody seen Monsieur Dennery?—Monsieur Dennery was in Antibes. . . ."

"Did it dawn on the poor wretch that he had been tricked?"

"Only when he staggered back into the dining-room. There were only two people left—Saint-Victor, who was fast asleep and snoring loudly, and Théophile Gautier, who was savouring his eleventh brandy. The Mayor tapped the critic on the shoulder and asked the fateful question: 'What do you think of my play, Monsieur Gautier?'—To which the furry-tongued, heavy-headed critic made the immortal reply: 'I'm not Gautier. . . . I'm Bigouroux. . . . Who the hell are you?'"

Magny, who had been listening with growing embarrassment to Saint-Victor's story, stepped forward, coughed discreetly, and said:

"Gentlemen, I regret to say that I can bear out all that Monsieur de Saint-Victor has just told you. On the occasion in question I confess that I was astonished to overhear Monsieur Bache addressing gentlemen who were strangers to this establishment by the names of some of my most distinguished customers. However, I dismissed the whole affair as simply one of Monsieur Bache's practical jokes, and I sincerely hope that nobody here has been inconvenienced or embarrassed through any fault of mine."

He gave a stiff bow and limped swiftly out of the room.

"Just let me get my hands on Bache!" roared Gautier. "And on Bigouroux too! Send for my great knife with the ivory handle, and I'll open their bellies, take out their entrails, and slowly unwind them till they reach down to the Seine!"

"I don't care what you say about Bache," muttered Claudin, "I still think he's a marvellous artiste. I've lost count of the number of times I've been to see him in *Orpheus in the Underworld*."

"You surprise me, Claudin," said Edmond de Goncourt. "I would have thought you'd have disapproved of that sort of operetta, and protested with Janin at such a 'profanation of holy and glorious antiquity'. . . ."

"Or joined with Léo Lespès," added Jules, "who went home from the Bouffes to 'console himself with his old Homer'— Lespès who doesn't know a word of Greek!"

Saint-Victor coloured up.

"The same can't be said of any of us here," he snapped, "and I for one don't like the present-day mockery of antiquity—or your sneers at Homer either."

"After all," remarked Taine, "no nation on earth has done more for human civilisation than the Ancient Greeks, and no race on earth has formed a saner concept of life and the universe."

"Oh, come now," said the Goncourts with one voice.

Taine adjusted his pince-nez firmly on his nose and gazed sternly at the brothers.

"What I have just said," he retorted, "is beyond dispute. The Ancient Greeks were exempt from the moral deformation which the grandeur of religion or the State impose on human nature. Everywhere else, civilisation has disturbed the natural equilibrium of the faculties, oppressing some and developing others. It has sacrificed the present life to the future life, man to God, the individual to the State. It has made the Indian fakir, the Egyptian or Chinese functionary, the Roman jurist, the medieval monk, the modern citizen and bourgeois. And under that pressure man has been alternately crushed and intoxicated. He has either become a cog in a vast machine, or considered himself a cipher in the face of infinity. But in Ancient Greece he subordinated his institutions to himself, instead of subordinating himself to his institutions."

"As for Homer," said Sainte-Beuve, pressing home the classical attack on the two modernists, "to love and admire his work is to rise above all literary superstitions and all the barbaric crudities in common admiration."

"But you all admire Homer," said the elder Goncourt, "simply because he comes at the beginning of world literature. . . ."

"Which," said Jules, "is rather like proclaiming primitive man, the antediluvian troglodyte drawing animals on cave walls, a greater artist than da Vinci."

Saint-Victor threw up his hands in despair.

"It's hopeless," he groaned, "to try to convince you of Homer's greatness. But if you can't appreciate Greek literature, what about Greek art and architecture?"

"Greek architecture is absolutely contrary to Nature," declared Edmond. "It's based on the straight line, and the straight line doesn't exist in Nature; it's a human invention."

"And Greek art," said Jules, "is utterly boring—a photographic deification of the human body, the product of a materialistic civilisation."

"No," murmured Renan, "it's a mistake to level the charge of materialism at the Greeks. Antiquity was neither materialistic nor idealistic: it was human. Life in Ancient Greece had no opening on to the infinite; it was all rest and peace, with images of happiness and pleasure on every side. And that isn't enough for us any more; we can no longer imagine life without sadness. With our thirst for the infinite we find the Greeks' limited art and simple morality cold and boring, we grow tired of their sense of proportion and their perfect taste; we long for the strange, the superhuman, the supernatural."

"Not I, Renan," said Gautier playfully. "I just love those Greek statues with their innocent little cocks, and their tiny balls like a couple of olives."

"I have reservations, though," said Veyne, "about their female statues with the pubis shaved."

"That's because they used courtesans as their models," explained

Saint-Victor, "and they were obliged to shave their bodies."

"Horrible!" exclaimed Saint-Beuve. "And I understand that depilation is still imposed on women in the Orient. A barbaric practice! A mutilation!"

"And unattractive into the bargain," admitted Saint-Victor. "It must look like a priest's chin!"

"Fortunately," said Charles-Edmond, "we treat our prostitutes nowadays in a much more civilised way. We house them, license them, pay them, look after them—*and* we allow them to keep their pubic hairs. What more could they want?"

"Nonsense!" retorted Sainte-Beuve. "The poor creatures are hounded from pillar to post by the wretched police. Their lives are made quite impossible by the so-called vice brigade. It's high time that somebody stood up in the Legislative Body and spoke in their defence."

"Good for you, Uncle Beuve!" cried Gautier. "I've always considered that prostitution was the natural state of woman."

"And an admirable institution as well!" boomed Flaubert. 'If there's one thing I hate in a man—apart from an admiration for Béranger, perfumes, and a fringe beard—it's an aversion to brothels. I've known dozens of worthy young men who had a pious horror of 'houses of ill-fame' and yet picked up the loveliest cases of clap you can imagine from their so-called mistresses. It may be a perverse taste, but I love prostitution—and for its own sake, quite apart from what lies beneath. I've never been able to see one of those women in a low-cut dress walking in the rain under the gas-lamps without my heart beating faster, just as the sight of a monk in a robe and a knotted girdle touches some deep ascetic corner of my soul. The idea of prostitution is a meeting point of so many elements—lechery, bitterness, the futility of human relationships, physical frenzy and the clink of gold—that a glance into its depths makes you dizzy and teaches you so much! It makes you so sad, and fills you with such dreams of love!"

"But one can live a full life," suggested Claudin, "without frequenting prostitutes."

"No, you can't!" thundered Flaubert. "A man has missed something if he has never woken up in an anonymous bed beside a face he'll never see again, and if he has never left a brothel at dawn feeling like jumping off a bridge into the river out of sheer physical disgust with life. If there's nothing else, there's something about their shameless clothes, the temptation of the unknown, the age-old poetry of venality and corruption! During the first years I was in Paris, I used to sit outside Tortoni's on hot summer evenings, admiring the sunset and watching the street-walkers pass by. At times like that I used to bubble over with Biblical poetry. I used to think of Isaiah, of 'fornication in high places', and I walked back along the Rue de La Harpe repeating the verse: 'And her mouth is smoother than oil.'"

"Flaubert's right," the elder Goncourt declared sententiously. "I find nothing repugnant in prostitution—on the contrary. Prostitutes relieve the monotony of decent society, the dullness of propriety and morality. They put a little madness into the world and slap the banknote on both cheeks. . . ."

"They are naked, unbridled caprice," Jules continued, "free and victorious, in a world of sober-sided lawyers and measured joys."

"My only complaint about prostitution," remarked Flaubert, "is that it no longer exists. The kept woman has invaded the field of debauchery, just as the journalist has invaded poetry, and there are no more courtesans, only varieties of semi-prostitutes."

"Don't you believe it, Flaubert," said Robin. "At the latest count there were about eighty thousand registered prostitutes in Paris, and the number's constantly increasing."

"Yes," agreed Charles-Edmond, "I was chatting to a tart only today who complained to me that her business was being ruined by the railways. 'Imagine a country girl,' she said, 'who's bored with life. She saves up to buy a railway ticket, comes to Paris, and gets a job as a maid to an old gentleman. The old gentleman does her up and gives her a few francs for her trouble, and she buys herself a silk dress with the money. The first time she goes for a walk on the boulevard in her new dress she picks up a twenty-franc man. And on her way home she tells herself she's a fool to work as a parlour-maid for twenty francs a month when she can earn twenty francs any evening on her back. So she saves up again to rent a hotel room for a week. She takes the room, gets a

dressmaker to rig her out on tick, goes off to the Bal Mabille—
and there's another one in circulation!'"

"I understand," said Edmond, "that there are hundreds of male
prostitutes at work in Paris too. Lagier was telling me of one
called André who dresses up as a woman and makes 1,800 francs
during the season of Opera balls."

"Ah," said Sainte-Beuve, "now *that* sort of thing can be terribly
confusing. I remember one day meeting a tightrope walker and
going to her rooms. I started fumbling up her skirts, and she said:
'You won't love me any more.' And then I found something. . . ."

"What did you do?" asked Saint-Victor.

"Oh, I pretended that I wasn't surprised. In a case like that, you
know, you must never look surprised. . . . I didn't walk out on her
straight away, but stayed on to make conversation, and I even
promised to come back. . . . Odd, isn't it: whenever I saw her in
the street after that, I always bowed to her as I would to a woman.'

"Those poor creatures have their problems like anyone else,"
observed Veyne. "They make their bosoms out of sheep's lights,
you know, boiling them first and then cutting them into the
required shapes. Well, one of them complained to me the other
day that a cat had eaten one of his breasts which he'd left to cool
down in his attic."

"The very thought of people like that makes me sick," snorted
Claudin.

"My dear boy," Sainte-Beuve said in his suavest voice, "it is
just as natural to feel and even express attraction towards a man
as towards a woman. I remember one day when I was coming out
of the Academy, I saw a young man, a charming young man,
in the street. . . . Well, if I had been in Ancient Greece, I'd have
gone after him just as you go after a woman."

"What I'd like to know," grumbled Flaubert, "is where the
good old-fashioned brothels have gone?"

"Oh, they still exist," Charles-Edmond assured him, "with
prices to suit every pocket. Bracquemond actually told me
recently of a military brothel he visited at Vincennes where the
charge was only four sous a time."

"And what were the women like?" somebody asked.

"He never found out. The place was a barn with a ladder leading up to the loft. Bracquemond climbed the ladder, but when his head came level with the floor of the loft, and he saw twenty military backsides all going up and down in the hay, his heart failed him and he fled."

"That sounds just the place for a boot-shaker," said Robin.

"For a what?" asked several voices.

"A boot-shaker. It's a profession I heard about at the Prefecture of Police. They had a lad of twenty there some time ago applying for a passport, and when they asked him for his occupation he said he was a boot-shaker. They didn't know what that was any more than you do, and they asked him to explain. 'You know,' he said, 'they've got one in every brothel. . . . Ain't you never been to a brothel? . . . When you don't want to pay, and they says as how they'll send for the pimps, and you hear boots clattering on the stairs outside, that's no pimps . . . that's me with a pair of boots and a bit of string.'"

There was a roar of laughter from Robin's listeners, but Jules de Goncourt shook his head impatiently.

"You can laugh," he said, "but our brothels are wretched places, even when you've got a bed instead of a hayloft and there's no boot-shaker on the stairs. I went to Farcy's some time ago— the best-known brothel in Paris, the paradise foreign diplomats talk about as if it were a dream out of the *Arabian Nights*. God, what a place! The drawing-room is like a dentist's waiting-room, with floral wallpaper, red velvet divans, a couple of cupids on the ceiling, and on the mantelpiece an imitation bronze of a young man feeding a goat. The women lie sprawling on the divans, cooing at you and begging you for a drink. And the bedroom I went to looked like a room in a broken-down inn in a small country town where the coaches don't stop any more. . . ."

"You must admit," his brother continued, "that we aren't very particular about the setting for our pleasures. I may criticise the Ancients on some scores, but at least their brothels were palaces, with fountains and flowers, paintings and baths, a whole décor calculated to charm and excite you. Whereas our nineteenth-century senses have to make do with a seedy little hotel. Why, if

Montmartre were *vesuvified* tomorrow, and dug up like Pompeii
centuries from now, posterity would take us for a nation of
porters bedding kitchenmaids in a setting from a Paul de Kock
novel."

"You're right, Goncourt," replied Charles-Edmond. "But why
should we confine ourselves to improving the décor? Instead of
the same old horsemeat, why shouldn't our brothels be staffed with
girls from every country in the world—Japan, China, America,
India?"

"And Egypt, I hope!" boomed Flaubert, flushed with wine and
enthusiasm. "Because the most intense physical sensation I've
ever experienced was with an Egyptian courtesan. . . . Imagine it
for yourselves. . . . On a pitch-black night, to the barking of dogs
that want to tear you limb from limb, you're led through an
Egyptian village to a low-roofed hut. Inside, right at the back, you
find a woman in a shift lying on the ground, a woman with a heavy
gold chain twined seven or eight times round her body, a woman
with buttocks like ice and a brazier inside. And with that woman,
who couples without moving, you experience infinite pleasure,
indescribable joy. . . ."

"That's just literature!" said a voice.

Turgenev had closed his eyes while Flaubert was speaking. Now
he opened them and smiled gently at the French novelist.

"Shall I tell you the most intense moment in *my* life?" he asked.
"It was in Russia, with a young woman I had courted in my youth,
and who had married someone else. I had returned home one
July after eight years in Germany, and I was staying at her
mother's house for the three days of balls and parties her mother
was giving to celebrate her birthday. She was staying at the house
too, but without her husband, who was something of a hypo-
chondriac and had been left at home.

"One evening I invited her to dance a mazurka with me and
she accepted, but then I suggested we should sit the dance out
instead. Next to the ballroom there was a series of rooms where
people were playing whist, and farther on, some more rooms
which were lit only by the moon, and where dancers were always
coming in and out. We sat down on a divan in one of those rooms,

facing an open window. Every now and then a group of dancers came into the room, spun around, and disappeared.

"All of a sudden the woman turned towards me and looked at me with her huge eyes. The next moment—and heaven knows how it happened, because I had to be unbuttoned and her skirts pulled up—she was on me and she was mine. I can still remember our teeth meeting as we kissed, the touch of her icy lips, the burning heat of all the lower part of her body. Then she had gone, and I ran out into the garden to get some air and cool my face in the wind.

"The next day I was told she had left. I saw her again, years later, on several occasions, but I never dared to mention that evening. Sometimes I even wonder if it ever happened. . . ."

There was a long silence, broken by a laugh from Charles-Edmond.

"Well, that settles it!" he said. "We'll have an Egyptian girl *and* a Russian in our ideal brothel! Any other suggestions?"

"How about some geisha girls from Japan?" asked Robin. "They're the only women of the Orient with the sort of liveliness and gaiety and love of pleasure that we appreciate in the West."

"But they're far too complicated," objected Saint-Victor. "A Japanese of my acquaintance told me once that nobody in his country could ever be so vulgar as to tell a woman that he loved her. All that etiquette allows a Japanese to say to the woman he loves is that he longs to occupy the place of the mandarin duck beside her—the mandarin duck being the Japanese love-bird. And I imagine that geisha girls can be a little difficult too."

"I'd certainly advise against having any Spanish girls," said Robin. "They tend to be rather emotional. An attaché at the Spanish embassy was telling me the other day that they have a statue of Saint Antony, a *San Antonio*, in every Spanish brothel. When there are plenty of customers, the girls say prayers to the saint, genuflect to him, offer up thanks to him. But if the men stay away, they break off one of his fingers, then one of his arms, and finally, if the run of bad luck continues, flush him down the latrines and buy another."

"On reflection," remarked Veyne, "I don't think there's any

future for the brothel, even if it's redecorated and re-staffed. Tarts are becoming much more independent. Only last week a little girl in the street offered me her sister, a child of fourteen. Her job was apparently to breathe on the windows of the carriage so that the police couldn't see inside."

"Tarts are also becoming richer," said Jules de Goncourt. "A young cousin of ours who came to see us this morning had a rendezvous with a cocotte who was going to take him out to Asnières in her carriage. Apparently there now exists a type of high-class prostitute who finds her custom among adolescent schoolboys, emptying their wallets and building up a stock of men who'll keep her in later years. . . ."

"After the boy had gone," Edmond went on, "we discussed the course that love had taken during our three generations. At our cousin's age, I had a girl who stitched shoes for a living. Jules had a tart who always had a few sous hidden away in her chest of drawers. And this youngster has a woman who keeps her own carriage and horses. And there you have the three periods we've lived through: the July Monarchy, the 1848 Republic, and the Second Empire."

"The explanation is simple," said Veyne. "Money has become the be-all and end-all of our society. Have you noticed that in every marriage settlement nowadays the dowry is given in trust? Well, there you've got another symptom of our times. The present-day father and mother are perfectly willing to hand over their daughter's body, health and happiness to a suitable suitor, but they insist on keeping control of her money."

"You can see the same symptom in the theatre," observed the elder Goncourt. "Look at the plays of other times and other countries, and you'll find dramatic conflicts about anything and everything—except money. Look at our present-day theatre, and you'll find that money is the subject of every play, and a financial document—a marriage contract or a will—the device used in every *coup de théâtre*."

"I'm sorry to say that I have to agree with you," remarked Robin. "Money is such a force nowadays that people will stoop to anything to get it, provided the price is high enough."

"That may be true of the lower classes," said Saint-Victor, "but there are limits to what a person of breeding and education will do, just to line his pockets."

"That's nonsense," retorted Flaubert, "and I'll prove it. Let me tell you a story about Hoppe—you know, the Dutch banker who died back in '55—which I heard from his lawyer the other day. . . . It seems that Hoppe took a fancy to a married woman and made her his mistress, but he wanted to enjoy her in peace and quiet whenever he felt like it. So he made enquiries, and found that she was the wife of a colonel who was loaded with gambling debts. He sent him a bawd who told the colonel that Hoppe was in love with his wife and was willing to pay all his debts and give him 50,000 francs a year into the bargain. The colonel threw the woman out, but a week later he wrote to Hoppe accepting his terms."

"I don't see that that story proves your point," said Saint-Victor. "The colonel was obviously a cad, selling his wife like that, but I wouldn't say he'd plumbed the depths by any means."

"I haven't finished yet," snapped Flaubert. "Once the terms had been agreed, the colonel invited Hoppe to his house and introduced him to his wife as a friend. After that, the banker went to bed with the wife whenever he liked, warning the colonel of his visits in advance. Unfortunately, knowing nothing of the bargain between the two men, the wife kept worrying that her husband might discover her infidelity, and one night she pestered Hoppe so much with her fears that he told her everything. She refused to believe him. So then he rang for the maid, told her to summon her master to the bedroom, and asked the colonel to confirm his story. Well, faced with the actual sight of his wife's adultery, the colonel hesitated . . ."

"You see?" said Saint-Victor.

". . . but only for a moment. Because Hoppe picked up his wallet from the bedside table, held it out to the husband, and said: 'Here are 500,000 francs. To remove all doubts from your wife's mind, you're going to get down and suck me off in front of her.'"

"And did he?" asked three or four voices in unison.

"He did."

The Goncourts' eyes were shining with delight and fascination.

"What a splendid story!" exclaimed Edmond. "I doubt if even the most cynical of Roman Emperors ever thought of putting human nature to a test like that."

"Some day," Jules chimed in, "we should write a novel about an imaginary emperor who feels the same curiosity about the limits of human degradation—an emperor who makes his senators debase themselves and forces his State Council to worship his excrement."

"You're putting me off my dinner, Goncourt," complained Claudin. "In any case, I don't see that the colonel dishonoured himself any more than a common prostitute, but you don't talk about prostitutes in terms of human degradation."

"It was the banker's mind that interested us," retorted Jules, "not the colonel's dishonour. And besides, there are all sorts of prostitution. Did you know that a foreigner or a *parvenu* who wants to have a stylish housewarming can have the cream of Paris society as his guests—at a price? He applies to one of four or five well-known women, and gives her a present—if he wants first-class company—or a thousand francs—if he wants a second-class crowd. The lady sends out invitations to all her friends and acquaintances and receives them in the gentleman's apartments, which she has previously inspected to make sure they're suitable. As for the gentleman, he looks as if he's just one of the guests. In that way, in our mercenary society, anybody who has made a million in some way or other can wager that he'll have *tout Paris* in his home, and win his bet."

"But for prostitution at its dearest and best," said Edmond, "you've got to go to the theatre. At any *première* you'll find the Grand Circle resplendent with demi-mondaines, and a dazzling array of whores in the boxes. It's amazing what a centre of debauchery the theatre is. From the stage to the auditorium, from the wings to the stage, and from one side of the auditorium to the other, invisible threads criss-cross between actresses' smiles, dancers' legs and men's opera-glasses in a network of pleasure and intrigue. It would be impossible to gather together in a smaller space a greater number of sexual stimuli, of invitations to copulation. It's like a Stock Exchange dealing in women's nights."

"Our beloved Emperor found that out long ago," said Charles-Edmond, "when he took a fancy to little Fix of the Théâtre-Français. That was in the days when Houssaye was doing his pimping for him. Do you know how the wily devil arranged it that time? The Emperor was leaving on his tour of France, and it so happened that Fix was booked to appear in Blois when he was passing through. The trouble was, he needed a plausible pretext for spending a day, and above all a night, in that one-horse town, and it was here that Houssaye came to his rescue. He rigged up an art gallery the town had been asking for with a couple of dozen ghastly daubs, and arranged for the Emperor to open it at an official ceremony. The Emperor must have had an enjoyable night with little Fix, because he rewarded Houssaye with a diamond tie-pin in the shape of an N, which you always see him wearing."

"The trouble with those actresses," Saint-Victor chimed in, "is that once they've bedded His Imperial Majesty, or indeed any man of distinction, they become absolutely insufferable. I was at some official ceremony or other this summer, and a little soubrette came flouncing in and sat down in the front row next to a portly Minister's wife. The good lady drew her skirts aside and said in a loud voice to her other neighbour:

"'I'm dining this evening with Prince Napoleon: I shall complain about the disgraceful way in which the seats here are distributed.'

"'Madame,' said the little soubrette, '*you're* dining with him, but *I'm* sleeping with him, and that's why I've got a seat!'"

Everybody burst out laughing, but Claudin added with a serious expression:

"Yes, and look at the way that Menken creature treated poor old Dumas in the spring."

"Who is 'that Menken creature'?" asked Turgenev.

"Adah Menken, a young American actress. You must have been away, Turgenev, when she hit Paris, because she was a sensation as *Mazeppa*, dressed in pink tights and tied to a horse's back. Dumas fell for her, and she had herself photographed sitting on his lap, with him in his shirt-sleeves. The photographer had copies of his work of art displayed all over the city, and Dumas *fils* still hasn't forgiven his father—or Adah Menken."

"But what about your beloved Schneider, Claudin?" said Veyne. "She isn't exactly innocent of the sin of pride, either. Did you hear how she drove her carriage into the Exhibition—a privilege reserved for royalty and heads of state—calling out: 'Make way for the Grand Duchess of Gerolstein!'?"

"At least she can sing and act," retorted Claudin, "which is more than you can say for that English trollop Cora Pearl. I've never been so disgusted as I was on that evening in January when she played Cupid in *Orpheus*. We're accustomed to seeing women of her profession take to the theatre to advertise their charms, and use the stage as a boarded pavement, but that was the first time I've known any theatre engage a woman whose only claim to fame is the money she earns in her alcove! Why, do you know that she had diamonds all over her costume—such as it was —and even on the soles of her boots? She dropped two of them on the stage and told her dresser she could keep them. They turned out to be worth four thousand francs—twice as much as the dresser earned in a year."

"Oh, she could spare them," said Charles-Edmond. "Her lovers have always been very generous to her. One of them once gave her a box of *marrons glacés*, with every chestnut separately wrapped in a thousand-franc note. And another sent her a sort of Trojan horse made of silver, and full of silver and gold. You can't wonder that the woman gets a little conceited at times."

Claudin choked on a grape he was eating, and had to drink some Sauternes to recover.

"A little conceited!" he spluttered. "Do you know what she said the other day to a friend of mine? 'Your princes and kings,' she said, in that dreadful English accent of hers, 'I trample all over them, and then they go for consolation to the Tweeleries. Yes, the Tweeleries is my lumber room!'"

"Frankly," said Jules de Goncourt, "I don't mind the extra-vagance and arrogance of the great courtesans—after all, their profession demands that they put on a display. What I detest is the hypocrisy some of them show. You remember when we dined with you, Saint-Victor, at Jeanne de Tourbey's place, and she started criticising the slang in Feydeau's latest serial. That sometime whore from a Reims brothel—why, she can't even read! And did you hear that when she rented a house from Prince Napoleon at Bellevue she flew a tricolour from the flagpole? A national mistress—that's all the country needed!"

"But what about my good friend Lagier?" asked Flaubert. "You can't accuse *her* of hypocrisy or prudery!"

"Heaven forbid!" said the elder Goncourt. "She's a splendid, jolly, foul-mouthed, good-natured creature, so honestly vulgar that there's nothing disgusting about her. She's the sort of woman who ought to be served up at a banquet garnished with watercress, like a Regency mistress."

"I'll always remember," said Jules, "the evening we went to her dressing-room after she'd appeared in *La Tour de Nesle*, and she walked around stripping off in front of us, telling us how she'd masturbated three times that day, she needed a man so badly, and promising us that any one of us who went to bed with her that night would have the best fuck of his life. . . ."

"But she had the honesty to say that she could never fall in love. I remember her lighting a cigarette, and sitting astride a chair so that she showed one knee all puffed up with rheumatism, and saying: 'Oh, what I'd give to be able to love a man! I'd like to be able to run my hand through my hair and say to myself: "*I'm in love!*" But I couldn't say that to myself and look in the mirror without my conscience laughing in my face!'"

"We have a soft spot in our hearts for Anna Deslions too. She used to live across the landing from us, you know, nearly twenty years ago, in a fourth-floor apartment in the Rue Saint-Georges, and I remember how every afternoon she'd send a set of nightclothes round to the home of the man of that night, all in his favourite colour. . . ."

"We went a few years ago to her Champs-Élysées apartment to see the furniture she was selling off. Most of it was the usual luxurious stuff you'd expect, but there were two pictures that caught our attention—one a Bonvin of a man sitting in a tavern which seemed like a family portrait of her father, and the other a Breton of gleaners in a field which struck a peculiar note of honest toil in that whore's interior. . . ."

"And looking at a showcase full of her jewels," concluded Jules, "three hundred thousand francs of dazzling light which used to play on her amber skin, I seemed to see her as she was in the old days, when we were giving a dinner-party, coming across to our apartment while we were out and asking our maid if she might look at the table laid for dinner, to feast her eyes on a little luxury."

"At least," said Claudin, who had been looking increasingly disgusted, "we can be sure that our foreign visitors will find every satisfaction for their sexual needs."

"We certainly seem to have become the brothel of Europe," said Saint-Victor. "And 1867 looks like being the 1815 of the phallus."

"By all accounts," remarked Robin, "the English are the hungriest of all for the pleasures Paris offers, from the humblest tourist to the Prince of Wales. One of the women he's slept with told me that His Royal Highness simply gobbles them up."

"Perhaps their own women don't satisfy them," suggested Edmond. "Though that would be surprising considering the splendid women at the English buffets in the Exhibition. With their glorious beauty, their crude pallor and their flaming hair, they're like whores of the Apocalypse, magnificent, frightening animals. . . ."

"It may be," said Taine, "that the English only abandon their reserve when they leave their country. Because I always found them very discreet when I was over there. There isn't a single drawing of a prostitute in their best satirical journal, *Punch*, whereas they are legion in ours. And you won't find an immoral woman in any of their novels, which could all have been written by clergymen."

"Perhaps they haven't got any whores in England?" suggested Gautier.

"No, prostitution does exist over there. But I believe that the

English are more continent than ourselves. As a northern race, their senses awaken later than ours; they are a very shy people; their religious beliefs last into maturity, acting as a brake; their minds are concentrated on making money to maintain a comfortable standard of living, so that their imagination has no leisure; and finally, they indulge greatly in physical exercise, which proves a wholesome distraction."

"Turgenev," said Gautier, "what do *you* think of the English?"

"Oh, they have a great many good qualities," replied the Russian gravely, "but all of them, however rich or intelligent they may be, lead a terribly hard life. And you have to get used to that, just as you have to get used to their climate. No, life in England isn't cheerful, but it's very interesting. For one thing, they have this passion for precedence and hierarchical order. Herzen told me once of a rich English friend of his who was given notice by his valet, his coachman and his groom on one and the same day. He asked his housekeeper for an explanation, and she said: 'If I hadn't been in your service for fifty years, I'd have gone too. Just look at the kitchen. . . .' Well, he looked at the kitchen, and saw a perfectly clean and tidy room. 'Can't you see what's wrong?' said the housekeeper. 'The table's round, so that one day the coachman sits next to me, another day the groom. Now if it was a square table, the valet would always sit beside me, in his rightful place.'"

An incredulous titter went round the table.

"You may laugh," said Turgenev, "but the English take that sort of thing very seriously. I once engaged an English servant for the Viardots who handed in his notice after a week or two. And when I asked him why he'd left such a good position, he said: 'They aren't the right sort of people, sir. It's bad enough when the mistress of the house speaks to one at table, but here the master does it too.'"

"That bears out something I've often noticed on my travels," said Edmond de Goncourt, "and that is that the Englishman always gets the wing of the chicken at a *table d'hôte*. The waiter rushes to serve him and ignores the Frenchman beside him. I couldn't understand this at first, but then I realised why it is. It's

because the Englishman doesn't regard the waiter as a man, and
any servant who feels that he's being considered as a human being
despises the person who looks at him in that light."

Sainte-Beuve suddenly spoke up from the head of the table.

"I'd like to be an Englishman," he said. "At least an Englishman is *somebody*, whereas a Frenchman is nothing, counts for
nothing . . . a citizen of a country swarming with policemen. . . .
As a matter of fact, I have some English blood in me. I was born
in Boulogne, you know, and my grandmother was English."

"You're a credit to the race, Sainte-Beuve," Jules de Goncourt said teasingly. "But then, I've always admired the English-
men I've known. The English seem to me to be honest as
individuals and crooked as a nation, while the French are crooked
as individuals and honest as a nation."

"Whether England is honest or crooked," said Renan, "her
destiny lies with us. By the great law which dictates that a
country's primitive race eventually dominates alien elements,
England is becoming more Celtic and less Germanic every day,
and in the struggle of the races she is on our side."

"At least the English are rather more civilised than their
cousins across the Atlantic," said Saint-Victor. "The vulgarity of
those Yankees is beyond belief."

Renan wagged a reproving finger at him.

"American vulgarity may be the price we shall have to pay one
day for our happiness. After all, American vulgarity wouldn't have
burned Giordano Bruno and wouldn't have persecuted Galileo.
Oh, I know that a stupid democratic régime can be exasperating,
but we should remember that intelligent people manage to live
in America by not being too exacting. *Noli me tangere* is all that
you can ask from a democracy."

"Speaking for myself," said Jules de Goncourt, "I think the
Americans are destined to be the future rulers of the world. Do
you know where I came to that conclusion? At our embassy in
Rome, when Edmond and I were dining there one evening in
April. I was sitting next to the wife of the United States minister
in Brussels, and I was amazed by the free, self-assured grace of
that spirited example of a young race, and the charming coquetry,

the unconquerable flirtatiousness of that young girl who was also a wife. And thinking of the drive and energy of our American friend Harrisse, whom some of you have met here at Magny's, I said to myself that these men and women were fated to be the conquerors of the world. They are going to be the Barbarians of our civilisation, who will devour the Latin world just as the Barbarians of old devoured it in the past."

"They haven't a hope of conquering the world," retorted Saint-Victor. "Why, they haven't even got enough imagination to find names for their streets: they call them by numbers and points of the compass!"

"I think you're wrong to underestimate the Americans," said the elder Goncourt. "They're a strong people, as tough as tempered steel—and small wonder when you think of the climate of their country, which goes from the torrid heat of Senegal to the freezing cold of Siberia."

"Personally, I'd put my money on the Germans as world conquerors," said Saint-Victor.

"The *Germans*?" exclaimed Claudin. "But they're just too funny for words! I mean to say, look at those you meet in Paris. You know the archaeologist Froehner—the assistant keeper at the Louvre? Well, I knew him when he was a humble student, playing a piano in his garret like all German students. Then I met him again a few weeks ago, wearing a neck-tie with pink spots and an absolutely incredible suit, the sort of suit you can imagine a German scholar turned dandy would wear. 'I suppose you find me changed,' he said. 'The fact is that I discovered that hard work and application and all that was just a lot of nonsense. Hase told me that the only way to the top in Paris was through women, so I'm trying his method.' And taking me into a corner of the room, he asked me whether I thought a German like him would ever be able to talk smut to women as Frenchmen did. He said he'd tried, but that what he said always sounded so coarse and filthy that he could never finish it properly. . . . Just think of it . . . a clod-hopping native of the land of innocence trying to succeed with the methods of delicate corruption of Paris society!"

"Yes, they're so earnest, so naïve," said Jules Goncourt. "In the reading-room of the Bibliothèque Impériale the other day I saw a man reading a book while holding the hand of a young woman sitting next to him. I went by two hours later, and he was still reading, and still holding the young woman's hand. They were a German couple of course. Or rather they were Germany itself."

"You mustn't be taken in by that idea of Germany," said Saint-Victor. "We've got to rid ourselves of the notion we've always entertained of Germany, simply on the strength of her poetry, as the land of innocence and good nature, the home of sentimentality and platonic love. We ought to remember that the fictional country of Werther and Charlotte, of Hermann and Dorothea, has produced the toughest soldiers, the ugliest diplomats and the craftiest bankers in the world. Oh, yes, we should stay on our guard against that childlike race of blond innocents: their fair hair is the Teutonic equivalent of the sly hypocrisy of the Slavs."

"What worries me more than the Prussians," said Flaubert, "is the sabre-rattling of our own bellicose bourgeois. It reminds me of 1840—the same talk of 'national dishonour', the same desire to add to our territory without it costing us a single soldier or a single centime."

"I quite agree," said Sainte-Beuve. "That's why I was horrified when Princess Mathilde came to see me the day after the big parade in June and told me what she'd said to Bismarck the previous evening. 'Well, Monsieur de Bismarck,' she boomed at him, 'you didn't think we were as strong as that, did you?'"

He shook his head sadly.

"The silly woman. People like her who make fun of Bismarck don't realise that he's a great minister. And they don't understand that the Prussians are the Macedonians of modern times."

"Then what do you suggest we do?" asked Claudin.

"I suggest that instead of provoking one another—because, after all, we *are* the two leading nations in the civilised world— we should set up a couple of schools, one in Berlin, one in Paris. Our young scientists would go and study in their laboratories, which are superior to ours, and the Prussians would come here to acquire a little of our French grace and culture."

Saint-Victor gave a muffled groan, burying his head in his hands, and as his fellow-diners gradually got up and left the room, chatting quietly among themselves, he remained hunched over the table. The Goncourts stayed behind with him, and when only the three of them were left, Edmond spoke up.

"Tell us, Saint-Victor," he said, "do you really think we are in danger from Prussia?"

The critic raised his head and gazed at them sadly.

"Yes, I do," he replied, "and let me tell you why. I was talking to Haussmann the other day, and he told me of something that happened while the King of Prussia was here in June. He'd taken William and his party up to the Buttes Chaumont to show them the view over Paris, but the King was more interested in something else. He pointed out the fortifications and said to Bismarck and von Moltke: 'That's the gate we came in by in 1815.' And all three of them smiled. . . ."

CHAPTER FOUR

1 March 1869

THE SENSE OF foreboding which had afflicted Paris in 1867 deepened during the following year, as the threat of war with Prussia increased while dissension and unrest grew at home. Political agitation was encouraged by a relaxation of the Press laws, which allowed the emergence of a host of new journals, the most prominent of which were Hugo's *Le Rappel* and Rochefort's *La Lanterne,* the latter making an instant reputation with the opening sentence of its first number: "The Empire contains thirty-six million subjects, not counting the subjects of discontent." At the same time Bismarck could only be heartened by the news that both sides in the Legislative Body—the Conservatives for reasons of economy and the Republicans out of a traditional distrust of standing armies—had virtually crippled a new plan for a mobile National Guard which could be incorporated in the regular army in case of war.

Despite their determination to remain aloof from contemporary political events, Magny's *habitués* were affected by the general disquiet, and they were also saddened by the obvious deterioration in the health of three of their most eminent members, Jules de Goncourt, Gautier and Sainte-Beuve.

The younger of the Goncourt brothers had begun to suffer from agonising headaches which were the first signs that the syphilis he had contracted in 1850 had entered its final stage. In September 1868 the Goncourts moved into a house which they had bought in Auteuil in the hope that Jules would benefit from the peace and quiet of a suburban home, only to find that the house on their left was full of noisy children, the house on their right had a horse stabled in it, and the trains which roared and whistled by in front kept them awake all night. At the beginning of 1869, in a desperate attempt to stave off the encroaching disease,

Jules agreed to submit to hydrotherapy; but the cold-water treatment, which he described as a "rain of torture which makes you scream at the anguish of your every nerve and dance in the enamel bowl the St. Vitus's dance of the madman's shower", was more than he could bear, and he abandoned it after only three days. From now on his mental and physical faculties would decline with increasing rapidity until his death eighteen months later.

Gautier's health was worsening too. In March and April 1868 he suffered two heart attacks and the newspapers published such alarming reports about his condition that his friends hurried round to see him and the Emperor sent a courier to his home. He himself was sufficiently alarmed to plan a new bourgeois existence for himself, which he outlined to his mistress Eugénie as "a good house, well kept, good living, hard work, the Academy and then the Senate". Alarmed at the effect which overwork was having on his constitution, and perhaps also a little conscience-stricken at the way she had neglected her veteran Romantic, Princess Mathilde hit on the idea of appointing him her official librarian, with an annual stipend of 6,000 francs. The day after the public announcement of the appointment, Gautier met the elder Goncourt on the staircase of Mathilde's Paris house and asked him: "Tell me honestly, does the Princess have a library?" "Let me give you a word of advice," replied Edmond: "behave as if she hadn't. . . ."

As for Sainte-Beuve, his bladder condition grew steadily worse, despite two operations for stone, and he was forced to take to his bed for long periods. These, the last months of his life, were darkened by two unfortunate incidents which caused him considerable embarrassment and distress. First, on 10 April 1868, which happened to be Good Friday, he entertained Prince Napoleon, Flaubert, Renan, Taine, Robin and About at his home in the Rue du Montparnasse to a dinner which included *filet au vin de Madère* and *faisan truffé*; and the clerical press promptly accused him of organising an insulting demonstration of atheism with his friends from the notorious Magny Dinners. Then, at the end of the year, he left the *Moniteur,* the official Government organ, after a disagreement with the editor, and moved to the *Temps*, the leading opposition paper, provoking Princess Mathilde to storm round to the Rue du Montparnasse and remind him that he was nothing but "the vassal of the Emperor". The first incident was dismissed with a mild if inaccurate quip—"What a fuss about a ham omelette!"—but the second cost Sainte-Beuve one of his most precious friendships and filled him with a resentment which burned fiercely till he died.

At the Magny dinner of 1 March 1869—a dinner graced by the presence of an eminent newcomer, the famous physiologist Claude Bernard—the Goncourts waited anxiously for Sainte-Beuve to appear, for they were impatient to hear his verdict on their latest novel, *Madame Gervaisais,* which had just been published. At last he came in, supported by Magny, his features white and drawn beneath the inevitable skull-cap. Charles and one of the waiters helped him into his chair, where he sat moaning gently under his breath, his eyes half-closed. At last he opened them, saw the Goncourts gazing expectantly at him, and hurriedly shut them again. Two minutes later he made another effort and looked the elder Goncourt straight in the face.

"Your novel . . . *Madame* . . . *Madame* . . ."

"*Madame Gervaisais.*"

"I know the title of the book, thank you. . . . I'm having it read to me at the moment. . . . Now, I don't say that some parts of the novel, read aloud by a very good reader in a suitable setting, might not have a certain effect. But the two of you are still being too ambitious, forcing your qualities, trying too hard to be unusual. . . For all I know, your novels may be given as *excerpta* to the schoolboys of the future. . . . But in my opinion they aren't literature any more, but music or painting. You want to render things in prose. . . . You want to go further than Rousseau, Bernardin de Saint-Pierre, Chateaubriand and Hugo. . . . You want to convey the movement in the colour of the soul of things. . . . Well, that's impossible. . . . I can't say what novelists will do in the future, or how far they'll go, but at the moment you really must tone your writing down. . . . .

"*Neutre-alteinte,* for instance," he muttered, going off at a tangent. "What's a *neutre-alteinte*? It isn't in the dictionary. I suppose it's a painting term, but not everybody's a painter. . . . It's like your tea-rose-coloured sky. . . . . Tea-rose! Who the devil knows what a tea-rose is? . . . Tea-rose-coloured, indeed! There's rose-coloured, and that's all. . . ."

The Goncourts had sat silent and motionless during this muttered monologue, with nothing but a slight flush in their cheeks to show their annoyance, but this final reproach was too much for Edmond.

"But, Sainte-Beuve," he exploded, "we wanted to convey to the reader the impression that the sky was *yellow*—that pinky-yellow colour of a tea-rose, a *Gloire de Dijon* for instance, and not the pink colour of an ordinary rose."

Sainte-Beuve ignored the explanation.

"In art, a man must succeed," he declared, "and I would like to see you succeed, believe me. But to do that, you must learn to write for the public, you must bring your books within reach of the public's intelligence and understanding. . . ."

"I told you so," Jules hissed in his brother's ear. "He's going to slate us."

The old critic's head jerked up angrily.

"I do not slate people," he snapped. "I have never slated anybody in my life. That would be bad literary manners. I simply tell the truth as I see it. . . . You should remember that very often, as a man grows older, when he seems kind he is false, and when he seems cruel he is kind."

"Yes, Uncle Beuve," sighed Gautier, "but you may be kind at heart and still ruin a man with a cruel word. I've often been asked why I've always been so indulgent in my criticism, and many people have attributed that indulgence to a complete lack of interest in any work produced nowadays. What they forgot was that I was writing for the official government paper, and that the judgements I passed in that paper accordingly took on a very special character. If I had condemned a work of art—whether picture, play or statue—too harshly, I would have harmed the artist's career and often deprived him of his livelihood. Besides, I knew what artistic creation involved, and I didn't judge it lightly like Sarcey and his kind, who think that a critic's task consists in pointing out the flaws in a work of art, and who in ten years or so will have dried up all the springs of creative talent by dint of discouraging every artist in the country. Besides, if the idea of being spiteful *had* occurred to me, I'd have been restrained by the memory of my pastrycook."

"What pastrycook?" asked Flaubert.

"You mean to say you don't know the story of my pastrycook? I'd written in some article or other in the *Moniteur* that somebody was "as stupid as a pastrycook". That was pretty harmless, wasn't it? You all think so, and so did I. But I was wrong. The article happened to be read by a highly susceptible pastrycook who took offence on behalf of himself and his corporation. He decided to get his revenge, and very nearly succeeded. He slyly bought up all the I.O.U.'s which I'd given my creditors and which were quietly circulating in Paris, and when he had them all in his possession he told me he was going to sell me up. I offered to pay him in instalments, but he refused. I put the whole sum at his disposal, and he replied that he didn't want my money, but that he'd decided to sell me up and sell me up he would. I was obliged to call in *a bailiff*—think of it, *a bailiff*, to force him to accept his due. . . . Oh, no, Uncle Beuve, we must weigh every word we write."

Just then the door opened and Magny came in, followed by Charles and the waiters carrying the next course. Robin seized the opportunity to change the conversation. "Let's turn our attention to serious matters," he suggested. "Such as Magny's splendid *chateaubriand*."

"Chateaubriand?" murmured Sainte-Beuve, rousing himself from his torpor at the sound of the great man's name. "Did I ever tell you that when a warrant was issued for his arrest back in 1832, Chateaubriand was found in bed with a couple of whores?"

"Monsieur Sainte-Beuve!" Magny said in a tone of melancholy reproach. Everybody turned to look at him, thinking he had been shocked by the disrespectful reference to the author of *The Genius of Christianity*.

"Monsieur Sainte-Beuve," he repeated, "how many times have

I told you that this dish, which was created in this very restaurant, is not named after Monsieur de Chateaubriand, who never dined here, but after Monsieur de Chabrillan?"

"When he was in Geneva," Sainte-Beuve went on, ignoring the interruption, "he decided one fine day that Mont Blanc was a suitably grandiose place for him to die—*Argentem frigidus Œtnam* and so on—or at least he said something which gave that impression. Madame de Chateaubriand and Madame Récamier were terrified, and they took it in turns to watch the old *poseur* and follow him around until he decided to put off dying until another day."

"Dying, dying—nobody talks of anything else," complained Charles-Edmond. "As if the papers weren't bad enough with the execution of that murderer yesterday!"

"I never read the papers," Robin said blandly. "Haven't time. In fact, I only knew it was happening because of a stonemason whose wife I had treated years ago. He came to see me, roaring drunk, and said that because I'd been so good to her, his wife wanted to offer me a seat at one of the windows in her house, which overlooks the guillotine."

"You didn't accept?" asked Gautier.

"No, I didn't. Why should I want to watch an execution from a distance, surrounded by drunken spectators, when I've seen so many from close quarters—and conducted experiments on the corpses afterwards?"

"You've experimented on guillotined bodies?" exclaimed Claudin.

"Yes, frequently . . . and with fascinating results. You know, I've known headless men who after forty-five minutes of death have moved their hands to touch their chests at the place where they were being pinched. Which suggests that the heart and the brain are . . ."

There was a sudden clatter as the young waiter who was serving Flaubert dropped a spoon on the floor. He stood for a moment, staring at Robin, open-mouthed and unnaturally pale, before bending down to retrieve it.

"You're upsetting Magny's staff with your stories, Robin," said his colleague Veyne drily. "But then, there's something about decapitation which horrifies the human mind more than any other form of death. I remember a plump, pink-cheeked old man who used to take his meals in a corner of the Restaurant Véfour—he had a special liking for sugary dishes—and who was always pointed out with horror because during the Revolution he'd carried the Princesse de Lamballe's head through the streets of Paris on a pike. And Marshal Sébastiani used to tell a blood-curdling story of his stay in Constantinople. . . .

"He had just repelled the English attack on the city, and the Sultan Selim asked him what reward he would like, promising to give him anything he wanted. Sébastiani asked if he might visit the harem, and the Sultan duly showed him the harem and all his wives. When the visit was over, Selim asked him if he had noticed a woman he liked. 'Yes,' said the Marshal, and indicated which one. And that evening Sebastiani received the woman's head on a platter, together with a message from the Sultan saying: 'As a Moslem, I could not offer you, a Christian, a woman of my faith. But this way you can be sure that the woman on whom you set your eyes will never belong to any other man.'"

"I can't match that story for horror," said Saint-Victor, "but I remember my father telling me that when he had to go through the Tuileries during the Terror, he used to hear the blade of the guillotine fall with a thud four or five times before he got out of earshot."

"Did you know," asked the elder Goncourt, not to be outdone, "that the present executioner drinks a jugful of milk on the eve of an execution, and can't bring himself to eat meat for a whole week afterwards?"

"Or that he's paid for the job in cash," said Jules, "and doesn't give a receipt for his fee? Bracquemond—you know, the engraver—was invited recently to watch the payment ceremony, in order to make a study of the man's hand. The Public Prosecutor sat at a table with the five-franc pieces in a pile on one corner. The executioner came in and bowed, and the Public Prosecutor pointed to the money without saying a word. And then Bracquemond saw the coins disappear in a flash under the biggest, thickest hand he had ever laid eyes on."

The Rue Mazet in 1870, showing Magny's at the far end of the street
(Jacques Buchholz)

Edmond de
Goncourt

Jules de
Goncourt

Gustave
Flaubert
by Nadar

Ernest
Renan

Claude
Bernard

Théophile
Gautier

Marcelin
Berthelot

Guillaume
Chevalier
("Gavarni")

Sainte-
Beuve

George
Sand
by Nadar

Hippolyte
Taine

Ivan
Turgenev

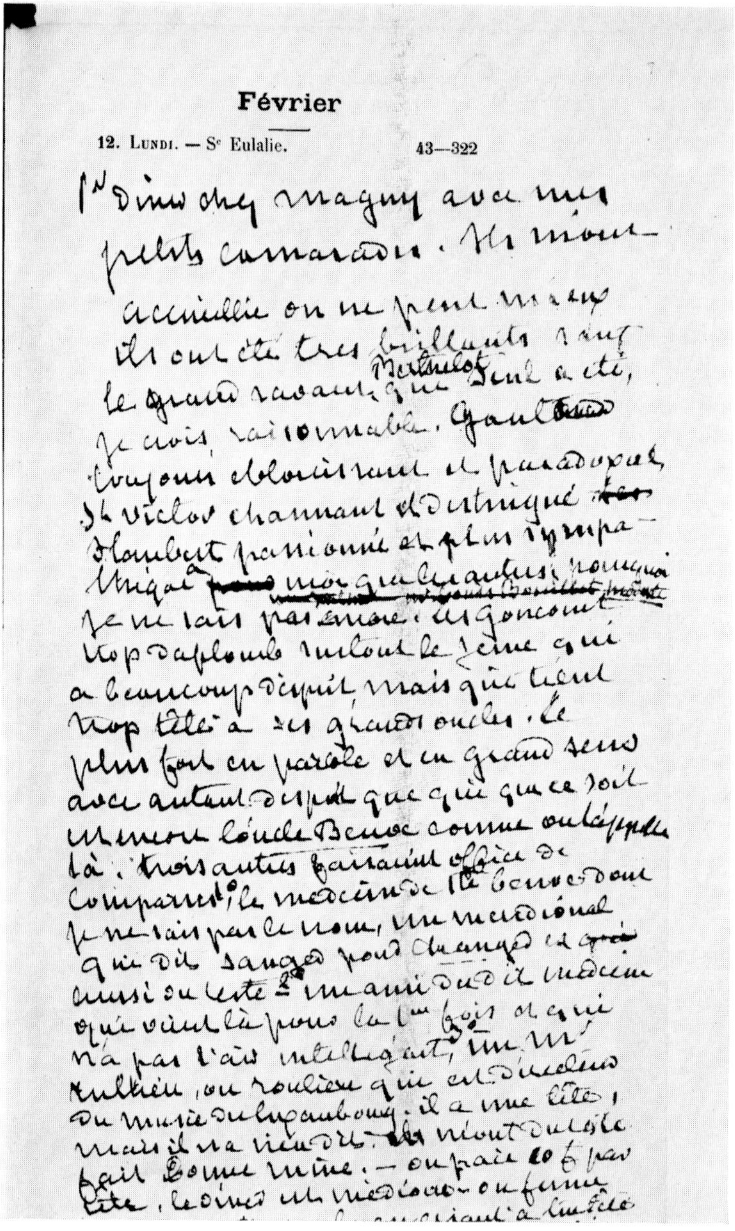
Février

12. Lundi. — Se Eulalie. 43—322

1er dîner chez Magny avec mes
petits camarades. Ils m'ont
accueillie on ne peut mieux
Ils ont été très brillants sauf
le grand savant Berthelot qui a été,
je crois, raisonnable. Gautier
toujours éblouissant et paradoxal,
St Victor charmant et distingué
Flaubert passionné et plus sympa-
thique à moi que les autres, pourquoi
je ne sais pas encore. Les Goncourt
trop d'aplomb surtout le jeune qui
a beaucoup d'esprit, mais qui tient
trop tête à ses grands oncles. Le
plus fort en parole et en grand sens
avec autant d'esprit que qui que ce soit
est encore l'oncle Beuve comme on l'appelle
là. trois autres faisaient office de
comparses, le médecin de Ste Beuve dont
je ne sais pas le nom, un méridional
qui dit sangé pour changé et qui
aussi du reste, un ami dudit médecin
qui vient là pour la 1re fois et qui
n'a pas l'air intelligent, un Mr
[illegible] ou [illegible] qui est directeur
du musée du Luxembourg. il a une tête,
mais il n'a rien dit. Ils m'ont du reste
fait bonne mine. — on paie 10 f par
tête, le dîner est médiocre — on fume
[illegible]

Page from George Sand's diary (Bibliothèque Nationale)

"Turgenev," Gautier called out, "how about giving us a spine-chilling story of a Russian execution?"

The gentle giant looked up from his plate and made a wry grimace. "I can tell you the story of an execution," he said, "but not a Russian one. You see, I was there yesterday morning."

"You saw the fellow guillotined?"

Turgenev nodded.

"I was dining a few days ago at a friend's house," he explained, "with some other guests, including Maxime Du Camp, and he invited me to attend the execution, not as an ordinary spectator, but as a member of a privileged party admitted to the prison itself. I was taken by surprise and accepted the invitation without thinking, and later a feeling of false pride prevented me from going back on my word. I was punished for my vanity, and I warn you that what I saw and experienced that night doesn't make a pleasant story."

"Never mind," said Gautier. "We've all got steady nerves and tough stomachs."

Turgenev took a sip of wine and leaned his elbows on the table.

"Well," he began, "I arrived at the agreed time and place—eleven o'clock at night at the statue of Prince Eugène, on the boulevard of the same name—to find a small group of people waiting for me: Monsieur Claude, the chief of police, his assistant, some other privileged visitors like myself, and a few journalists. Du Camp had warned me that we should have to spend a sleepless night in the prison governor's quarters, because although executions in winter don't take place until seven in the morning, you have to be at the prison before midnight or you might not be able to push your way through the crowd. As you know, it's about half a mile from the statue of Prince Eugène to La Roquette prison, and for the first part of the way we saw nothing out of the ordinary. There were just rather more people on the boulevard than usual. We did notice one thing, though; nearly all the people were walking—and some of them, mainly women, actually running—in the same direction; and all the cafés and pot-houses were lit up, which struck me as unusual at that late hour in a

E

remote district of Paris. It may have been my imagination, but I think most of us—apart from Monsieur Claude and his assistant, and possibly Du Camp—felt a little awkward and ashamed as we walked jauntily along, for all the world as if we were on a shooting expedition.

"The closer we got to the prison, the more crowded the streets became, and a bunch of street-urchins started circling round us, with their hands in their pockets and the peaks of their caps pulled over their eyes. And then one of them suddenly shouted: 'There he is! That's him!' and pointed to me. . . ."

"Don't tell me!" said Gautier. "He thought you were the executioner."

"Right, Théo. Du Camp told me I'd obviously been mistaken for *Monsieur de Paris*, and when I met the executioner later I understood why, because he has the same build and the same grey hair as I.

"Well, on we went, and soon we came to the prison, where a space in front of the gates was cordoned off by a squad of soldiers drawn up in a line four deep across the square. As we approached the gates a young police officer—he turned out to be the chief inspector of that district—rushed over to us with such an arrogant manner that it reminded me of the good old days in my beloved Russia; but as soon as he recognised his superiors he calmed down and let us all into the prison with infinite precautions. We were politely received by the governor, a tall, sturdily built man with the typical appearance of a French infantry officer, and shown to his quarters, where we sat around the fire for a while talking in a desultory way. Somebody raised the question of capital punishment, but everything we said seemed so platitudinous that we soon dropped the subject, although talking about anything else was impossible out of ordinary respect for the man who was about to die. We were all overwhelmed by a feeling of uneasiness and irritation—not boredom, but something a hundred times worse—and it came as a positive relief to us to hear the clatter of heavy wheels outside and to be told that the guillotine had arrived."

"Did you watch it being put up?" asked Flaubert.

"Only for a little while: it takes quite a time to unload it all and set it up. When we went out on to the square, we found a huge closed van drawn by three horses standing outside the gates, with a smaller van which looked like an oblong box drawn by a single horse a little farther off. That one, I was told, was to carry the dead man's body to the cemetery after the execution. A few workmen in smocks began unloading the component parts of the guillotine from the larger van, while a tall man in a round hat with a white necktie and a light coat thrown over his shoulders stood beside them giving orders in an undertone."

"*Monsieur de Paris?*"

"Yes, the executioner. Our group went over to the van to be introduced to him, and some of us—probably just to show off—even shook hands with him. His hands, by the way, were very beautiful and remarkably white; I was reminded of Pushkin's lines about *the executioner . . . playing with his snow-white hands*. He behaved very courteously and gently towards us, with a sort of patriarchal dignity, and we all treated him very respectfully. He was, after all, the second most important person there that night, and in a sense the condemned man's prime minister.

"There was already a great crowd of people in the square, and the uninterrupted din of human voices rose from behind the lines of troops. I walked over to the soldiers, who were standing motionless, their faces expressing nothing but cold, submissive boredom, and even the faces I could see behind the soldiers' shakos and the policemen's three-cornered hats—the faces of the workmen and women—showed the same boredom, with just the addition of a kind of indefinable irony. I watched the base of the guillotine being assembled, with two lanterns moving about just above the ground, casting bright circles of light on the cobblestones, and then went back to the governor's apartments, where our host was regaling the others with mulled wine. He showed us a whole pile of letters which had been sent to the condemned man, who apparently refused to read them. Most of them were full of jokes, but some were serious and urged him to repent and confess. A Methodist clergyman sent a twenty-page theological thesis, and there were also little notes from women, some of them enclosing marguerites and immortelles. I couldn't help feeling that the governor was at a loss to understand the interest we took in the condemned man, whom he regarded as just a disgusting animal, and probably put it down to the idle curiosity of rich civilians."

"Did you talk all night," somebody asked, "or did you manage to get any sleep?"

"Oh, after a little talk we all curled up on chairs or divans, but I don't think any of us dozed off for even a moment. Most of the time we were wandering about like souls in torment, going out on to the square now and then to see how the guillotine was getting on. By three o'clock, according to Monsieur Claude, there were over twenty-five thousand people outside, and the noise they were making sounded like the distant roar of the sea: it had the same kind of endless Wagnerian *crescendo,* not rising all the time, but with long intervals between the ebb and flow. The shrill notes of women's and children's voices rose in the air like spray above that enormous rumbling noise, which would die down for a moment and then swell and grow as if it were going to sweep everything away, only to quieten down again a little later. I asked myself what the noise signified—impatience, joy, malice? —and finally decided that it didn't express any separate human feeling: it was simply the rumble and roar of an elemental force."

"Did you see the mob itself at any time?" asked Flaubert.

"Yes, when I went out for a breath of air just after three. The guillotine was ready by then, the two uprights standing out dimly against the dark sky with the slanting blade between them. For some reason I'd imagined the uprights would be farther apart than they were—there was only two feet between them—and their proximity gave the whole apparatus a sort of sinister shapelessness, the shapeliness of a long, slender swan's neck. The large, dark-red wicker basket in front of it filled me with a feeling of disgust, because I knew that the executioners would throw the murderer's head into it and the warm, still-quivering body. . . . I walked across to one of the lines of soldiers and gazed for a long time at the people crammed behind it. There was one man I noticed in particular, a young workman of about twenty: he stood there grinning, his eyes staring at the ground, as if he were thinking of something funny, and then he would suddenly throw his head back, open his mouth wide, and start shouting wordlessly; then his head would drop again and he'd start grinning again. I wondered what was going on inside that man's head, why he'd condemned himself to a sleepless night, to nearly eight hours' immobility, and what all the other people behind him were thinking. Now and then an argument would break out, or some women would start screaming, and a heavy smell of alcohol came from the crowd: it was not for nothing that the pot-houses and cafés glowed with red light in the background. The sky had become completely overcast, and there were ghostly dark patches in the trees; these were street urchins who had climbed up into the branches and were whistling and screeching like birds. One of them had fallen out of his tree and broken his spine, but he only aroused loud laughter, and that for a short time.

"On my way back to the governor's quarters, I passed the guillotine and saw the executioner on the platform, surrounded by a small crowd of inquisitive people. He was carrying out a rehearsal of the execution for their amusement. First he threw down the hinged plank to which the murderer was fastened, and which touched the semi-circular slot between the uprights with one end as it fell into place. Then he let the knife fall, and it ran down heavily and smoothly with a swift roar. I didn't climb on to the platform, because the feeling that I was committing some unknown crime was growing stronger within me. Possibly it was because of this feeling that the horses harnessed to the vans and quietly chewing their oats in their nosebags struck me at that moment as the only innocent creatures among all of us."

"Turgenev," said Saint-Victor, "I thought you were going to tell us about the execution."

"I'm coming to that," the Russian retorted gently. "The last few hours of waiting, oddly enough, go much more quickly than the first, so that we were all surprised at the news that it had struck six and there was only one hour to go to the execution. Every trace of sleep vanished from our faces straight away, but I felt sick at heart. Some new faces appeared, including a short, grey-haired priest in a long black cassock and a wide-brimmed hat. A collation was served for us in the drawing-room, though I for one had no stomach for it; and while he was sipping his chocolate one of the journalists asked if the condemned man was still asleep.

"'Yes, he's fast asleep,' the governor replied.

"'What, in spite of this terrible din?' somebody asked—because the noise had grown tremendously loud and turned into a sort of hoarse roar, no longer *crescendo*, but rumbling on triumphantly.

"'His cell is behind three walls,' the governor explained.

"Then Monsieur Claude looked at his watch and said: 'Twenty-past six', and, shuddering inwardly, we all put on our hats and set off after our guide.

"We went out into the prison courtyard, where a sort of roll-call was held, then through an empty room with a leather stool in the centre, where we were told the *toilette du condamné* would take place, and then along two corridors and down a spiral stair-case to an iron door which led into the murderer's cell. The bed was empty: the condemned man had woken up before we arrived and was standing behind the table on which he had just written a farewell letter to his mother. He was a young man with a mop of brown hair, and as we came in, his huge, dark round eyes swept from left to right, gazing at each one of us in turn.

"'We have come to inform you,' Monsieur Claude said in his soft, dry voice, 'that your appeal for a reprieve has been dismissed and that the hour of retribution has come for you.'

"The condemned man turned and looked at him calmly, almost sleepily, but without saying a word.

"'My child,' said the priest, coming up to him on the other side, 'be brave!'

"The man looked at him exactly as he had looked at Monsieur Claude.

"'I knew he wouldn't be afraid,' said the chief of police, rather like a schoolmaster showing off his prize pupil. 'Now that he has got over the first shock I can answer for him.'

"'Oh, I'm not afraid!' said the condemned man, bearing out what Monsieur Claude had just said. 'I'm not afraid!'

"The priest took a little bottle out of his pocket.

"'Won't you have a drop of wine, my child?'

"The condemned man shook his head and politely declined. In answer to questions from Monsieur Claude and the prison governor, he protested his innocence of the murder of which he had been convicted, but refused to name the accomplices he claimed had done the killing.

"'All right, all right,' said Monsieur Claude, as if to imply that his questions had been a mere formality and that there was something else to be done now.

"Two warders went up to the condemned man and began taking off his prison strait-jacket, a sort of smock of coarse blue cloth with belts and buckles behind and long sleeves tied with tape at the waist. He stood quite calmly while this was being done, breathing evenly and keeping his eyes cast down. Once or twice he shook his head as if to dismiss a troublesome thought, glanced up at the ceiling and heaved a scarcely perceptible sigh. Apart from these slight movements, nothing about him betrayed, I won't say fear, but even anxiety, and I'm sure that the rest of us were all more agitated than he. When his hands were released from the sleeves, he held the strait-jacket in front of him with a pleased smile, while it was being undone at the back—behaving just like a little child being undressed. Then he took off his shirt, put on a clean one, and carefully buttoned the neckband. It was strange to see the easy grace with which his bare limbs moved against the yellowish background of the prison wall—a grace which amounted almost to elegance. Indeed, one of my companions, whom I happened to meet later in the day, told me that all the time he had been in the condemned cell he had kept imagining that the year was 1794, that we weren't ordinary citizens but Jacobins, and that we were taking to his execution not a common murderer but an aristocrat, *un ci-devant*.

"Meanwhile the condemned man had been putting on his boots, cheerfully knocking the soles and heels against the floor and wall to make sure his feet were in properly. Then they put the strait-jacket on him again, and Monsieur Claude asked us to go out and leave him alone with the priest. The last confession and absolution

didn't take long, because in less than two minutes he joined us,
and the whole group, with him in the centre, set off up the narrow
spiral staircase we had descended a quarter of an hour before. A
moment later, we were plunged into darkness: the night-light on
the stairs had gone out. It was an awful situation: we were rushing upstairs, we could hear the clatter of our feet on the iron steps,
we were bumping into one another and treading on each other's
heels, one of us had his hat knocked off, and behind me somebody
shouted angrily: '*Sacré Dieu!* Light a candle! Let's have some
light!' And there among us, in our midst, in the pitch darkness,
was our victim! I wondered for a moment whether he might not
take advantage of the darkness to escape to some remote corner of
the prison and try to knock his brains out against a wall. But
eventually our group emerged into the corridor with the condemned man still in our midst, and we continued on our way to
the guillotine.

"Our progress was more a flight than a procession, with the
murderer almost bounding along and the rest of us hurrying
after him. Some members of our party, anxious to have another
look at his face, actually ran ahead to the right and left of him,
while he took the next flight of stairs two at a time. At last
we reached the room I mentioned earlier, where the *toilette du
condamné* was to be carried out. We entered through one door, and
through the opposite door there came the executioner, in his
white necktie and black suit, looking rather like a diplomat or a
Protestant pastor. He was followed by a short, fat old man in a
black coat, who was his chief assistant, the hangman of Beauvais.
The condemned man went up to the stool, where the old man
knelt behind him and started hobbling his legs with some rawhide straps he had taken out of a small leather bag. Then two other
assistants came over, removed the murderer's strait-jacket, tied
his hands behind him and began tying more rawhide straps round
his body. There weren't enough holes in the straps for the prongs
to go through, and after rummaging in all his pockets the old man
finally brought out a small crooked awl. He started laboriously
boring holes in the straps, but his fingers were swollen with gout
and the hide was new and thick. In the meantime the priest, who

was reading prayers in French out of a breviary, realised that something was amiss and began to draw out his prayers to give the old man time to remedy matters. At last the operation was over and we all heaved a sigh of relief—not knowing that yet another operation had to be performed. . . ."

"The cutting of the murderer's hair," Robin said knowledgeably.

"Yes," said Turgenev. "The condemned man was asked to sit down on the stool, and the Beauvais hangman started cutting off the collar of the shirt he had only just put on. The scissors were none too sharp and he had some trouble slicing through the coarse, pleated cloth. Then the executioner had a look and complained that the space left bare was not big enough. He indicated with his hand how much more he wanted cut off, and the old man set to work again. A few minutes later the top of the condemned man's back was completely exposed, and he shivered slightly, for it was cold in the room. Then the old man put his puffy left hand on the murderer's head and started cutting his hair with his right. Thick tufts of wiry, dark-brown hair fell on the floor, and one of them rolled up to my boot. I couldn't take my eyes off the slender, youthful neck which the scissors were laying bare, and imagining a line cut straight across it. There, I thought, a five-hundred-pound axe would fall in a few minutes' time, smashing the vertebrae and cutting through the veins and muscles, and yet the neck looked so smooth and white and healthy, as if it didn't expect anything of the kind.

"At last the hair-cutting operation was at an end, and the condemned man stood up, shaking his head. This was the moment when prisoners about to die addressed final requests to the prison governor or sent last messages to relatives or friends, but this young man scorned such sentimentalities and didn't utter a single word. The executioner took him by the elbow, Monsieur Claude said: 'Let's go!' and we all went out into the prison courtyard.

"It was five to seven, but the sky was still barely light, and a dull mist covered everything. As soon as we crossed the threshold we heard the noise of the crowd, an unbroken, ear-splitting, thunderous roar. The condemned man hobbled forward, his shackles interfering with his walk, and suddenly the two halves of the gate opened before us like the enormous mouth of an animal. A huge howl went up from the mob, which at long last had caught sight of what it had been waiting for, and we saw the monster of the guillotine staring at us with its two slim black uprights and its slanted axe.

"I suddenly felt cold and sick, and my legs gave way under me. Glancing at the condemned man, I saw him recoil, throwing his head back and bending his knees, as if somebody had hit him in the chest. 'He's going to faint,' somebody whispered, but he recovered his composure straight away and hobbled on. Those in our party who wanted to see his head roll off rushed past him on to the square, but I hadn't the courage to do that and stopped at the gates.

"I saw the executioner rise up suddenly like a black tower on the left of the platform. I saw the condemned man scramble up the ten steps to the guillotine and two men pounce on him from both sides, like spiders on a fly. I saw him fall forward suddenly with his heels kicking in the air. . . .

"At that point I turned away, the ground heaving up and down under my feet, and waited for what seemed a terribly long time, although I was told later that only twenty seconds elapsed between the murderer putting his foot on the first step of the guillotine and his headless body being flung into the basket. I noticed that the roar of the crowd had rolled up into a ball, so to speak, and a breathless hush had fallen over everything. In front of me there was a sentry, a red-cheeked young fellow who stood looking at me in perplexity. I just had time to think that he probably came from some decent, law-abiding family in the country, before I heard the knock of wood on wood—the noise made by the top part of the yoke, with the slit in it for the knife, as it fell into place above the murderer's neck. Then something suddenly swooped down with a dull growl and stopped abruptly with a thud. . . . It was just as if some huge animal had retched. . . . I felt dizzy, and everything swam before my eyes. I would probably have fainted if Monsieur Claude's assistant hadn't seized me by the arm and offered me a drink of water. But I declined and went back into the prison yard, which seemed a haven of refuge from the horrors outside the gates. . . ."

Turgenev stopped speaking, but nobody said a word. After a few minutes' silence he continued:

"I joined our group later in the guard-house to take leave of the governor while the crowd was dispersing, and there I was told that during the confusion immediately after the execution two men had forced their way through the lines of soldiers, crawled under the guillotine, and soaked their handkerchiefs in the blood that had dripped between the planks. I listened to all that in a sort of daze, feeling utterly exhausted. Indeed, all my companions looked tired, while none of them—and this is the interesting point—looked as if he were aware that he had been present at the performance of an act of social justice. It was the same with the crowd outside: all the people I saw were silent, with glum, sleepy faces wearing expressions of boredom, fatigue and disappointment. Yes, there was dissatisfaction and disappointment on every face—but not a trace of edification.

"About fifty yards from the prison, Du Camp and I hailed a cab and drove off together, discussing what we had just seen. We talked about the senseless barbarism of all that medieval procedure—the undressings and dressings, the hair-cutting and strap-tying, the journeys along corridors and up and down staircases—which had dragged out the murderer's agony for half an hour, from twenty-eight minutes past six to seven o'clock. We asked ourselves what purpose such an appalling routine could possibly serve, and then, inevitably, what justification there could be for capital punishment itself, or at least for public executions. Of the fifty thousand people on the Place de la Roquette that morning, we estimated that no more than fifty or sixty could have seen anything in the half-light at a distance of 150 feet and through the lines of soldiers and horses. And what benefit, however small, could the rest have derived from that drunken, sleepless, idle night? I recalled the young workman who had stood there shouting senselessly and whose face I had studied for several minutes. Would he start work that morning as a person who hated vice

and crime more than before? And what about me? What had I
got from it, apart from a feeling of involuntary astonishment at
a murderer who could show such contempt for death? Is that
really the impression our law-givers want us to have? And if not,
what is the point of it all?"

There was a long silence after he had finished, which was broken
by Claude Bernard muttering sadly:

"All that blood going to waste. . . . Because you can't get
enough of it nowadays. . . . Nobody goes in for bloodletting any
more. In my day there were buckets of it in all the hospitals, but
when I needed some the other day for my lecture, I couldn't get
any. And if it hadn't been for that old doctor who attends all my
lectures—you know the fellow, Robin?—I'd have had to do
without. . . . He's an old pupil of Broussais's and keeps up the old
traditions. 'I bleed myself every day,' he told me, 'and use it to
water my flowers. . . .' "

"Oh, the human body can always be put to some use or other,"
said Veyne. "A naval captain I know was telling me yesterday
that when he was fighting at Sebastopol, one of the wheels of a
cannon stuck and he ordered a marine to grease it. There wasn't
any grease there, so the marine took an axe, split open the head
of a dead man lying nearby, picked up his brains in his hands, and
simply plastered them on the axle."

Flaubert growled his appreciation of this anecdote, although
some of his neighbours had turned a little pale.

"What interested me about Turgenev's story," he said, "was
the vicious curiosity of the crowd. I remember hearing about
something similar at Provins about fifteen years ago. A young
man was going to be executed, who had murdered a man of
property and his wife, raped their maidservant, and drunk their
entire cellar. To witness the guillotining of this eccentric, over
ten thousand people from the surrounding countryside arrived
in Provins the day before, and since the inns couldn't hold them
all, many of them actually slept all night *in the snow*. Oh, you
can sneer at the gladiators, make laws, reform the wild beast;
but even when you've pulled the tiger's teeth and he can only
eat pap, he'll still remain bloodthirsty at heart. Working clothes

don't conceal the cannibal, nor can the bourgeois's skull-cap hide his Carib skull. Progress, indeed! Universal suffrage! Tcha!"

"I wouldn't mind betting," said the younger Goncourt, "that the crowds on both occasions were largely made up of women. Executions of any sort seem to hold a morbid fascination for the gentle sex. I've still got a piece of hangman's rope which a mistress of mine gave me years ago for luck. It was the real thing too: it had been used to hang a man she had known."

"But then," said his brother, "women are obsessed with death in all its forms, judicial, violent or natural. And when it strikes somebody they love, they change from being merely garrulous to being positively eloquent. All of them, whether they're illiterate or educated, whores or marchionesses, find words and phrases and gestures which are the envy and despair of any novelist or dramatist. I've never seen a single tragedy on the stage which contained anything to touch those unrehearsed sorrows, those spontaneous tears, those stammered words springing straight from grief. And yet, underneath it all, behind the most sincere and poignant grief, you'll always find, right from the start, a preoccupation with mourning clothes. There's hardly a single case of bereavement in which the woman doesn't say to you: 'It's a good thing I didn't buy a summer dress!' "

"It isn't just women who are obsessed with death," remarked Gautier. "I think about it all the time. The fact is, nothing interests me any more. I've a feeling that I've ceased to be a contemporary. I'm perfectly prepared to talk about myself in the third person, as if I were already dead."

"I know the feeling, my dear Théo," said Turgenev. "I sometimes remind myself of the shades of the Elysian Fields in Gluck's *Orfeo*, and I expect I have their look of deep indifference. They say that a man dies several times before his death, and that has happened to me. I look on my happiness as I look on my youth, as on the youth and happiness of a stranger. I am here, and all that is there, and between this *here* and that *there* lies a gulf which no eternity can ever bridge."

Sainte-Beuve, breathing heavily and obviously in pain, spoke from the head of the table.

"The future," he said, "has certainly nothing more to promise *me*. I expect nothing more from life, either in the way of happiness or in the way of ambition. I don't regard myself as called to any useful vocation, and I'm no longer sustained by the chimera of public good. I've reached the stage of complete indifference, where nothing matters any more, so long as I do *something* in the morning, and go *somewhere* in the evening."

"With me," continued Turgenev, "it's an almost physical sensation. You know how sometimes in a room there's an almost imperceptible smell of musk that you can't get rid of? Well, all around me, all the time, there's a smell of death and decay. And one night not long ago I had a constriction of the heart together with a nightmare vision of a large brown stain which I recognised, half-way between sleep and wakefulness, as death."

"You're a cheerful lot, I must say," remarked Robin. "If any of you are interested in discovering exactly how you are going to die, and of what, I can recommend you to my colleague Axenfeld, the specialist in nervous diseases. I was at a dinner-party at his house recently at which the guests got rather drunk and started talking about the uncertainty of the deaths that lay in store for them. Our host suddenly stood up and announced that he was going to die of a cerebral haemorrhage, and after that gave his neighbours details of the diseases that were going to kill them, together with a grisly description of their final sufferings. I've never seen people sober up so quickly."

"Thank you for the suggestion, Robin," said Saint-Victor. "But some of us might prefer to find our own way out of this world, without waiting for Axenfeld's diagnosis to be proved right."

"I agree," said Renan. "Dying is nothing in itself when a man is sure that the work to which he's devoted is going to be continued. What is shameful is suffering, ugliness, the gradual weakening of the body, the cowardice which fights with death over a candle-end which was once a torch. The only acceptable death is a noble death which is not a pathological accident, but a deliberately chosen end."

"Suicide," murmured Sainte-Beuve, "is a legitimate, almost

natural form of death. It's far better to leave this life suddenly and deliberately, in the manner of the Ancients, than to preside over the disintegration of all the organs, the death of all the senses. My only regret is that I haven't the courage to kill myself."

"We've often discussed the matter," said the elder Goncourt; "and we finally decided that the best way to go would be after dinner one evening, when one was old and famous, in the middle of the sexual act, so that one arrived on the other side still ejaculating, at the foot of a gigantic throne, to hear God the Father's voice booming: 'Hold it down, Monsieur, you're wetting me.' "

Everybody laughed, and a a spasm of something resembling mirth passed over Sainte-Beuve's face.

"Alas," he whispered, "I may still admire the flowers, but I can't pick them any more."

"I'm in the same plight," confessed Turgenev. "And there perhaps lies the explanation for the scent of death that I can smell around me. For various reasons—my white hair and so on— I cannot make love any more. I am quite incapable of it. And when that happens to a man, he is as good as dead."

Saint-Victor slapped him on the back.

"You mustn't give up too easily, old man. Look at old Louis Bonaparte, Napoleon's brother. Near the end of his life he couldn't stand up and his hands were paralysed, but he wanted to marry a pretty little thing he met in Florence. And when Princess Mathilde scoffed at him and pointed out that he couldn't even blow his nose, do you know what he said? 'What of it? I'd ring for my valet and he'd come and turn me over.' "

"That's the spirit!" laughed Robin. "Even in hospital, you know, the sick don't give up making love till the very end. Did I ever tell you how they manage their love affairs in Saint-Louis? It's all fixed up during Mass at the hospital chapel. The patients of an amorous nature sit in the seats next to the aisle, the women dressed up to the best of their ability in their grey coats, and the men wearing their cotton caps with a jaunty air. They pick the side which allows them to display an undamaged profile, because many of them are in a bad way from scrofula, and each of them holds his missal in such a way as to show the number of his bed marked on it. It costs them money too, because they have to pay five sous for a seat on the aisle. . . ."

"No, it's no use deceiving myself,' said Turgenev. "After forty there's only one word which sums up the basis of existence: renunciation."

"Yes, this is certainly the worst stage in life," Gautier lamented. "I find that women won't grant me the privileges of youth any more, but I don't qualify yet for the privileges they give old age. I'd like to be declared a person of no consequence, to enjoy the immunity that goes with that status."

"Have you been smoking too much, Turgenev?" asked Jules de Goncourt. "Because there's a fundamental opposition between tobacco and woman, and one diminishes the other. . . ."

"Tobacco, we find," said his brother, "has a deadening effect on sexual desire and the sexual act. Though I must say we feel that love is gross and material compared with the spirituality of the pipe."

Turgenev shook his head, and was about to speak when Charles-Edmond chimed in with another suggestion.

"Have you tried making love to a woman who's fully dressed?" he asked.

"But that's so insipid!" declared the elder Goncourt. "If one must indulge in copulation, it has to be with a woman who is naked. . . ."

"A woman," added Jules, "one can roll on top of and cover with kisses."

"Not necessarily," replied Charles-Edmond. "I know that Morny would have disagreed with you, or so young Daudet assures me. He says that Morny never slept with a woman, but paid homage to Venus every morning on a divan in his office, with a caller dressed in all her petticoats and pantaloons. He found that terribly exciting, and I was thinking that if Turgenev . . ."

"Oh, leave the poor man alone!" Gautier broke in. "I sympathise with him, because I'm having the same trouble. There's only one type of woman that can excite me now—the sort I saw at the Tuileries last Monday. Gaunt, emaciated, bony women in fantastically low-cut dresses, flat-chested and sallow-faced, with something ghostly and unhealthy about them, and so little body that you'd have to fuck them standing up. Oh, I know that they don't correspond to the conventional idea of beauty, but I find them terribly exciting, and utterly *modern*."

"I know the type you mean," said Veyne. "But you're talking about society women, women of the upper classes. I remember a few years ago, during a smallpox epidemic in Paris, I was called to a big house where the ladies had decided to have a second vaccination. Well, cutting into their arms was like cutting into parchment. But after the ladies of the house it was decided to give a second vaccination to the chambermaids, and *that* was a very different story. The steel went into their flesh as if it were a juicy apple. Yes, a juicy apple. . . ."

"But it isn't a matter of class," the elder Goncourt protested; "it's a question of period and fashion. Woman's body changes with every civilisation, every age. Her body in the time of Phidias was utterly unlike her body in our own time. Other days, other ways, other lines. That's why Ingres's famous *La Source* is such a failure: it's a polished, painstaking, ridiculously naïve reconstruction of a girl's body in antiquity, and unless an artist paints the woman of his own day—like Boucher with his plump eighteenth-century courtesans—he's doomed to be forgotten."

"You may be right about Ingres not painting the women of our times," said Robin, "but the old boy certainly took a keen interest in them to the very end. You know, whenever he was at the Opera with his wife and started getting excited at the sight of one of the dancers, he'd cry: 'Back to our carriage, Madame Ingres!' and he'd fuck her on the way home."

"The sight of a little ballet-dancer wouldn't be enough to stimulate old Prince Demidoff," remarked Flaubert. "Do you know how *he* manages? He sits in an armchair with Julie Duverger naked in front of him and two lackeys behind him, one of them holding a pair of silver-gilt sugar-tongs to put his tongue back in his mouth. (Duverger says his tongue's always popping out, but never his cock.) A doctor takes his pulse, and then they bring in a big St. Bernard that pounces on Duverger. Old Demidoff gets an erection, the doctor shouts: 'Quick, quick!' and Duverger sets to work."

"If you'll excuse me, gentlemen," Sainte-Beuve said suddenly, "I think I'll leave you to your discussion. I'm feeling rather tired and not too well."

"Let me take you home, Uncle Beuve," said Gautier, getting up to help the old critic out of his chair.

"That's very kind of you, Théo, very kind. . . . No, you stay here, Veyne—my nephew in literature will see me safely home."

Leaning heavily on Gautier's arm, he limped slowly and painfully towards the door, turning on the threshold to take a last look at the room in which he had spent so many enjoyable evenings. He gave the company a benign smile which was like a final benediction.

"Goodbye, gentlemen," he said, and the door closed behind him.

Nobody spoke for a few minutes, and then Saint-Victor voiced the general opinion.

"That," he said, "is probably the last we shall see of Sainte-Beuve. I'm no medical man, but I wouldn't imagine he's very long for this world."

"And I can think of a lot of people," said Claudin, "who'll heave a sigh of relief when he's gone."

"Oh, come now," protested Veyne. "Sainte-Beuve wouldn't do anybody any harm."

"Not while they're alive, perhaps. But I'd hate to die knowing that he was going to produce one of his poisonous obituaries—written or spoken—about me."

"I must say I agree with Claudin," said the elder Goncourt. "Whenever I hear Sainte-Beuve talk about a dead man, with his little anecdotes and epigrams, it's as if I'm watching a colony of ants attacking a corpse: in a few minutes he'll pick a reputation clean for you, leaving nothing but the bare bones of the skeleton neatly laid out."

"You're just annoyed, Goncourt," suggested Saint-Victor, "because of what the old boy said about your novel."

"Certainly not!" Edmond retorted indignantly. "We simply find it revolting to watch that envious old man crawling round the statues of the great and clinging with his stumpy little arms to their feet of clay."

"Do you know *why* he's so hard on great men?" asked Claudin.

"I can think of quite a few explanations," said Flaubert. "But what's yours?"

"You know that he spent his childhood at Boulogne, don't you? Well, one day when the first Napoleon came to Boulogne to inspect the troops who were going to invade England, little Sainte-Beuve caught sight of him passing water. And it's in that position, so to speak, that he's seen and judged all great men ever since."

"There's another explanation for his envy," said Jules de Goncourt, "and for his lack of virility, the feminine nature of his talent, the tortuous, shifty, despicable sides of his character."

"You mean his impotence?" asked Claudin.

"No—because I don't believe he *is* impotent. But I understand that he finds it so difficult and embarrassing to perform the acrobatics of love that it amounts to the same thing. He's a fascinating example of a deficiency in character produced in a man by the imperfection of his genitals."

"He may not always have been impotent," said Saint-Victor, "but he certainly hasn't been able to indulge in sexual pleasure for the last two years. He told me once that he'd had a serious accident in the winter of '66 which had shortened his days and condemned him to an invalid life. One of the springs in his machine is broken—that was how he put it. But Veyne can tell us more about that."

"Veyne could but won't," the doctor retorted with a smile which took the sting out of his reply. "You forget that Sainte-Beuve is a patient of mine, and I owe him the usual discretion."

"Poor old chap," mused Saint-Victor. "Even in his heyday he can't have had much fun with his whores and his housekeepers. Levallois was telling me only the other day about that house-keeper-mistress of his, Madame de Vaquez, whom he firmly believed to be Spanish and always consulted when he was writing about Spanish literature. She'd convinced him of her nationality, first by telling him she was Spanish, and then by going to bed with a dagger. But when she died in his house of consumption, her papers showed that she was a native of Picardy."

"And to make matters worse," said Veyne, "he used to get terrible scoldings from Princess Mathilde about his immoral way of life. 'Your house is a house of ill-fame,' she told him once, 'a home of loose women—and I've set foot in it, I've sat on the same chair as Madame Ratazzi!' "

"Is it true," asked Robin, "that the Princess has broken with him completely?"

"I'm afraid so," replied Flaubert. "What happened was that old Beuve left the *Moniteur* in a temper and went over to the *Temps*. The Princess begged him not to, and he refused to listen; that's the whole story in a nutshell. My own opinion, for what it's worth, is that the first offence was committed by the Princess, who was too sharp, but that the second and graver offence lies at the door of Sainte-Beuve, who behaved anything but gallantly. When you have a friend such as the Princess who gives you an income of thirty thousand francs a year, you owe her a certain consideration. If I'd been in Sainte-Beuve's place, I think I'd have said: 'You're displeased at what I've done: let's say no more about it.' His manners and his attitude were both at fault. . . . But then, I can't understand old Beuve. Why should anybody write for the newspapers when he can write books and isn't dying of starvation? I think what he wants is to be given a national funeral, like Béranger. . . ."

"Poor Gautier looks as though he'll be needing a funeral himself pretty soon," observed Claudin.

"Yes, I've rarely seen Théo so sick and depressed," said the elder Goncourt. "You know that he's making another attempt to get into the Academy? . . ."

"Yes, and that's another thing I can't understand," growled Flaubert. "When a man is *somebody*, why the devil does he try to become *something*?"

"Well, the other day he was in the Princess's drawing-room, sitting on the carpet at Sacy's feet like a poor, tired court jester, and fawning on him with a dreadful obsequious servility. Every now and then he was racked by a fit of coughing, and a cruel remark went round the room to the effect that he was coughing to get into the Academy."

"Has he any hope of getting in this time?" somebody asked.

"Not if Sacy has anything to do with it. Because Théo started telling him and the other guests about that panther-woman of his, describing his bestial relations with the creature in terms calculated to shock the old puritan out of ever giving him his vote. Théo's son was sitting next to me, and I asked him why he didn't go and give his father a nudge. 'Oh, you don't know him,' he said. 'He's perfectly capable of turning to me as he does when I wake him up at the theatre, and saying: *Merde!*' "

"If Gautier goes as well as Sainte-Beuve," said Bernard, "there'll be nobody left of the Romantic generation but Papa Hugo and old Dumas."

"How is Dumas, by the way?" asked Flaubert.

"Very down in the dumps, I gather," replied Saint-Victor. "He was badly shaken when Adah Menken died last year, and since then he seems to have withdrawn into his shell. Dumas *fils* told me the other day that the old man had started re-reading all the books he had written. Said something about being a tree with its foliage full of birds, and the birds waking up and singing in the evening of his life. . . . Apparently one day he found him deep in a book and asked him what he was reading.

" '*The Three Musketeers*,' he said. 'I always promised myself that when I was old I'd find out for myself what it was worth.'

"So Dumas *fils* asked him how far he had got.

" 'I've finished it,' he said.

" 'And what's your considered opinion?'

" 'It's good.'

"But when he got on to *Monte-Cristo* he said: 'It isn't a patch on the *Musketeers*. . . .' "

"And he was right, as usual," said Veyne. 'What a splendid old boy he is—and what a poor thing his son is in comparison! I doubt if Dumas *père* has spent a single night since the age of twenty without a woman in his bed, and he has to put up with his son pontificating about the moral decadence of France and preaching chastity in every play he writes. . . ."

"But not practising it," said Charles-Edmond. "Take that Russian wife of his, the ex-Princess Naryschkine. Well, he lived with her for years while he was condemning the rest of us for our immoral ways, and he even offered her to his friends."

"I don't believe it!" exclaimed Claudin.

"But it's true—I had the whole story from Feydeau. He went to Luchon a few years ago to spend a holiday with Dumas *fils*, and the day he arrived, Dumas took him to dinner at his mistress's house. The woman kept hinting that she wanted to be alone with her lover, and Feydeau finally excused himself, but Dumas left the house with him, explaining that he'd come to Luchon for his health and that making love always gave him backache.

" 'But why don't *you* go to bed with her?' he said.

" 'You really wouldn't mind?' said Feydeau.

" 'On the contrary,' said Dumas, 'you'd be doing me a service.'

"So for a while Feydeau laid siege to the woman, reporting to Dumas every day on his progress: one day putting his arm round her waist, the next day caressing her breasts, and the day after that taking the rest, which she gave up without much resistance. . . . He went back to Luchon the following year and learnt that all winter she had been the mistress of the local mayor, a Monsieur Fron, who told him all about it. Then he lost sight of her, and forgot all about her until he got a letter from Dumas telling him they were married!"

"But she *was* Dumas's mistress for some time," Claudin pointed out, "and he *did* marry her in the end. So you can't say there's any proof that he's immoral."

"Can't I just!" retorted Charles-Edmond. "Feydeau told me that at Luchon there were three little girls who used to do their rooms, and one morning Dumas threw off his dressing-gown and danced naked in front of them, making them cry with fear and disgust. And that's the pillar of rectitude, the defender of morality, the champion of womanhood who looks down his nose at his wicked old father!"

"Talking of Feydeau," said Flaubert, "did you ever hear the story of how he nearly lost his virginity?"

"You mean to say he's still a virgin?" exclaimed Claudin, eyes wide open in astonishment.

Flaubert threw his arms up in the air.

"Good God, no, man! Dammit all, he's got a son—at least, we must suppose that little Georges is his. I was talking about when he was sixteen."

A chorus of voices begged him to go on.

"Well, at sixteen, young Feydeau was in love—not with anybody in particular, just generally in love, and waiting for somebody he could make the woman of his dreams. Now his mother used to take him to the Musard concerts every Tuesday, and there he saw a girl about his own age, an absolute angel—an angel's hair, an angel's eyes, an angel's face. Young Feydeau promptly fell in love with her, sat as close as he could to her, made sheep's eyes at her, and once even followed her at a distance, panting with emotion. The girl looked so pretty and demure that even Feydeau's mother was taken by her, and she told her son that the two of them would make a lovely couple if only he had some money. But as he hadn't, and the girl was always being watched over by her mother, there was obviously nothing to be done, and he gave up hope."

"Is that all?" asked a disappointed voice.

"Have a little patience, will you?" growled Flaubert. "As I was saying, Feydeau was working at this time at Laffitte's, and because he was a virgin he was always being twitted by a fat clerk in his office, a big red-faced, bull-necked fellow with hair on his hands. I need scarcely say that the other fellow wasn't a virgin: in fact, he was so hot-blooded that he kept pulling out his cock and banging it three or four times against his desk to cool it down.

"Well, one day, he said to Feydeau: 'If you weren't such a fool, I'd let you in on a bargain: for ten francs you could be sucked off by a pretty tart.' Now young Feydeau thought that being sucked off wasn't just horrible, it was impossible, and he refused to consider the idea. But after a while he decided that the clerk must be having him on, and he plucked up his courage and agreed to try the experience.

"The clerk took him round to a house in the Rue Poissonnière, where a maid showed them into a little drawing-room. 'I'll go first,' said the clerk, and disappeared into the next room. Feydeau listened hard, heard voices talking, then the sound of heavy breathing, then nothing. The clerk came back into the drawing-room, pale-faced after the operation, and whispered to him: 'She's rinsing out her mouth.' Then Feydeau went into the bedroom, just as the woman was coming through the opposite door. He fell flat on his back in a dead faint, and when he came to he was being driven away in a cab the clerk had sent for. You see, the woman was the angel of the Musard concerts. . . . And the poor fellow was so disgusted that for three years after that he couldn't help shrinking away every time a woman came near him."

"One can never tell about women," mused Turgenev. "I can never forget the two daughters of the steward who lived near my mother's house in Russia. They were incredibly beautiful, and every young man in the neighbourhood was in love with them. I often used to pass their house when I was out walking or hunting, and one day I felt an urge to pay them a call. The family told me that the younger girl, the more beautiful of the two, was suffering from a fever, and that I couldn't see her. Well, as I was leaving I heard the sound of words through the wooden walls, and though I couldn't make them out they aroused my curiosity. So when nobody was paying attention I went back into the house and into the girl's bedroom. She was lying on her bed, fully clothed, with her head thrown back and her eyes half-open, and out of her pretty mouth were pouring all the impurities, indecencies and obscenities you could imagine, like a torrent of filth. An old aunt of hers was sitting by the bed with her head buried in her hands, weeping her heart out. . . ."

"We made a similar discovery about the opposite sex a few years ago," said the elder Goncourt, "when our housekeeper died. We found that that woman whom we had known for twenty-five years, who tucked us up in bed at night, opened our letters when we were away, knew all our business and made all our decisions for us, had led a secret life we knew nothing about. She'd had a whole series of lovers whom she'd kept on our money and fed on our food. She'd indulged in wild, drunken orgies and made love with a frenzy that prompted one of her lovers to say: 'It's going to kill one of us, me or her!' She'd even had two children while she was in our service. . . ."

"You mean to say you didn't notice that she was pregnant?" asked Veyne.

Goncourt gave him a black look which would have quelled a lesser man.

"She must have disguised the fact," he snapped. "And when she had the children, she simply told us she was going into hospital."

"We forgave her, of course," said his brother. "Indeed, seeing something of what she must have suffered at the hands of those working-class pimps, we felt genuinely sorry for her. But she's left us with a deep suspicion of the entire female sex for the rest of our lives, a horror of the duplicity of woman's soul, of her prodigious gift, her consummate genius for mendacity."

"I've always maintained that a bottle is better than a woman," Robin said jokingly as he got up to go. "When the bottle's empty, it's finished. It doesn't ask you for money or a wedding-ring. It doesn't ask you for gratitude or love or even politeness. And above all, it doesn't give you a child."

"Yes, that's a point," said the elder Goncourt. "We've often thought that women ought to be provided with a key in the navel, a key that you'd turn to prevent them from having children if you didn't want to have any by them."

"But that would be immoral!" cried Claudin. "It's wrong to even consider preventing conception. If children die, they die, and that's that, but you've got to have them. . . ."

"Nonsense!" said a voice. "Snuff out the candle!"

"Oh, that's selfish!" said Charles-Edmond.

"What—not to ejaculate?"

"Yes."

"Is your mistress sterile?" asked Veyne maliciously.

"Yes."

There was a roar of laughter.

"What do *you* think about it, Renan?" asked Charles-Edmond. "Are you for Malthus or against?"

Renan folded his podgy hands across his stomach, leaned back in his chair, and closed his eyes for a moment before replying.

"I can only say," he murmured at last, "that the sight of an ugly child makes me very sad. By now I think the possibility of giving birth to a Caliban ought to have been guarded against by law. After all, we have societies for the prevention of cruelty to animals, women and children. Don't you think it's cruel to children to endow them from birth with hereditary ugliness? I do, and by heaven"—he made a bitter grimace—"I speak as one who knows!"

"I agree with Renan," said Taine. "My feeling is that I love children too much to give them life."

Berthelot shook his head emphatically.

"Have a care, gentlemen," he said. "With all your fine sentiments you're forgetting two important facts. Not only is France at this moment the country in which the fewest children are born, but it's also the country with the highest number of old people—four hundred for every fifty-eight in Prussia."

"But that doesn't matter," said Veyne, "provided we don't go to war with Prussia. . . ."

"Which is exactly what we're going to do."

Renan nodded in sorrowful agreement, as more of his companions got up from the table, and the waiters came in with their coats.

"I think so too," he said. "The nation is an animal which lives on glory. But once it has grown accustomed to that fodder, you have to give it the same every day. . . . Yes, we shall go to war. . . ."

"And be defeated?"

"I fear so."

"Why not?"

The question rang out so clear and sharp that every head turned to look at Taine, who was sitting with his hands on his knees, stiff and erect, the gaslight gleaming on his pince-nez.

"Why not?" he repeated. "Our human race was flung on to this globe, no one knows when or where or how. Races have replaced races, empires have destroyed empires, civilisations have grown and fallen like harvests on a plain. And now, perhaps our turn has come. Yes, gentlemen, why shouldn't it be our turn now to die?"

CHAPTER FIVE

24 January 1871

Less than two years later, with the Empire in ruins and the Teuton hordes investing the darkened, starving *ville lumière*, Taine's dismal prophecy seemed about to be fulfilled.

For most Parisians, even after a winter of hardship under siege conditions, the suddenness and amplitude of the disaster which had overtaken France was still difficult to comprehend. With Bismarck on the one hand eager to goad an ill-prepared France into war, and on the other hand leading French personalities assuring a bellicose public that "there must be a struggle for supremacy, and until this collision has taken place everybody will feel that nothing has been decided", both sides had spent long months waiting for a pretext for war. That pretext had come in 1870 with the affair of the Hohenzollern candidature for the Spanish throne and the famous Ems telegram, and on 19 July Napoleon III had declared war on Prussia. Hastily mobilised French troops marched through Paris by torchlight to shouts of "*À Berlin!*" and the Minister of War declared that his armies were "ready down to the last gaiter button", but defeat followed on defeat, and on 2 September, after the most humiliating débâcle in French history, the Emperor surrendered with eighty thousand troops at Sedan.

Two days later a new Republic was proclaimed in Paris and the Empress Eugénie fled to England. For a little while the population of Paris forgot the advancing German armies in their joy at the overthrow of the Empire, and they gave a delirious welcome to Victor Hugo, his prophecies of "little Napoleon's" downfall thoroughly vindicated, when he arrived in the capital on his return from exile. Their euphoria, however, was short-lived. On 19 September the investment of Paris by the German armies was completed, and a few days later the capital's last link with the outside world—apart from carrier pigeons and balloons—was cut.

The rest of Europe waited with a certain *Schadenfreude* for the pleasure-loving city of corruption and debauchery to surrender within a matter of days, but to everyone's astonishment Paris held out for several months, in spite of shelling, starvation, and the cold of one of the worst winters of the century. Her resistance was all the more surprising in that it was organised by an ineffectual general, Louis-Jules Trochu, the Governor of Paris and President of the Government of National Defence, who had no liking for the régime he was expected to support and a deep distrust of the National Guards; while they for their part regarded his Government as defeatist and incompetent. The suspicions on both sides were shown to be partly justified, first in October, when an unsuccessful attempt was made to establish a revolutionary Commune pledged to the idea of a *levée en masse*, and again towards the end of January, when Trochu resigned and the Government agreed to capitulate on the 28th.

It was on the 24th, with surrender in the air, that the *habitués* of the Restaurant Magny came to the Rue Mazet through the shell-scarred streets of the Left Bank, to compare notes and discuss the latest news. There was a comparative newcomer present in the person of Auguste Nefftzer, the political editor of the *Temps*, but the company seemed sadly depleted: Flaubert and George Sand were at their homes in the country, Turgenev was in Russia, and Sainte-Beuve and Jules de Goncourt were dead.

The old critic's health had improved slightly during the spring of 1869, and in April he had been well enough to lunch at the Café Véfour and go to the Academy to vote—in vain—for Gautier. In the summer, however, his condition worsened, and on 12 October a last, desperate operation was performed on him. When the surgeon asked him afterwards if he was still in pain, he replied with a touch of his old spirit: "But I'm no longer alive— I just happen to be here." He died the next day, and was buried in the Cimetière Montparnasse. "So there's that bright spirit extinguished," wrote his "nephew" Gautier, "that star of intelligence vanished for ever. He was fond of me and I certainly returned his affection. Our old guard grows smaller every day, and there aren't many veterans of *Hernani* left. Happily our emperor Hugo still stands on his rock, but today he is a captain without any army. . . ."

Jules de Goncourt had followed him to the grave only a few months later. His morbid sensitivity had been exacerbated by his disease, and towards the end of his life he suffered excruciating pain from noise, notably on a weekend he and Edmond spent at Saint-Gratien when the local villagers celebrated Princess Mathilde's gift of new church-bells by ringing them almost without a pause for forty-eight hours. In January 1870 he made his last entry in the *Journal*, and complained to his brother that he felt sure he would never do any work again. He took to reading Chateaubriand's *Mémoires d'outre-tombe,* a sinister choice which distressed Edmond; but by May 1870 he was incapable of holding a book, let alone reading one, and soon he could not remember the title of a single novel he had written. In June he was afflicted with paralysis, and on the 20th he died, aged only thirty-nine, leaving behind a brother so overwhelmed by grief that Barbey d'Aurevilly cruelly nicknamed him "the Widow".

As the surviving members of the Magny club arrived at the restaurant on 24 January, each holding a hunk of bread to eat with his meal—for only two days earlier, the Government had issued a decree prohibiting caterers from serving bread to their customers —they looked round the dining-room with almost morbid curiosity, to find out who was still in Paris and how they had weathered the rigours of the winter. A group gathered in front of the fire, while Renan sat by himself at the table, reading a newspaper and occasionally throwing his hands up in a gesture of despair. When Saint-Victor came in, he slumped heavily on a chair and quoted:

"And I looked, and behold a pale horse; and his name that sat on him was Death. . . ."

Renan peered at him over the top of his spectacles and asked drily:

"Does that apocalyptic remark have any topical significance?"

"Simply that things look very black indeed."

"Is there any news about the capitulation?" asked Robin.

"Just rumours that negotiations have started. We'll have to wait till Berthelot arrives to find out if there's any truth in them. As President of our precious Scientific Defence Committee, he should know if anyone does—though the Government may not let him into all their secrets. They probably think as little of him as he thinks of them."

"He's the only one still to arrive—unless of course Goncourt decides to turn up. Does anybody know if he's coming?"

"I've no idea," replied Saint-Victor. "You must ask Magny. All I know is that he still hasn't completely got over his brother's death."

"He took it very hard, did he?" asked Claudin. "I was out of Paris at the time, and I haven't seen him since."

"He was shattered by it," said Gautier. "In fact, I was convinced he'd follow his brother within a few weeks, and when I saw the three places in his family vault, with two of them filled by his mother and Jules, I remember thinking that the third place wouldn't be empty for long. You should have seen the state he was in, Claudin! As soon as I arrived at Auteuil for the funeral, he threw himself into my arms and burst into tears, and soon I was weeping with him. He'd gone completely to pieces, and he looked like a ghost. The horrible thing was that his hair, which had been dark the last time we'd met, had turned quite grey, and as the funeral went on, it whitened before our very eyes. No, I didn't imagine it—other people saw it too. By the time we left the cemetery it was completely white. His face had grown emaciated too, and his neck looked suddenly thinner, with the dewlaps and tendons of a man of seventy. . . ."

He shook himself, as if to banish an unpleasant memory.

"That was the saddest day in my life," he went on, "and not just on Edmond's account. I was near the catafalque in the church at Auteuil, and on the black velvet drapings there was a big silver G—which is my initial too—so that I had a vision of my own funeral. I thought to myself that the friends who were there for Goncourt would turn up for me when my turn came—and it can't be long now."

"Come now, Gautier," said Veyne, "none of your gloomy ideas. Things could be a lot worse, you know."

"Could they?" Gautier asked bitterly. "Not for me, I can tell you that. The revolution last September was the end of me, the *coup de grâce*. But then, I've always been a victim of revolutions. . . . Yes, I mean that! When the 1830 Revolution broke out, my father was a Legitimist, and he'd gambled heavily on the July Ordinances: we lost all our fortune at one stroke, fifteen thousand francs a year. I'd been destined for the life of a gentleman of leisure, but instead I had to earn my living. . . . Still, after years of work, things had worked out pretty well for me: I had a little house, a little carriage, a pair of little horses. February '48 put an end to all that. . . . I picked myself up again, and I was going to be elected to the Academy, appointed to the Senate. With Sainte-Beuve dead and Mérimée on his last legs, it was more than likely, wasn't it, that the Emperor would want to appoint another man of letters. I was home and dry. And then the Republic loused everything up. . . ."

"Oh, you've come out on top before, old fellow," said Claudin kindly, "and you'll do it again."

"No, I won't," the old Romantic murmured. "This time I'm finished. At my age a man can't begin his life all over again. . . . What makes it worse is the hypocrisy I've got to put into everything I write: I'm supposed to produce tricolour descriptions. . . . And where's that famous French courage we were always told we were born with? It doesn't exist any more—everybody runs for his life. Look at those soldiers they marched through the streets with their coats inside out, for the people to spit at: they were an official declaration of the French Army's cowardice!"

"That's the fault of the cynics," said a voice from the doorway, "with their never-ending *blague*. People made such fun of our silly old-fashioned heroism that they killed it all off, and a nation without any heroism is doomed to die."

The speaker was an almost unrecognisable Edmond de Goncourt, his hair completely white, his face pale and drawn, his hands fumbling nervously with a white silk scarf he was carrying. He walked over to the group by the fire and shook hands with everyone, receiving the condolences of those who had not seen him since his brother's death.

A few moments later, Berthelot came in, to be bombarded immediately with questions about the Government's plans.

"I can tell you this in confidence," he said, after making sure that there were no waiters in the room. "Favre left Paris yesterday afternoon to open negotiations with the Prussians. He had to be smuggled out, of course, because if the National Guards had recognised their Foreign Minister on his way to parley with the Huns, they'd probably have lynched him."

"And could you have blamed them?" asked Robin. "Look at the lies the Government has told them! 'Not an inch of our territory, not a stone of our fortresses,' said Favre—and half France is probably in Prussian hands. 'Dead or victorious,' said General Ducrot—and he's both alive and defeated. 'The Governor of Paris will not capitulate,' said Trochu—and . . ."

"And the Governor of Paris hasn't capitulated," Nefftzer broke in. "Nor will he, for the very good reason that he's resigned to let Vinoy and the others do his dirty work for him."

"I must say," remarked Goncourt, "that Vinoy taking the place of Trochu looks to me like a change of doctors by the bedside of a dying man."

"There's a doctor here," Veyne complained, "who's going to be a dying man unless we sit down to dinner soon. Let's drink our soup of adversity and eat our bread of affliction."

"Bread of affliction is right," remarked Claudin, who had taken a bite out of his ration while the others were sitting down. "What in heaven's name do they put into it?"

"Are you sure you haven't got a bit from the end of the stick?" Saint-Victor asked knowledgeably. "I always insist on a hunk from the middle, because I once saw a dog piddling on some sticks standing in a corner of the baker's shop."

"Berthelot," Taine called out from the far end of the table, "you've been close to our rulers ever since September. Can you explain to us why we've been defeated? What went wrong?"

Berthelot considered the question for a few moments before replying.

"To a large extent," he said at last, "it's a question of artillery. Ever since the beginning of the war, the Prussian guns have out-ranged our own guns by seven or eight hundred metres. They've been able to stay one or two hundred metres beyond our reach and blow us to smithereens at their leisure. Major Potier's new gun would have evened things up, but naturally General Guiod, the same man who opposed the introduction of the *chassepot*, wouldn't have anything to do with it!"

"It's the same with the gunners," Nefftzer broke in. "Every-body said that we hadn't got enough trained men, but it wasn't true—the Army wouldn't have them. A friend of mine took along a retired artillery officer he knew—a very capable man—to see General Guiod. Well, do you know what that old fool said to him? 'Monsieur, I don't like untimely enthusiasm!' "

"They don't like enthusiasm at all," Berthelot remarked bitterly, "and Guiod must have been surprised to find it in an old man. They certainly did everything they could to avoid encouraging it—calling retired officers back to the colours instead of looking for budding military talent among the young. What they should have done was to make a lot of small *sorties* under the command of young captains. The captain who did best should have been promoted to colonel, and then, if he distinguished himself several times, to general. Like that we'd have had a nursery of officers, a forcing-house for military talent. But what did the Army do? It decided to reserve all promotion for the army of Sedan. Yes, I'm not joking—for the army of Sedan!"

"So it wasn't just our guns that were at fault," said Taine; "it was our generals too?"

"Yes. And like the guns, they've always been inferior to their Prussian counterparts—not just in strategic skill but in sheer application. When a Prussian general is ordered to move an army corps to a certain point at a certain time, he gets out his maps and studies the lie of the land; he works out exactly how long every unit will take to cover a certain distance, making allowances for any slope that might cause a delay. By the time he turns in for the night, he's found all the routes he needs for his troops. But a French general doesn't do anything like that: he goes out on the

F

town all night, and when he arrives on the battlefield the next morning, he asks whether his troops have arrived and where he should attack. From the beginning of the war—and that's the cause of all our defeats from Wissemburg to Montretout—we've never been able to mass our troops at a given point in a given time."

"That bears out what my friend Tessié Du Motay told me the other day," said Robin. "He was on the spot when General Vinoy sallied out to try to take Chelles on the 21st of last month. Vinoy had been given orders to attack at eleven in the morning, but it was two o'clock in the afternoon when he showed up, with all his staff officers a little tipsy after a good lunch, and asking where the devil Chelles was. And the very same day, I think, Du Motay saw General Le Flô arrive on the plateau of Avron and heard him ask somebody if that was in fact the plateau of Avron!"

"In my opinion," said Claudin, "it isn't so much a matter of generalship or guns as a question of national character. Fighting today is all done with precision weapons, and precision weapons are contrary to the French temperament. Shooting fast and charging with a bayonet—that's what the French soldier is good at doing. If he can't do that, he's paralysed, absolutely paralysed. Mechanised warfare isn't for him. And that's where the Prussian soldier is superior, at present at least."

Renan looked up from his plate.

"But that shouldn't surprise you, Claudin," he said. "In every subject I've studied, I've always been impressed by the superiority of the German mind and German workmanship. So it's only natural that in the art of war—which is an art after all, inferior but complicated—they should have achieved the same superiority. . . . Yes, gentlemen, the Germans are undoubtedly a superior race!"

"Nonsense!" shouted several voices.

"Yes, they're very superior to us. And shall I tell you why? Because we are a Catholic country: Catholicism cretinises the individual; the education given by the Jesuits or the brothers of the Christian School arrests the faculties or constricts them, whereas Protestantism develops them."

"Exactly!" agreed Nefftzer. "It's the Massacre of St. Bartholomew's Eve which is killing France just now. If France had turned Protestant, she'd have become the greatest nation in Europe for evermore. You see, in the Protestant countries there's a graduation between the philosophical views of the upper classes and the spirit of enquiry in the working classes, whereas in France there's an unbridgeable gulf between the scepticism at the top and the idolatry at the bottom. Believe me, that's what's killing France!"

"Our present situation certainly suggests a degree of what Renan calls cretinisation," remarked Veyne. "And I can't say that I was impressed by the brilliance of those schemes for defeating the enemy you told me about, Berthelot. Wasn't there one crackpot plan to raise the siege by infecting dogs with rabies and then turning them loose to bite the Prussians and make them all raving mad?"

"Yes, and did you see the idea Jules Allix put to that crazy bunch of female soldiers, the Amazons of the Seine? He suggested that every Amazon should wear a little indiarubber thimble on one finger, topped by a pointed tube containing prussic acid. Then if any amorous Prussian should try to sully the honour of a fair Parisienne, she would just have to prick him and the monster would drop dead. 'No matter how many of the enemy assail her,' Allix told us, 'she can prick them one by one and remain standing pure and holy in the midst of a circle of corpses!'"

"That does sound rather ridiculous," Goncourt conceded, "but even I, the least scientific of men, have found myself dreaming up the craziest devices for defeating the Prussians. I've invented a chemical which dries up all the hydrogen in the atmosphere and kills the Prussians by making the air around them unbreathable. I've also devised a little flying chair which can be wound up like a watch for twenty-four hours and used to rain death down on the enemy. It's astonishing what a fillip hatred and despair can give to the imagination."

"I see that I should have asked you to advise our Scientific Defence Committee," Berthelot said gravely, somehow managing to keep a straight face.

"What annoys me," declared Veyne, "is that our late Emperor should be safely out of harm's way, enjoying himself in some comfortable refuge, while we have to suffer the consequences of his folly."

Goncourt shook his head.

"No," he said, "you can't blame all our troubles on the Emperor. If our generals have been inefficient, our officers incompetent and our soldiers cowardly, that isn't the Emperor's fault. Besides, no one man can have so great an influence on a nation, and if the French nation hadn't been disintegrating, the Emperor's mediocrity wouldn't have robbed it of victory. A sovereign always reflects the nation he rules over, and he wouldn't stay on his throne for three days if he were at variance with the nation's soul."

"You mean that you consider he bears no responsibility for the country's plight?"

"I didn't say that. I just don't agree that it's all his fault. And I must say that I find all these pamphlets about the Empress's alleged lovers and so-called orgies extremely distasteful."

"But what about the examination of Napoleon's correspondence? Surely, as a historian, you can't complain about an objective investigation like that?"

"I can't say I approve of the spirit behind it. I went to the Tuileries in October to see Burty at work on the archives, and it made me feel rather sick. There were some National Guards playing cards in the courtyard, and a horrid-looking canteen woman had set up her table under the peristyle, next to a pile of camp-beds. Burty looked disgustingly proud and happy as he showed me round the palace, and in every step he took you could sense the base satisfaction of the shopkeeper's son who'd moved into the home of royalty. You could see the same virtuous satisfaction in the ugly faces of the clerks working on the correspondence. They were sitting at trestle-tables sagging under heaps of papers and letters, with their instructions hanging from a nail hammered into the gilt frame of a mirror. I felt as if I'd wandered into a secret chamber of the Revolutionary Inquisition, and I found that unsealing of History odious and repugnant."

"Did you see anything interesting, though, among the papers they were reading?"

"I didn't look at any of them. . . . No—that isn't true: when I was in the Salle Louis XIV, where the final sorting of the documents is done, I picked up one of the documents at random. It was a bill showing that that monster of extravagance and luxury, His Imperial Majesty Napoleon III, used to have his socks darned at a cost of 25 centimes a hole. . . ."

"But there are some fascinating things in the archives," said Saint-Victor, "and some that are just too funny for words. Do you know what I spotted when I was over there? A letter from Monsieur Dudevant, Madame Sand's husband, asking for the Legion of Honour, and quoting as a qualification his situation as a deceived husband. Yes, I'm serious—he said that he deserved the cross for being a cuckold. What else could he mean by 'domestic misfortunes which belong to history'?"

Claudin was the only person who failed to join in the laughter.

"I agree with Goncourt," he said gravely, "that there's too much mud-slinging at the Emperor. He may have made a few mistakes, but you can't deny that he meant well, or that he was an intelligent man."

"Oh, well-meaning he may have been," retorted Goncourt, callously spurning Claudin's approval, "but not intelligent. You see, stupidity is usually garrulous, whereas his was silent. That was his great strength, because it allowed people to suppose that he was intelligent. But you mustn't be taken in, Claudin, you really mustn't."

"You knew him personally, Renan," said Gautier. "What did *you* think of his intelligence?"

"His intelligence? I would say it was of a very low order—so low that the man wasn't even conscious of his own iniquity. Do you know that when he was writing his book on Caesar, he used to read it out to Maury—old Alfred Maury, the librarian at the Tuileries—like a schoolboy reading an essay to his master? Well, Maury told me that with the same pen that had signed the order for the *coup d'état* he had actually written this statement: 'Nothing which is founded on violence can endure.' And when

Maury showed that he found this a little hard to stomach, the
Emperor didn't bat an eyelid. He simply didn't understand."

"Jules and I saw him once at close quarters," said Goncourt,
"at a reception at Princess Mathilde's. He was going towards the
buffet, with the slow, mechanical gait of a sleepwalker and the
eyes of a lizard that seems to be asleep and isn't. He looked sleepy,
dull-witted, and sinister in a shifty sort of way."

"Yes, that's the word for him—sinister!" said Gautier. "I
always used to think he looked like a circus artiste who'd been
fired for drunkenness."

"What struck me about him whenever *I* saw him," remarked
Veyne, "was how little he resembled his uncle. But then, the
first Napoleon probably wasn't his uncle anyway."

"What do you mean?" asked Claudin indignantly.

"Why, Claudin, didn't you know that, before he abdicated, King
Louis of Holland made a public declaration that the last two sons
Hortense had given him weren't his at all? They say the real
father of our late Emperor was a Dutch admiral called Verhuell—
which would explain his phlegmatic, expressionless features."

"It explains his shilly-shallying too—his chronic inability in the
last few years to make a decision and keep to it. The first Napoleon
was never like that."

"I've a different theory about that," said Robin, "namely that
the Emperor lost his grip when Orsini made that attempt on his
life back in '58. A few days after that attempt, somebody com-
mented to Louis-Philippe's son on how well the Emperor had
behaved. 'Just like my father," he replied, 'every time somebody
tried to assassinate *him*. But it had its effect on him. Not a week
went by after the first attempt without my father committing a
serious blunder.' "

"We've got to remember too," said Saint-Victor, "that
Napoleon has been ailing for quite a few years. The astonishing
thing is that he knew he was going to pieces, and knew his people
knew too, and yet never let it worry him. Ollivier told me that
in one of his conversations with the Emperor, Napoleon asked
him to tell him frankly what people were saying about him.
Ollivier finally plucked up the courage to tell him that it was

widely believed that his faculties were declining. And all the Emperor said was: 'That is consistent with all the reports I've received.' Now, whatever you think of the man and his policies, you can't help admiring the sheer impersonality of that remark. . . ."

He broke off as the main course was brought in, and everybody gazed with a mixture of eagerness and suspicion at the small pieces of dark meat on each plate.

"What in God's name is this, Charles?" asked Gautier.

"Saddle of mutton, Monsieur," the old waiter replied gravely.

"What are you going to serve us next time, Charles—the shepherd?" said Veyne. "Because this saddle of mutton is a very good saddle of dog."

"*Dog?*" shrieked Claudin. "You say this is *dog*? Charles—tell me it isn't true!"

"Claudin, don't be ridiculous," said Robin. "Of course it's dog—and if you gave me a few minutes I could probably tell you which breed. Haven't you seen the women outside the food-shops clutching their little doggies in their arms all the time? That's because they know damned well that if they put them down for a moment, they'd be lying on a butcher's slab within an hour."

Claudin refused to be convinced.

"It can't be true! Magny's an honest man—he'd tell us if he were serving us anything like that! Besides, dog's an impure meat: horse is all right at a pinch, but *dog*. . . ."

"What on earth have you been eating these last few weeks," asked Veyne, "to turn up your nose at some of the best meat on Magny's menu? Dog is very tasty. Now, I could understand your complaining if it were rat . . . though I've eaten that lately, and it's quite good too. It tastes like a cross between pork and partridge."

Renan, who had been looking very thoughtful during this conversation, suddenly turned pale, put his handkerchief to his mouth, and rushed out of the room, to return, white-faced and subdued, a few minutes later.

"Renan must have a private stock of food to be so queasy about the mention of a rat," said Nefftzer while he was out of the room. "The rest of us have certainly had to eat stranger things than that in order to stay alive."

"Some of them very strange indeed," said Robin. "Renan should have had dinner with me at Voisin's on Christmas Day. Saint-Victor was there, and he can jog my memory if I forget anything. As far as I can remember, the only normal things on the menu were things like radishes and sardines, and most of the other dishes came straight from the zoo. The *hors-d'œuvre* consisted largely of stuffed donkey's head, and the soup was elephant consommé. . . ."

"Then there was kangaroo stew and roast camel among the *entrées*," said Saint-Victor. "But I thought they sounded just a bit *too* outlandish, and I plumped instead for roast bear. . . ."

"And then we had a choice between wolf in roebuck sauce, antelope with truffles, and plain, ordinary cat with a garnishing of rats."

"Didn't you have any elephant steak?" Veyne asked mischievously.

"Not on Christmas Day. That wasn't on the menu at Voisin's till New Year's Day. I had some then, and it tasted delicious."

"Are you sure it was genuine?" asked Claudin. "I grant you that those two elephants in the zoo—Castor and Pollux they were called, weren't they?—were a corpulent pair, but you met so many people in the New Year who had eaten a piece of them or were going to eat a piece of them that the miracle of the multiplication of the loaves and fishes seemed to have been repeated. There wasn't a single restaurant in Paris that didn't put elephant steak on its menu, and you kept meeting people who said: 'We're going to have some elephant sausages or elephant black pudding for dinner.' I began to wonder whether the whole population had been taken in and there weren't any elephants at all."

"Like those German helmets you saw in all the shops in November?" said Robin. "Did you see that they found a factory in the city where they were making hundreds of chocolate-coloured Bavarian helmets and those classic Prussian helmets with their spread-eagle lightning-conductors? The owner was genuinely astonished when the police arrested him: he said that he was just trying to meet the public demand for trophies from the battlefield. He didn't confine himself to helmets either: one room in his house was littered with forged letters in German from non-existent mothers, sisters and wives which he was going to sell as taken from the pockets of German corpses."

"There may not have been many genuine German helmets or love-letters in Paris in November," said Saint-Victor, "but there was plenty of elephant-meat around in the New Year. I happened to go into Roos's, the English butcher's on the Boulevard Haussmann, at the time, and there on the wall, in the place of honour, was young Pollux's trunk. Roos had bought both elephants from the zoo, and was complaining to a group of women customers that Pollux had yielded only two thousand three hundred pounds of meat when he had been counting on three thousand. But he wasn't exactly giving the meat away. He was charging twenty francs a pound for the feet, and forty francs a pound for the trunk. And heaven knows how much for his black pudding, because he was telling the women that an elephant's blood was the richest there is. . . ."

"At that sort of price," said Veyne, "there can't have been many people who could afford to buy elephant, even as a special treat. How things have changed in only a few weeks! Do you remember how, at the beginning of the Siege, those of us who weren't accustomed to eating horse-meat made self-conscious jokes about it? Like that one about the *bouillon* running away because the meat came from a race-horse? Well, now the joke has gone sour on us, and we're moving fast towards starvation. There's hardly any horse-meat left in the city, vegetables are a terrible price, and every sort of fat except candle-fat and axle-grease has disappeared. The greater part of Paris is living on coffee, wine and bread."

"And many people haven't even got that," said Robin. 'The other evening in the street a prostitute came up behind me and said: 'Monsieur, would you like to have me for a bit of bread?' "

"I know," murmured Goncourt, "Even I, who have enough money to buy myself an occasional meal, have been reduced to eating almost anything at home. A week ago, with nothing to eat, and no desire to come into town, I shot a starling in the garden for my dinner. And then I didn't eat it. I don't believe in metempsychosis, but for some reason I suddenly associated my dead brother with the dead bird. I remembered how it used to arrive at dusk every evening, give a shrill whistle as if to announce its presence, and perch on one particular branch of a sycamore in the garden before flying away. A sort of superstitious idea occurred to me that some part of my brother had entered into that little winged creature, and I was filled with horror at the thought that I had killed a friendly visitor from the other world, which had been watching over me and my house. I know that it was silly, ridiculous, insane, but the idea haunted me all night."

His voice quavered as he spoke the last few words, and there was a pause as he sat gazing unseeingly at the table and twisting his napkin in his hands.

"It's odd, isn't it," Saint-Victor said at last, "how every conversation nowadays is about food—how to make onion soup without onions, how to use arsenic to cheat your stomach, and so on—while the only shops with people outside them have got something edible on display, even if they aren't normally food-shops. Why, the other day I even saw some eggs in a jeweller's window in the Rue de Clichy, lying in cotton-wool as if they were precious stones."

"One thing that amazes me," said Nefftzer, "is the patience of the poorer classes in the face of insolent window displays like that. If I were starving to death and saw a display of food that reminded me that the rich need never go short, I think I'd smash the window and beat up the shopkeeper. But all the people do here is joke and laugh. They don't even lose their temper."

Goncourt nodded his agreement.

"When I was reading old copies of Marat's newspaper," he said, "for my book on the Revolution, I thought all his furious denunciations of the grocer class were just hysterical exaggeration. But now I know that Marat was right. Most of those shopkeepers are rogues and robbers. I wouldn't object if one or two of them were strung up outside their shops. At least that might stop the price of sugar going up two sous an hour as it does at present."

"Another thing I admire about the population of Paris,"

Nefftzer continued, "is their courage under fire, the patient good humour with which they put up with bombardment as well as starvation. The Germans certainly made a mistake with their so-called *psychological moment*; all that the shelling of Paris has done is to irritate the people instead of terrifying them."

"That's my impression too," said Goncourt. "The other day I went on a tour of the districts that have been shelled, and I found no panic or alarm. Everybody seemed to be leading his usual life, and the café proprietors were cheerfully replacing the mirrors that had been shattered by blast. And yet it isn't a case of a stray shell now and then any more, but a deluge of cast iron moving across the city. You've seen the damage here on the Left Bank, especially on the Boulevard Saint-Michel, and in my own district shells are exploding every few minutes, so that people have to cross the boulevard on all fours. A few days ago, when I was standing at my window trying to make out the Meudon batteries with my telescope, a shell-splinter sent mud splashing against my front door, and a woman had a foot blown off by a shell only twenty yards from me. . . ."

"You may find this hard to believe," said Berthelot, "but our precious rulers have no idea whatever of what the people are going through. Do you know what that insolent cretin Ferry replied when I complained to him about the bread-lines being installed where there were shells falling all the time, and the risks the poor women ran waiting for their rations? He said: 'Well, they shouldn't go there, that's all.'"

"No wonder the ordinary people distrust the Government!" exclaimed Veyne. "But would the revolutionaries who tried to set up a Commune last October have been any better than the men in power now?"

"Good Lord, no! You can't imagine the crapulous imbecility of the people who took over the Hôtel de Ville that day. There was one group that actually wanted Barbès in the Government: they didn't know that he was dead! And when I asked a sentry outside the council-chamber who it was that he was guarding, he had no idea which Government was inside! It was enough to make a strong man weep!"

"I wonder what Hugo thinks of his precious Paris now," mused Claudin. "Has anybody seen him since he returned from exile?"

"I have for one," said Goncourt. "I went to see him at Meurice's house last November to thank him for the letter of sympathy he sent me when my brother died. He received me in what I thought was a perfect setting: a little drawing-room where the ceiling and the walls were lined with old tapestry. In that old-fashioned room, in the half-light dulled by the old colours of the walls and turning blue with cigar-smoke, in which everything looked a little vague and uncertain, things as well as people, Hugo's head, lit up by the firelight, looked imposing and right. Some of his white locks were curling rebelliously like the hair of Michelangelo's prophets, and there was a curious, almost ecstatic tranquillity in his face. Yes, a sort of ecstasy, but with a gleam in his eyes which looked to me like cunning."

"What did the Grand Old Man talk about?" asked Veyne.

"Believe it or not, about the moon. He told me that ever since he'd spent a night in the Observatory years ago with Arago, he'd been curious to find out exactly what it looked like. In those days, he said, the lenses of telescopes were not very powerful, so that if there were a monument on the moon—and whenever he mentions a monument, he means Notre-Dame de Paris—it would have shown simply as a dot. But nowadays, with the new lenses three feet across, we ought to have something better than those photographs of mountain chains."

"And was that all he had to say?"

"No. I asked him whether he felt at home again in Paris and he replied that he liked the city as it is now, during the Siege. He said he wouldn't have liked to see the Bois de Boulogne in the days when it was crowded with carriages and landaus, but that now it was a quagmire and a ruin it rather appealed to him."

"I suppose he disapproves of everything Haussmann did under the Empire," said Claudin.

"I thought that too, but it isn't the case. He said that Notre-Dame and the Sainte-Chapelle had been beautifully restored, and there was no denying that there were some fine new houses. And although the city had been anglicised he said there were two things to distinguish it from England—a better climate and the absence of coal. But he doesn't approve of Haussmann's boulevards. As a matter of personal taste, he said, he preferred the old streets of his youth, and he pointed out that the Empire did nothing to provide a defence against foreigners: everything it did was designed to provide a defence against the population."

"I saw Hugo a few weeks ago," said Charles-Edmond, "at one of those public readings of his poems against the Empire. It was given by Frédérick Lemaître, Hugo's 'Ruy Blas' of thirty years ago. Old Frédérick has lost most of his teeth and he had to wear spectacles for the reading, but it was rather moving to hear that glorious voice declaiming Hugo's verse again. On the other hand, I must say I didn't like Hugo's patriarchal posturing."

"Oh, I didn't find him like that at all," said Goncourt. "He was very simple and kind with me, and full of sympathy for me in my loss. He compared my loneliness without Jules to his own isolation in exile, and urged me to find escape from it in work. And he tried to comfort me with the idea of a sort of posthumous collaboration with my brother, saying that he believed in the presence of the dead and calling them the Invisible Ones. . . . No, I didn't find him at all pretentious. And I liked his rather cold, almost aristocratic courtesy, which is positively refreshing in these casual times, when celebrities slap you on the back and call you 'old chap' the first time they meet you."

"The old boy isn't quite the noble patriarch you seem to have found him," said Robin. "I've heard some odd things about his habits from Madame Meurice herself. It appears that he's a classic case of acute satyriasis, only too willing to enjoy the homage the women of Paris want to offer him. Every night at ten he leaves the Hôtel Rohan, where he's installed the faithful Juliette Drouet, and goes back to the Meurice house, where there are always one, two or three women waiting for him—women of every sort and condition, from great ladies to dirty little sluts. His bedroom is on the ground floor, and every morning and evening, when Madame Meurice's maid is out in the garden, she catches glimpses of the Grand Old Man coupling with his latest admirer."

Gautier, who had been dozing gently in his corner, opened his eyes in sudden interest when he realised who was the subject of the conversation.

"I've been to see Hugo too," he said. "He told me he'd been back to the Academy to try to get Dumas *père* elected. But it seems there are only thirteen Academicians in Paris at the moment, and there have to be twenty-one for an election."

"By the time the Siege is lifted, it will probably be too late anyway," said Saint-Victor. "The old man was sinking fast in the autumn. Dumas *fils* seemed rather pleased at the collapse of his health—he said the moral to be drawn was to beware of women. But he told me a touching story about his father. Apparently he had two golden louis on his bedside table, all that was left of the fortunes he'd made in his lifetime. And one day he picked them up and said to his son: 'Alexandre, everybody says I've been a prodigal, and you've even written a play on the subject. Well, see how wrong people can be. When I arrived in Paris for the first time, I had two golden louis in my pocket . . . and look— I have them still.' "

"Dead or alive, he's well out of it," said Claudin. "I shudder to think what the Prussians are going to do to us when they occupy Paris."

"Oh, I'm not worried about what they'll do to *me*," declared Gautier. "If they come for me in my little attic in the Rue de Beaune, do you know what I'll do? I'll show them my letters patent stating that I'm a member of the St. Petersburg Academy, and *ipso facto* a general in the Imperial Russian Army. And not only will they run away with their tails between their legs, but they'll have to present arms to me as well."

He smiled sadly at a thought which had just occurred to him.

"Do you realise, gentlemen, that if I died in Russia, I'd have a whole division at my funeral? Whereas if I die here in France, all I'll get is a wretched little infantry platoon. . . ."

"*You* may be all right," said Saint-Victor, "but what about the rest of us? Because the Germans are a vicious people, full of hatred. They haven't many pleasures, and their principal joy in life is derived from hatred, from thinking out and perpetrating revenge. They still bear us a grudge for what we did to them under

Napoleon, and even under Louis XIV, and they won't forgive us for holding out against them in Paris for all these months."

"I believe I know what form their revenge will take," said Berthelot. "I think they'll strip us of our industrial equipment."

"And they'll empty our museums and art galleries," prophesied Charles-Edmond.

"*If* they find anything in them," said Goncourt; "but our greatest treasures have been hidden away. I met Chennevières in the Louvre in September, and he told me that he was leaving for Brest the next day with a third trainful of pictures from the Louvre, which had been taken out of their frames and were being sent to the arsenal or the prison at Brest to save them from the enemy. He said the packing operation was a melancholy, humiliating affair, with the Director crying like a baby over *La Belle Jardinière* lying in her crate, as if she were a loved one about to be nailed into her coffin. I saw some of the crates myself, and it was strange to think that they contained pictures one had imagined fixed to the walls of the Louvre for all eternity—pictures which were now nothing but anonymous parcels labelled *Fragile*. But at least they should be safe now from the Prussians. . . ."

"I don't share your fears of what the Prussians will do," declared Nefftzer. "I think they'll try to surprise us with their generosity, their magnanimity."

"Amen to that!" chorused some of his companions.

"Of course they'll be generous," said Renan. "As I've said before, they're a superior race, proud and independent, but fundamentally just."

"Nonsense!" snorted Charles-Edmond. "I met some of them when I went shooting in Baden, and all I can say is that we used to send your proud, independent German peasants to pick up the game with a kick in the arse!"

"Well, I'd rather have peasants you kicked in the arse than peasants like ours, whom universal suffrage has made our masters—peasants who saddled us with Napoleon III for twenty years!"

"So there's nothing left for us to do," asked Goncourt, "but rear a new generation to take our revenge?"

"No, no!" cried Renan, pounding the table angrily. "You mustn't talk about revenge! Let France die, let the Nation die: there's a higher ideal, an ideal of Duty and Reason!"

"No, no!" shouted his companions, and Saint-Victor bellowed louder than the rest:

"Let's have an end to fancy theorising. There's nothing higher than the Nation!"

Renan bowed his head until the storm had passed, and then looked up to reply quietly:

"Yes there is. The idea of the Nation or the Fatherland was quite natural in ancient times, but it was displaced by Christianity, and since the idealists of our times are the heirs of Christianity, they shouldn't give their allegiance to such narrow ethnographical concepts as the Nation."

"When I went to see Hugo," Goncourt insisted, "he said to me: 'We'll rise again one day. The world will never stand for that abomination they call Germanism. We'll have our revenge in four or five years.' "

"That word again!" groaned Renan. "Isn't our plight unhappy enough without making it worse with talk of hatred and revenge? Everything I've dreamed of, hoped for, advocated has come to nothing. I had made it my aim in life to work for the moral, intellectual and political union of Germany and France, and now the criminal folly of Napoleon's government, the political ineptitude of French democracy, the excessive patriotism of the Germans and the military pride of the Prussians have created a gulf between the two countries which will take centuries to bridge. But if the time has come when 'the kissing has to stop', I shall say no more. I cannot unsay what I have said all my life, and preach hatred when I have advocated love. Like Goethe, all I can say is: 'How can you expect me to preach hatred when I do not feel it in my heart?' "

"Then what do you suggest we do as a nation?"

"Accept defeat gladly. Because a victorious nation is always enslaved by those who have brought it victory. The victor is the worst of masters, the fiercest enemy of reform. It's after a defeat that a nation has the best chance of making progress. It's after a defeat that a people is free and happy. God preserve us from victory!"

"Since God appears to have preserved us from it only too well," said Veyne, "let's console ourselves with a heavenly gift I find it easier to appreciate. Théo, why don't you warm our hearts and cheer our spirits with Sainte-Beuve's delicious concoction? Charles . . . the rum and curaçao, please."

A few minutes later a sigh of appreciation went round the table as the company forgot war, siege and imminent defeat in the enjoyment of the *mélange About*.

"Thank heavens," said Gautier, "that I can still find pleasure in this delectable drink. I was beginning to think that my taste-buds had been ruined by the horrors I've had to ingurgitate during the Siege. . . . Incidentally, did I ever tell you of the book I want to write about taste? Really, of course, I should use some other term, like *dégustation*, because the metaphysical applications of the word have detracted from its purely physical meaning, and nowadays, when you say *taste*, the Classicists prick up their ears and say 'I beg your pardon', thinking that you're talking about *them*.

"Yes, I've often dreamt of explaining all the mysteries of taste, and describing the various sensations every dish produces as it passes over the papillae of the tongue. I don't think there's anybody else in the world who's capable of performing such a *tour de force*. Have you ever asked yourself why something which *you* consider delicious revolts the person sitting next to you at table, and why there should be such a difference between you, seeing that your palates are made the same way? And can you explain our habit of eating bread with every course and mixing a mouthful of that insipid paste with every portion of food we ingurgitate? If bread is a dish in itself, why don't we eat it on its own?"

"I suppose because it's the staff of life," suggested Claudin, "the essential foodstuff that accompanies every other."

"No, Claudin, no," sighed Gautier. "Bread is just a western invention, and a stupid, dangerous invention at that. It was thought up by avaricious bourgeois, and all that it has done for them is bring them revolutions. Philanthropists and humanitarians think they've very clever when they tell their governments: 'The people need bread! Give the people bread!' If they were taken at their word, they'd be in real trouble. You see, the people don't like bread: they like red meat, carnivorous animals that they are. If bread were abolished, there'd be no pretext for revolution any more, and the revolutionary song-writers would have to shut up. Besides, bread has another serious disadvantage: its insipid taste spoils the flavour of the fruits and other dainties provided by Mother Earth; it has spoilt our taste and encouraged the deplorable use of mustard, seasoning and spices. Abolish bread, and mustard will vanish, leaving man alone with Nature: after four thousand years of corrosive spices, he will finally recover full possession of that sense of his over which God racked his creative brains the longest. . . ."

Warming to his subject, he took another sip of his *mélange About*, and went on:

"Once I've duly established the fact that bread is the supreme corrupter of taste, I shall rehabilitate gourmandism and restore it to its place among the virtues: I shall take each of our traditional dishes in turn and explain its particular flavour; I shall describe its triumphant entry into the kingdom of the mouth and its ephemeral reign; I shall lay down the rules of that gastronomic poem they call a menu and study the divergencies of taste which separate convivial men; I shall divide mankind into fruit-eaters, flesh-eaters, fish-eaters and cannibals, and by means of that classification alone I shall provide the key to love and hate, war and history. . . ."

There was a long silence, and then he murmured in a barely audible voice:

"I shall never write that book, or any other. What's the use? Nothing matters any more. . . ."

He sat slumped in his chair, gazing at the table with unseeing eyes. At last Goncourt stood up and laid a gentle hand on his shoulder.

"Come along, Théo," he said, "It's getting late. I'll take you home."

"It's time we were all going home," said Veyne, and he and the others slowly got to their feet. They were silent and thoughtful as they put on their hats and coats and followed one another down the steep stairs.

Out in the street they gathered in a group on the pavement, as if reluctant to venture any further, turning up their coat collars and shivering in the bitter cold. The rumble of gunfire could be heard in the distance, together with an occasional explosion, and the sky towards the Luxembourg was bright with the glare of a burning building.

"Strange, isn't it," somebody said, "to think that two weeks from now there may be Prussians sitting on our chairs at Magny's and dining at our table!"

And with the sudden realisation that they might never dine together again, Magny's guests parted with silent handshakes and went their separate ways down the darkened street.

CHAPTER SIX

22 November 1872

IN THE EVENT, the fears expressed that night in the Rue
Mazet were not realised: no Prussian officers came to celebrate
their victory with a dinner at Magny's. Indeed, the conditions
of the peace preliminaries agreed in February—the cession of
Alsace and the northern part of Lorraine to the newly constituted
German Empire, and the payment of a war indemnity of five
milliard francs—were ratified so swiftly by the French National
Assembly that the German Army had no sooner staged its
triumphal entry into Paris, on 1 March, and occupied the area
surrounding the Place de la Concorde, before it had to be withdrawn again. But that ceremonial march, insisted upon by Bismarck as the only alternative to the surrender of Belfort, was
regarded by the poorer classes of Paris as another humiliation
inflicted on them by their fellow countrymen in the provinces.
For four months they had suffered hardship and even starvation,
pinning down a large investing army which would otherwise
have been free to ravage the provinces, and in return the provinces
had voted into power a reactionary Assembly which had ignored
the feelings of the capital. The more prosperous Parisians—
those whom Thiers, the head of the Provisional Government,
called "the decent people of Paris"—had left the city immediately
after the capitulation to "breathe some fresh air", and it was
chiefly the lower classes who were left to watch the victorious
enemy parade through their streets. To make matters worse, the
Assembly took a series of measures calculated to exacerbate their
injured pride—moving from Bordeaux to Versailles instead of to
Paris, suppressing six newspapers, and ordering the Army to
seize a cannon which the National Guard refused to surrender
to the Germans—with the result that on 18 March revolution
broke out in the capital, the Government fled to Versailles, and
the Commune of Paris was proclaimed.

For a few weeks Paris lived through a nightmare even more horrible than the winter's siege, for now it was Frenchmen who invested the capital under the amused gaze of the German occupation forces; it was Frenchmen who fired public buildings and shot hostages in the "Bloody Week" in May when the Versailles troops entered the city; and it was Frenchmen who shot and bayoneted twenty thousand real or suspected Communards, men, women and children, until the gutters ran with blood. And yet, within a matter of weeks an ignorant visitor could have been forgiven for thinking that nothing more serious had occurred than a series of unfortunate fires. Life swiftly returned to normal; tourists flocked to Paris from the provinces and abroad—for ten pounds one London agency offered "a week in a first-class hotel, evenings at the Opera and the Théâtre-Français, and tours of the ruins of Paris and the battlefields around the city"; and when Edmond de Goncourt came across a concourse of private carriages in the Rue de la Paix, he discovered that the important personage whom so many wealthy people had come to see was the great Second Empire couturier, Worth. Indeed, so rapid was the capital's recovery, and so complete its return to the prosperity and gaiety of the Second Empire, that after revisiting the city, the journalist George Augustus Sala entitled a book of his impressions: *Paris Herself Again.*

One Parisian institution, however, never regained the prestige and popularity it had enjoyed before the war: the Restaurant Magny. The drift of customers from the small, out-of-the-way restaurants on the Left Bank to larger, livelier, more luxurious establishments on the fashionable Right Bank, which had begun with the building of Haussmann's boulevards under the Second Empire, became more pronounced during the months immediately following the Commune. But the greatest blow to the restaurateur of the Rue Mazet was the defection of the Magny dining club to the Café Brébant owned by his brother-in-law. This move had been decided because of the problem of accommodation which had beset the club for years, but it was also a consequence of the death of most of the original founders—Gavarni, Sainte-Beuve and Jules de Goncourt—and the frequent absences of other members with a sense of loyalty to Magny's, such as Flaubert and Turgenev. Those veterans of the Magny Dinners who attended the gatherings at Brébant's found, as Sainte-Beuve had prophesied, that the atmosphere was completely different. The diners now included a preponderance of politicians, generals and men about town, and the conversation consisted of society gossip rather than discussions on literature and life. And then, in October 1872, one of the last links with the old Magny Dinners was broken by the death, at the age of sixty-one, of Théophile Gautier.

Flaubert was unable to attend Gautier's funeral, but he came to Paris the following month, and arranged to meet Goncourt at Magny's for a dinner *à deux* in memory of their old friend and of the many evenings they had spent there in his company. On 22 November, ten years to the day after the first Magny Dinner, Edmond de Goncourt accordingly took a cab to the restaurant in the Rue Mazet and once again climbed the familiar stairs to the first floor. Flaubert had not yet arrived, but Magny showed Goncourt into the small private room where they were to have dinner and poured him a glass of champagne.

"How are you keeping, Magny?" the novelist asked, in a gruff attempt to unbend.

"Quite well, Monsieur de Goncourt, thank you."

"And the restaurant? Prospering, I suppose?"

Magny shook his head sadly.

"Business is bad," he said disconsolately, "very bad indeed. It isn't just your friends going over to my brother-in-law's place— though I can't deny that that upset me, just like Monsieur Gautier dying last month. It's everybody wanting to dine on the Boulevards, and not caring what they eat provided there's lots of room and bright lights and famous faces. And then there's the problem of staff, Monsieur de Goncourt! Charles was saying to me just now that it's getting impossible to hire a good waiter. Any bungling idiot who's done a couple of seasons in a third-rate spa thinks he's capable of serving in a first-class Paris restaurant. I shudder to think what Monsieur Philippe would say about some of the men I've taken on."

"You worked for Philippe before you started this restaurant, didn't you?"

Magny nodded gravely.

"Yes, Monsieur de Goncourt, and for his son too. Now Monsieur Philippe *père*—he was a smart one, and no mistake. He bought himself a pot-house near the turn of the century, and I've heard tell he fooled the neighbours into thinking he was doing a roaring trade, just by rushing in and out with wine-jugs that had nothing but water in them. He started serving meals about 1820—and it was Mother Brodier, his shell-opener, who cooked them—and by '37, when he handed over to his son, he'd made a fortune."

He gave a bitter smile.

"I could have made a fortune too," he went on, "by putting up my prices and skimping on the food. If I hadn't loved my work, I'd have saved four thousand francs a year on butter alone: that's over a hundred thousand in the thirty years I've been here. And then I could have bought those newfangled contraptions that some customers are willing to pay more for. Have you seen that little press that some of my colleagues use to squeeze the blood out of a duck? It doesn't make any difference to the duck, but it doubles the price you can charge the customer."

"But surely," said Goncourt, "nobody goes to those new restaurants just for the sake of bright lights and elaborate contraptions?"

"Then I don't know why they do," retorted Magny. "It can't be for the *cuisine*. Take my brother-in-law, for instance. He may have a big place over there on the Boulevard Poissonnière, with lots of big rooms, but his cooking . . ."

He made an expressive grimace.

At that moment the door opened, and Charles ushered Flaubert into the room. Goncourt got to his feet and the two veteran novelists, both looking far older than their fifty years, clasped each other in a silent embrace.

"Monsieur Flaubert," said Magny after a while, when his guests had sat down, "it's a pleasure to see you again after such a long time."

"It's good to see *you* again, Magny, especially after all the trouble you had here. Did you have a hard time of it?"

"I survived, Monsieur Flaubert—which is much as any of us could hope for. I must admit that I felt a little nervous when the Rue Dauphine became a battlefield, but luckily for me I knew that fellow Ferré, who was in charge of the barricade. He was an old acquaintance of mine, and many's the time we'd played cards together in the Passage du Commerce just round the corner. In those days, of course, he wasn't a famous revolutionary, but just a quiet little lawyer's clerk who didn't even take an interest in politics. Well, when he took over the barricade in the Rue Dauphine, he came round to see me and said to me: 'Give me some wine for my men and keep out of the way.' So I followed his advice, and I'm still here to tell the tale."

"Good man!" boomed Flaubert. "But now tell us what you intend to give us to eat this evening."

"Since this is something of an occasion," Magny replied, "I thought that I should offer you the best I can provide, the specialities of the house. First, of course, my *petites marmites*. Then a dish I know you both enjoy—my *écrevisses à la Bordelaise*—followed by a *tournedos Rossini* . . ."

"Which Rossini invented with you in this very restaurant, didn't he?"

"He did indeed, Monsieur Flaubert. Ah, the *maestro* was such a wonderful connoisseur, such a dedicated gourmet! Do you know, when he was due to dine here, he would take nothing but one cup of iced coffee all day, to prepare himself for the meal? And one of his friends told me that of the three times he cried in the whole of his life, one was when he accidentally dropped a truffled turkey he was carrying into Lake Garda. . . ."

"And after the *tournedos Rossini*?" Goncourt asked a little testily.

"Another creation of mine, a *purée Magny*. . . ."

"That glorious *purée* we've had here time and again! You once promised to tell me how you made it, Magny; why not now? Or is it very complicated?"

"It's simplicity itself. You bake the potatoes in the oven, cut them in half and scoop out the pulp, pass it through a wire sieve, and mix with an equal quantity of the freshest butter you can find."

"Normandy butter, I hope?"

"That goes without saying, Monsieur Flaubert. . . . Then, after the *purée Magny*, there'll be salad, a *parfait de café*, and dessert."

"And the wines?"

"A Latour Blanche 1861, a Romanée Conti 1858, a Bellanger *frappé*, and a Grand Porto 1827."

"That sounds perfectly splendid, my dear fellow. Our mouths are watering already. Off you go, and set your minions to work. . . ."

As Magny left the room, Flaubert turned to his companion and raised his glass.

"Let me propose a toast, Goncourt," he said. "To the memory of our dear Théo."

"To Théo," Goncourt repeated, adding with a note of reproach in his voice: "I was sorry not to see you at the funeral."

"I was sorry not to be there, but that fool Mendès let me know too late. Was it as horrible as most funerals are?"

"It was very grand and pompous. Army bugles sounded for the Officer of the Legion of Honour, and opera singers chanted a Requiem for the author of *Gisèle*. And there was a horde of small-time scribblers there who were obviously escorting the journalist and not the poet. . . . Oh, I nearly forgot one thing that happened: the clergy, for some reason or other, disappeared when we got to the grave, taking their holy water with them. So Auguste Marc tore a branch from a tree and tossed it into the grave, covering the coffin with leaves."

"I knew something like that would happen!" Flaubert cried triumphantly. "It always does. When they buried my sister, the grave was too narrow and the coffin wouldn't fit in. They shook it and hit it and tried to lever it in, and finally one of the grave-diggers stamped on it, just where her head was, to push it down. . . . And this time it was the priests who spoiled everything. Still, I'd have been sorry if Théo hadn't had a Catholic funeral, because basically he was as Catholic as a twelfth-century Spaniard.

And in matters like that, you've got to respect the dead man's wishes. . . . Did you see him before he died?"

"No. I'd only just come back from a holiday in the Tyrol, and I was reading my paper over dinner—that's the only way I can eat when I'm dining alone—when I suddenly saw the announcement that he'd gone. I went to see him next morning, and Bergerat took me into his bedroom. You know, Flaubert, lying there with his pallid face framed in his long black hair, he had the fierce serenity of a barbarian who had fallen asleep for ever. There was nothing there to suggest a modern death. Memories of the stone figures outside Chartres Cathedral came back to me, mingled with stories of Merovingian times. And the room itself, with the oak bed-head, the red patch of a missal, the sprig of box in a simple vase, gave me the impression of being in a *cubiculum* in Ancient Gaul, a primitive, tragic Roman interior."

"Poor Théo!" murmured Flaubert. "You know, Goncourt, I'm convinced that he died of what he called the swinishness of the times we live in. The Fourth of September inaugurated an epoch in which people like him no longer have any place in the world. You can't expect orange trees to produce apples, and luxury craftsmen are useless in a society dominated by the plebs. He had two hates: hate of the Philistine in his youth— and that gave him his talent; and hate of the hooligan in his maturity—and that killed him. He died of suppressed anger, of rage at being unable to say what he thought. He told me himself several times: 'It's the Commune that's done for me. . . .' "

"It was the Siege as well," said Goncourt in a matter-of-fact voice. "I went to see him in those days in the attic which was all he could afford, and he looked as if he were dying of cold and hunger. . . . But now I come to think of it, I've never heard how *you* fared during the war. All I remember is hearing the news that Rouen had fallen to the Prussians, and hoping that you hadn't carried out your threat to blow yourself up. . . ."

"No, I didn't do that, but there were times when I thought I was going mad. I've had some bad moments in my life, I've suffered grievous losses and I've wept a great deal, but all those accumulated sorrows were nothing to what I went through then. And I still haven't got over it. . . . I didn't think I believed in progress and humanitarianism, but I had some illusions, and now they're all gone. Those officers who wore white gloves and smashed mirrors, who knew Sanskrit and guzzled champagne, who stole your watch and then sent you a visiting-card, those civilised savages horrified me more than cannibals. And now everybody's going to copy them, everybody's going to be a soldier. The whole of Europe will put on uniforms, and we'll make wholesale murder the aim of all our efforts. . . ."

"Did they behave badly at Croisset?"

"No, I can't say that they did. We had ten of them quartered on us there, and though they took a few things, they did no damage. But the whole thing aged my mother by ten years— if it hadn't been for the invasion, she wouldn't have died last April. And the humiliation of it all, the shame of it all! How can anybody believe in civilisation or science when a country full of scientists commits abominations worthy of the Huns—no, worse, because they're systematic, cold-blooded and deliberate, without the excuse of passion or hunger?"

"And then they're so arrogant," said Goncourt, "so sure that they're what Renan calls a superior race, and so hurt and puzzled that we should hate them. Renan told me the other day that Mommsen had written to him suggesting that it was time to pick up the threads of their work together, and hinting that the Academy might like to continue the Emperor's policy—in other words, go on paying the pensions Napoleon paid to foreign savants. Have you ever heard of such impudence? The Germans are like those obsequious clerks who come and ask for their jobs back from an employer they've robbed and ruined."

"I suppose we should try to remember that this has all happened before and will all happen again. I heard the other day of a Chinese envoy who arrived in Paris just in time for our national cataclysm. Somebody remarked to him that he must find what was happening very surprising, but he replied: 'Not at all. You're a young race, you Westerners, you have hardly any history to speak of. The world has always been like this: the Siege and the Commune are

everyday events for the human race. . . .' But I was forgetting—
you were actually in Paris all the time, weren't you?"

Goncourt nodded.

"I survived the Siege," he said with a bleak smile, "and then
nearly got myself killed in the Commune. Though that was my
own fault for letting my curiosity get the better of me. I'd spent
day after day longing for the Versailles troops to enter Paris,
and I'd almost given up hope when it actually happened. First
there was a rumour in the evening that they'd broken into the
city, then a vague murmur in the distance that I heard while I
was trying to get to sleep, and finally the sound of drums and
bugles, and shouts of 'To Arms!' amid the booming note of the
tocsin being rung in all the churches in Paris. That's a tragic,
sinister noise, Flaubert, but it filled me with joy, because it
sounded the death-knell of the odious tyranny oppressing us."

"You went out into the streets?"

"Not then, but the next day—and that was my mistake. A
shell exploded on the Madeleine as I was passing, and the streets
were full of National Guards who were either wounded or
demoralised. I dropped in on Burty, and found myself trapped in
his apartment for two days and nights, because the National
Guards were forcing anybody they found in the streets to build
barricades. Burty got on with his work and I started reading his
book on Delacroix, while the shells got nearer and nearer. One
shattered the porch of a house in the Rue Vivienne on the other
side of the Boulevard, another smashed the street-lamp opposite,
and a third exploded right outside during dinner, shaking us on
our chairs. A bed was made up for me, and I lay on it fully
dressed all night, listening fitfully to the drunken voices of
National Guards challenging every passer-by."

"And you stayed there all the next day?"

"Yes. We spent most of the day watching from the windows as
guns rumbled past, an ambulance picked up a wounded man, an
omnibus drove by full of National Guards, and some staff officers
galloped along the Boulevard, shouting to the men underneath
us to take care not to be cut off. And all the time Madame Burty
was putting away books and pictures and trying to find a corner

of the apartment where her children would be safe from bullets and shells.

"The sound of firing came nearer all morning, and suddenly a squad of workers appeared who'd been ordered to build a barricade under our windows. Luckily for us, their hearts weren't in it, and when bullets started raking the Boulevard they downed tools and disappeared down the Rue Vivienne. Then we saw the National Guards gradually falling back from the barricade in the Rue Drouot, first in good order and then in a general stampede, and the last defenders of the barricade—four or five boys of fourteen—ran past about six o'clock."

"Boys of fourteen, you say?" exclaimed Flaubert.

"Oh, yes—or even younger. Brave little devils too: I heard one of them shout to the others: 'I'll stick it out longer than you!' Once they'd gone, of course, the Versailles troops broke out of the Rue Drouot, spread out across the Boulevard, and opened a murderous fire in the direction of the Porte Saint-Denis. Their rifles sounded as loud as cannons between the buildings on both sides of the Boulevard, and the whistling of the bullets past our windows was like the sound of tearing silk. We'd all taken refuge with the children in the back rooms, but at one point I crawled on hands and knees into the dining-room and looked out through a gap in the curtains. I'll never forget what I saw then, Flaubert— one of the most dramatic scenes I've witnessed in the whole of my life.

"On the other side of the Boulevard there was a man stretched out on the ground of whom I could see nothing but the soles of his boots and a bit of gold braid. There were two men standing under a tree near the corpse, a National Guard and a Communard lieutenant, with the bullets making the leaves rain down from the branches above them. And behind them, in front of the closed doors of a carriage entrance, a woman was lying flat on the ground, holding a peaked cap in one hand. I discovered later that she was the wife of one of the three men, but I don't know which.

"The National Guard started gesturing violently, indignantly to the Versailles troops down the Boulevard, to indicate that he wanted to pick up the dead man, but the bullets went on whistling into the tree. So finally, flushed with anger, he slung his rifle across his back and simply walked forward, shouting abuse at the soldiers. All of a sudden I saw him stop, put his hand to his forehead, lean his hand and his forehead against a little tree for a moment, and then spin around and fall flat on his back with his arms spread out."

"Leaving just the lieutenant?"

"Yes. He had remained standing where he was, not moving a muscle except to brush away a twig which had fallen on to his shoulder. He looked at the dead National Guard for a moment and then, without hurrying, he tossed his sword behind him with a contemptuous slowness, and walked forward to pick up the first corpse. The dead body was very heavy and kept slipping out of his hands, but finally he managed to lift it and started walking back, holding it upright against his chest. Then a bullet hit him in the leg, shattering his thigh-bone, and the two men, the living and the dead, spun around together in a hideous pirouette before collapsing in each other's arms. I don't think I've ever seen anything as brave as that lieutenant's contempt for death, or anything as sinister as that terrible *danse macabre*. . . ."

"The fighting didn't go on much longer, did it?" said Flaubert.

"No—that was the decisive day, with the taking of Montmartre. Though of course the Communards also began setting fire to public buildings that day, and the next day it was as dark as in the middle of an eclipse. There was a cloud of smoke hanging over Paris, and a black rain of scraps of burnt paper from the Ministry of Finance fell all day from the sky, reminding me of the rain of ashes that buried Pompeii. I took advantage of a pause in the shelling to leave Burty's apartment and go back to Auteuil. My house was still standing, thank heaven, though a shell had blown a huge hole in the garden and another had gone through the roof and exploded on the top floor."

"You didn't go back to Paris that week, I suppose?" said Flaubert.

"Wait a minute—I can't remember. . . . Yes, I did. I spent the next day tidying up the house and wandering round what was left of Auteuil. But the day after that I went back into the city, because I remember seeing a huge detachment of prisoners at Passy station on their way to Versailles. I heard an officer say to a colonel as he handed over a piece of paper that there were four hundred of them, including sixty women. The men had been split up into lines of seven or eight fastened together with string around their wrists. They were just as they had been captured, most of them without hats or caps, with their hair plastered over their foreheads by the rain. The odd thing is that they came from every class of society: hard-faced workmen who'd made themselves head-coverings from check handkerchiefs, bourgeois clutching their overcoats to their chests, and National Guards who hadn't had time to change out of their uniforms."

"What about the women?"

"There was the same variety among them. Some of them were wearing kerchiefs and others were in silk dresses, and I noticed housewives, working-girls and prostitutes all together. The difference was that none of them showed the apathetic resignation of the men. There was anger and contempt on their faces, especially the face of one very beautiful girl, a girl with the implacable beauty of a young Fate. She had dark, curly hair, steely eyes, and cheeks red from weeping, and she stood there hurling insults at the officers and men from a throat so choked with anger that it couldn't form a single sound. Her twisted lips moved in absolute silence, masticating abuse without being able to spit it out.

"The only sign of weakness that any of them gave was that slight inclination of the head to one side that you see in women who've been praying in church for a long time. One or two of them covered their faces with their veils, but a sergeant flicked one of the veils with his riding-crop and shouted: 'None of that! Let's see your ugly mugs!' His men were kinder: a few of them felt sorry for the women and held out their water-bottles to them. Their hands were tied, of course, but they turned their heads with graceful movements and opened their parched mouths to drink. And then the signal for departure was given, and the pitiful column set off on the road to Versailles."

"On their way to be shot, I suppose?" said Flaubert.

"I suppose so. There seemed to be no end to the shooting that week. On the Sunday of that week I saw six thousand prisoners being marched along the Champs-Élysées, and I was told that five hundred others had been shot on the spot."

"Did you actually see any executions?"

"No, but I heard one being carried out. It was that same Sunday at the end of the Bloody Week. I'd met Burty on the Place de la Madeleine and we were strolling along the boulevards among the crowds of people who had come out of their cellars and hiding-places in search of light and sunshine, with the joy of deliverance on their faces. We hadn't got very far before we were accosted by Verlaine's wife, who wanted Burty's advice on how to hide her husband from the Versailles troops. I left Burty talking to her and went to see how much of Paris had been burnt by the Communards. There was still smoke everywhere, the air smelt of burning and varnish, and in many places there were still traces of the recent fighting: a dead horse, paving-stones from barricades, peaked caps swimming in pools of blood. I visited the ruins of the Palais-Royal and the Tuileries, admired the brand-new gold of the Sainte-Chapelle shining above the smouldering shell of the Prefecture of Police, and finally came to the Hôtel de Ville. That was a magnificent sight, Flaubert—all pink and green, and shining agate where the stonework had been burnt by paraffin. It looked like the ruin of an Italian palace, tinted by the sunshine of several centuries, a picturesque marvel which would have been preserved for future generations if this country weren't irrevocably condemned to the restorations of Viollet-le-Duc. And as a supreme irony, in the midst of all the ruins, on a marble plaque intact in its new gilt frame, there shone the lying inscription: *Liberty, Equality, Fraternity.*"

"But the executions . . . ," prompted Flaubert.

"I was forgetting. . . . I was walking back towards the Châtelet along the quays when I saw the crowd taking to its heels like a rioting mob being charged by the cavalry. And sure enough, some soldiers came riding up, brandishing their swords and forcing people off the roadway. In their midst a group of men were walking, led by a fellow with a black beard, with a handkerchief tied round his forehead. I noticed another man being almost carried along by his two neighbours, as if he hadn't the strength to walk. All of them were ghastly pale, with a vague look in their eyes which has stuck in my memory. A solid bourgeois standing beside me started counting: "One, two, three. . . .' There were twenty-six of them.

"'The escort hustled the men along to the Lobau barracks, where the gates were hurriedly slammed behind them. So far I hadn't realised what was happening, but I had an indefinable feeling of uneasiness. The worthy citizen beside me had finished counting, and said to a neighbour:

"'It won't be long now. You'll soon hear the first volley.'

"'What volley?' the other asked.

"'Why, they're going to be shot, of course.'

"And almost at that very instant a volley of shots rang out, with something like the mechanical precision of machine-gun fire. There was a first, a second, a third, a fourth, a fifth *ratatatat*, then a long interval, then a sixth, and finally two rapid volleys one after the other. At long last there was silence, and we were all heaving a sigh of relief when there was the deafening explosion of a single shot, then a second, then the last. Those were the *coups de grâce* being given to the prisoners who weren't dead.

"Just then the firing squad came out of the gate like a bunch of drunks, with blood dripping from some of their bayonets. They were followed by a priest who came stealing out and went off alongside the barracks wall, clutching an umbrella and walking a little unsteadily. And two covered wagons drove into the yard to pick up the dead. . . ."

"Poor devils," said Flaubert. "In my opinion, what we should have done was to condemn all the Communards to the galleys and force the stupid fools to clear up the ruins of Paris with chains round their necks, as common criminals."

"I don't know that I agree with you," replied Goncourt. "The day I saw those men going to be shot, Burty's wife told me a secret he'd been careful to keep from me. Apparently one of his friends on the Public Committee had told him a few days earlier that the Commune had lost all control over its troops, and that

G

they were going to enter all the houses in Paris, confiscate the valuables they contained, and shoot all the householders. . . . Oh, I grant you that the solution the Versailles Government imposed was a brutal one, but at least it saved us all from cowardly compromise. It taught the Army that it was still capable of fighting and restored its self-confidence. And finally, a bloodletting like that, done as thoroughly as that, and killing off the rebellious part of the population, postponed the next revolution by a whole generation. I believe that our old society has the chance of twenty years of peace before it as a result."

"I wonder," said Flaubert.

His companion's face fell.

"You may be right. I sometimes think that Thiers missed his chance just after the Commune, when he had the perfect opportunity to abolish universal suffrage, and that the whole thing is going to start all over again. Perhaps it would have been better for France if the Commune had enjoyed two or three months of absolute power, with time to put into practice all its anarchistic, antisocial plans. That might have given the present generation the courage to destroy both universal suffrage and freedom of the press. I don't say that my solution would have saved France from demagogy forever, but at least it would have given us a better chance of peace than the pathetic attempts we've made for the past seventy years to reconcile authority and freedom."

"To think," mused Flaubert, "that nothing of all that need have happened, if only people had read and understood my *Sentimental Education*. . . ."

"It was published when Jules was very ill," said Goncourt, "and though of course I read it and admired it, I didn't see what sort of reception it was given. Didn't the critics like it?"

"They positively hated it. The *Constitutionnel* and the *Gaulois* called me a cretin and a swine. Sarcey compared me to the Marquis de Sade, whom he admitted he'd never read, and Barbey d'Aurevilly said I soiled the gutter when I washed in it."

"And the public?"

"The public didn't like it either. You see, Goncourt, my novel didn't do this. . . ."

Putting his long, thin hands together, he formed a pyramid with his fingers.

"The public wants books which foster its illusions, whereas *Sentimental Education* . . ."

He turned his hands upside down and parted them as if to let all his dreams fall into a bottomless pit.

"But what did you mean when you said that your novel could have prevented the Commune?"

"Simply that it told the truth as I saw it, and France hadn't heard the truth for a long time. The country was in an extraordinary mental condition, a state of madness which was the result of extreme stupidity, and the stupidity came from an excess of humbug and falsehood. People had lost all understanding of good and evil, beauty and ugliness. Do you remember the critics of the day? They saw no difference between the sublime and the ridiculous, and simply flattered the latest opinion, the newest fashion. Everything was false—false realism, false army, even false whores. The genuine whores in the tradition of Sophie Arnould, like my dear friend Lagier, aroused horror and disgust. And everybody's judgement was warped. People praised an actress, not as an actress, but as a good mother. They wanted art to be moral, philosophy to be clear, vice to be decent and science to be intelligible to the masses. Whereas I told them the truth."

"And nobody understood?"

"Nobody. Not even my *chère maître* Sand, although she praised the book extravagantly. She was more concerned about my happiness, and still is. Why, only last month she was urging me to get married, and telling me that living alone was dangerous for me and cruel to those who loved me."

"Get married? You aren't going to take her advice, are you?"

Flaubert gave a roar of comical indignation.

"Good Lord, no! I told her that I found the idea of sharing my life with a woman too fantastic for words. I said that women had never fitted into my existence, that I wasn't rich enough, and too old, and too decent to inflict myself on somebody else for life. Besides, I've always considered that marriage is a sort of apostasy for the artist, because he's a monstrosity, something outside nature. You can only depict wine, love and women on condition that you aren't a drunkard, a lover or a husband. . . ."

"I entirely agree," declared Goncourt. "I've always felt that marriage is fatal to art, because in almost every marriage the wife is the solvent of the husband's honour, using honour in the loftiest and purest sense of the word. She's the adviser who, in the name of material interest, urges the advantages of weakness, of insipidity, of cowardice, of all the wretched little compromises one can make with one's conscience. I can understand a trades-man getting married, as a safeguard in case of bankruptcy, but an artist—never!"

He paused, then added:

"And yet . . ."

"Yes?" prompted Flaubert.

"And yet, I find myself more and more obsessed by the idea of sexual enjoyment. You know, Flaubert, I actually began this year trying to forget myself in the brutality of animal pleasure. . . ."

"If you mean that you celebrated the New Year in a brothel, I often used to do that. Sometimes I even kept my cigar in my mouth all the time, just to show that I didn't care. There's no need to worry about that, old fellow!'

"But it isn't just that. I keep finding it impossible to work because of this obsession with women, an obsession a husband or lover wouldn't have. I'm haunted by a picture which refuses to go away—a picture, not of a woman's body or breasts, but of the natural part, cut out and detached. It's worst of all when I'm travelling in a train. If I open my eyes, I see all the holes in the padded seats as so many female organs multiplied to infinity in an obscene hallucination. . . ."

"My dear chap," said Flaubert, "you mustn't take it so seriously. Don't think about it so much. You should do as I do: for years I've used women as mattresses for an ideal woman."

"And who was that?" asked Goncourt, forgetting his own problem in a sudden access of curiosity. "Your first love?"

Flaubert smiled.

"No. *That* was a little girl I fell in love with at a wedding when I was eleven. I remember I wanted to *give her my heart*—an expression I'd heard people use. In those days baskets were always being delivered to our house containing gifts of fish or game for my father from grateful patients. And as the conversation at home was often about surgical operations, I seriously thought for a long time of asking my father to cut out my heart, and sending it in a basket to the little girl. . . . But haven't I ever told you of my other love, the great love of my life?"

"No."

Flaubert took a sip of wine and half-closed his eyes.

"It all happened at Trouville in '36, when I was fourteen. I often went walking on the beach, and one day chance took me to the place where people used to bathe. Men and women used to go swimming together, changing on the beach or in the hotel, and leaving their wraps on the sand. That particular day I noticed a pretty red and black cloak on the beach and moved it farther away, out of reach of the rising tide. Apparently I had been seen, because at lunchtime, in the hotel dining-room, a young woman sitting with her husband at the next table thanked me for my kindness.

"How beautiful she was, Goncourt! She was tall and dark, with splendid black tresses tumbling on to her shoulders. She had burning eyes, admirably arched eyebrows, and a velvety golden skin. And she spoke slowly, in a sweet, musical voice.

"Every day I used to go to watch her bathing, and when she came out of the water, and walked past me, my heart pounded wildly, the blood rose to my cheeks, and I lowered my eyes. I can still see the place where I sat, the waves breaking on the sand, the beach festooned with foam. I can still hear the voices of the bathers talking among themselves, the sound of her footsteps, the sound of her breathing as she passed close beside me.

"I sat utterly still, as if Venus had stepped off her pedestal and started walking. You see, for the first time in my life I was conscious of something mystical and strange, something like a new sense. I was filled with tender emotions, and I felt tall and proud. I was in love. . . ."

"And did anything ever come of it?" asked Goncourt.

Flaubert made no answer.

"I loved that woman," he said, "from the time I was fourteen until I was twenty, without telling her, without touching her. . . . And I love her still."

Goncourt waited for a few moments, but when it became obvious that Flaubert was going to say no more, he decided to break the silence.

"I had a similar experience," he said, "when I was a young man. I've never told anyone about it, but the memory of it returns now and then to sadden me.

"I was about twenty-four at the time, and one evening at the Bal Mabille I met a girl of sixteen or seventeen called Marie. She had huge, sky-blue eyes, set very close to a long aquiline nose, and she was tall and thin and dressed in the humble clothes of a grisette. I danced with her that evening and again the following evening, and after seven or eight evenings dancing quadrilles and polkas with her, she granted me a rendezvous."

"In a hotel?" asked Flaubert.

"No, in a little apartment a cousin of mine had in the Rue d'Amsterdam. And there I muffed her twice—partly because I was put off by her silence and the angelic look in her eyes, and partly because I was impeded by what I supposed to be a physical malformation. Finally, as she was getting ready to leave, I threw her down on the sofa in the ante-room; and while I was kneeling over her, taking my pleasure with her, I heard a sound like that of a toy drum bursting, and I saw tears come into her eyes, although she didn't cry out or moan or even sigh. And when she got up, her light summer dress was covered in blood. It sounds incredible, but that girl, who went dancing every night at the Bal Mabille, was a virgin.

"Oh, she was a strange creature—pale as death when we made love together, and completely motionless, with no sign of life in her body but the pounding of her heart, and a curious expression in her big blue eyes, the perverse expression of an angel cast out of heaven."

For the first time in their long acquaintance Flaubert looked at his companion with sympathetic interest.

"Were you in love with her?" he asked.

"I can't say that," replied Goncourt, "but I felt a sort of tenderness for her, a certain curiosity about her, and a little of that pride and gratitude that any man feels towards a woman who has given him her virginity.

"We had met in the spring or summer, and in the autumn I remember that a friend of mine and I had arranged to go for an outing in the country with our mistresses, after a lunch at Véfour's. Well, my friend's mistress let him down, and he arrived late and completely drunk. The result was that when we got to the Gare Saint-Lazare, we had to ask for a room in the café on the corner, where my friend was violently sick, and where Marie and I spent the rest of the day melting ice over his head.

"Winter came, and carnival time, and my friend and I arranged to go with a party of other young people to the ball at the Opera. We were all to change into fancy-dress at the Hôtel de l'Étoile—that little hotel opposite the Académie de Médecine in the Rue des Saints-Pères—and go back there after the ball for supper. Marie wore a Pierrot costume in white silk that night, and I had never seen her look lovelier than she did in that light, floating material, nor her eyes look more strangely seductive. But, for some reason I couldn't understand, before we left and on our return, she resisted all my passionate attempts to possess her, gently but firmly repulsing all my kisses and caresses.

"In the spring I realised at last that my friend had become Marie's lover, and that my mistress's affection for him dated back to the day we had lunched together at Véfour's, and I was filled with a cold contempt for that girl, for that love of hers born in the midst of a fit of drunken vomiting. You see, Flaubert, I didn't know much about women at that time: I didn't understand the hold which illness has over them, or the intimate ties which caring for the sick creates within them. So the contempt I felt for the girl banished the indignation I felt about my friend, and I never spoke to him about his treachery."

He lit a cigarette and continued:

"The years went by. My mother died. My brother left school and was painting and writing with me when I met Marie again. She asked me up to a little room in a house behind the Stock

Exchange, where she worked during the day. She told me that she had broken with my friend, and gave herself to me again with the same casual abandon as a German girl whom you simply push back on to a bed.

"My brother had not yet got a mistress of his own, and had spoken to me only a few days before of the disgust aroused in him by a streetwalker who had removed half of her hair and half her teeth before going to bed with him. I don't know why I acted as I did—whether it was to give Jules a pretty mistress I was no longer in love with, to test the poor girl's frailty, or to some extent to degrade her in my eyes—but I invited her to dinner at the Café d'Orsay, and after dinner I told her that I had an appointment and that she was to give herself to my brother as she had given herself to me.

"My brother made frenzied love to her for several weeks, but then he decided that she was too melancholy for his taste, and even rather frightening, with the lethargy into which love-making plunged her, and the strange far-away look which came into her great blue eyes. And he dropped her."

There was a long silence. Finally Flaubert asked gently: "Did you ever see her again?"

A look of pain passed briefly over his companion's face.

"Never," he replied. "Some time afterwards, one morning after a night when Jules and I had worked until three o'clock, our housekeeper put a letter on my bedside table which had come by the first post. I glanced at the address, didn't recognise the handwriting, and went back to sleep. When I woke up again, I opened the envelope and found inside a black-edged funeral invitation and a note from a friend of Marie's saying that Marie had just died of consumption and that on the eve of her death she had asked for me to be informed, saying three times that she desperately wanted me to be at her funeral."

"And did you go?"

"The invitation," said Goncourt, "stated that the funeral was to be held that very morning. And it was half-past twelve . . ."

Flaubert reached across the table and placed his hand on Goncourt's in an affectionate gesture.

"I know how you feel," he murmured. "I often find myself thinking about the past, about my childhood and youth, about everything that will never come back. When one's mind no longer turns naturally towards the future, one has become an old man. And we are both old men. . . . Lonely old men. . . . I have been to so many funerals of late that I feel choked with coffins, like an old cemetery. Sainte-Beuve, my old friend Bouilhet, your brother Jules, our beloved Théo . . . and, of course, my mother. Strange, isn't it, Goncourt: it was only after she had died that I realised that that poor dear woman was the human being I loved the most. It was as if part of my entrails had been torn away."

"Jules's death had the same effect on me," said Goncourt. "But then, even when he was alive, we had an impression of incompleteness when we were parted. Each of us would feel the lack of the other half of ourselves, as if we were a book in two volumes of which the first had been lost. We were each left with nothing but a half-sensation, a half-life. . . . And then I was left with that half-life for the rest of my days. . . ."

He paused, as tears welled up in his eyes.

"The funeral was a nightmare, with everything as vague as things seen in a swoon, and my ears filled with a sound like the roaring of great waters. But what came after was even worse. Whenever I read an interesting article, I'd say to myself: 'I must show this to Jules.' Whenever the street door opened, I expected to hear him asking the maid: 'Where's Edmond?' It was a little easier during the Siege and the Commune, because they were so to speak distractions to my grief, but then it started all over again, until I wondered whether life was worth living."

"Especially in this age and this society! What a world we live in, Goncourt! The bourgeoisie is so confused that it has even lost the instinct of self-preservation, and its successors will be worse. I'm filled with a sadness like that of the Roman patricians of the fourth century, because I can feel an irresistible flood of barbarism rising out of the depths. I hope I'll be dead before it sweeps everything away, but the waiting period isn't very pleasant. Never have the things of the mind counted for less. Never have the hatred of all greatness, the scorn of Beauty, the execration of literature been so obvious. The only solution that makes sense is a government of mandarins, provided the mandarins know something—indeed, a great many things. Our only chance of salvation lies in a legitimate aristocracy, by which I mean a majority composed of something other than mere numbers. But have we any hope of seeing such a thing? Never in a thousand years!"

"You are at least fortunate to be able to escape to Croisset," said Goncourt, "because Paris has become impossible, a Babylonian antheap, full of unkind, impatient people. There aren't even any chairs now in the bookshops along the quays. Nowadays books are bought standing up. A request for a book and the naming of a price: that's the sort of transaction to which the mania for money has reduced bookselling, which used to be a matter for dawdling, chatting and browsing."

"And the people's faces are so stupid! I assure you, Goncourt, that I've reached such a degree of sensibility that the idea of having an unpleasant-looking gentleman opposite me in a railway compartment is unbearable. In the old days I wouldn't have cared. I'd have said to myself: 'I'll go and sit in another compartment.' And if I'd been unable to avoid my unpleasant gentleman I'd have relieved my feelings by bawling him out. But now that won't do. . . . The very fear of the thing is enough to set my heart pounding. . . . No, a trip to Paris has now become a serious undertaking. Besides, now that Théo's dead, who is left here that I could want to see—apart from you and Turgenev?"

"Have you seen him this time?"

"Not yet—the poor fellow's confined to his rooms with gout. Now *he's* another one like Sand who keeps trying to raise my spirits. He either suggests taking me to Russia to eat strawberries and wander in the ryefields, or urges me to fight harder against what he calls the sinister cloud of old age. And Sand for her part tells me to go out and live in the world. . . . But even as a child I knew that life was like a bad smell coming from a kitchen ventilator: you don't need to taste the food to know it will make you sick. . . ."

The litany of laments continued a little longer, then silence fell.

Coming into the room with some more coffee, Charles found the
two novelists sitting motionless at the table, gazing moodily
into space.

When they finally got up to go, they were the last customers
in the restaurant. They took leave of their host—Flaubert slapping
him on the back, and Goncourt giving him a limp handshake—
embraced briefly in the street, and climbed into the waiting cabs.
Charles watched them drive away in opposite directions, then
turned to put the shutters up on Magny's, and on an entire
epoch.

Epilogue

EPILOGUE

THE MAGNY DINNERS were over, but some of the *habitués*, like Flaubert and Goncourt, occasionally dropped in to the restaurant for a meal, for old times' sake. There were now only a handful of them left, and by the end of the century death had claimed all but one.

The first to go was François Veyne, one of the founders of the dinners, who died in 1875 at the age of sixty-two. He was followed the next year by Auguste Nefftzer, and also by the only woman ever to attend the Magny Dinners, George Sand. She died at Nohant, deeply mourned by Flaubert, who was writing his *Three Tales* for her and wept like a child at her funeral, and by Turgenev, who wrote to his great friend: "What a sweet woman she was, and what a fine man! And now she is there in that horrible, insatiable, silent hole, which doesn't even know what it devours. . . ."

Claude Bernard died two years later, and in 1880 Flaubert himself, who had often been compared to Bernard as a "physiologist of the heart", succumbed to what was probably a cerebral haemorrhage. His last years had been saddened by loneliness and poverty—he had sacrificed nearly all he possessed to save his niece's husband from bankruptcy—although he had found some consolation in writing his unfinished comic masterpiece, *Bouvard and Pécuchet*, and in guiding the first literary steps of his young disciple Maupassant.

Saint-Victor died in 1881, and Turgenev in 1883. The Russian had remained a dedicated writer to the very end, telling a friend after an operation on his stomach: "All the time I was searching for the words with which I could give you an exact impression of the steel cutting through my skin and entering my flesh . . . like a knife cutting a banana." His funeral, according to Goncourt, "brought out of the houses of Paris a swarm of creatures with gigantic bodies, squashed features and God-the-Father beards: a little Russia whose existence in the capital nobody had ever suspected."

In 1885 the anatomist Robin, the most entertaining and informative of the doctors who had dined at Magny's, died at the age of sixty-four. His last words earned the admiration of all his scientific friends, for he had expected to be carried off by a heart disease, and murmured in surprise as he expired: "Apoplexy? . . . Curious!"

Renan and Taine died within a few months of each other, the former in October 1892 and the latter in March 1893. Both had been elected to the Académie française in 1878, and both had spent their last years bringing monumental works to completion: Renan his *History of the People of Israel* and Taine his *Origins of Contemporary France*. The press mourned them as two of the greatest writers of modern times, but their memory was viciously attacked by Edmond de Goncourt, who could neither forget nor forgive the protests they had made when he had published records of their conversations at Magny's in the first, abridged version of his and Jules's *Journal*. Yet by general consent Goncourt had come out best in the public quarrel which had taken place on that occasion, and all France had laughed at his tart rejoinder to Renan's description of him as "an indiscreet individual": "Monsieur Renan has been so 'indiscreet' about Christ that he really ought to allow a little indiscreetness about himself."

Goncourt himself died in 1896—the same year as Gustave Claudin—a lonely, embittered old man. While his own novels, like those he had written with Jules, had never won public approval, Émile Zola, whom he regarded as an upstart pupil, had obtained world-wide fame and immense wealth by means of what Goncourt considered the unscrupulous exploitation of the brothers' literary techniques. Baulked of success and recognition, robbed by death of the companionship of his contemporaries, and deprived by his own decision of the comforts of marriage and paternity, he had devoted the last twenty years of his life to securing immortality for himself and his brother through the eventual publication of the unexpurgated Goncourt *Journal* and the foundation of an Académie Goncourt which was to award an annual prize to an outstanding fictional work. Even so, he had been haunted to the end of his life by fears that his will might be annulled and the manuscript of the *Journal* destroyed, and in 1893 he had made the pathetic admission: "I shall die not knowing what is to become of the two great projects of my life intended to ensure my survival."

After the death of Charles-Edmond in 1899, only one of the *habitués* of the Restaurant Magny remained: Marcelin Berthelot. Since the time of the Magny Dinners the great chemist had risen in office and honour in both academic and public life. In 1876 he had been appointed Inspector-General of Higher Education; in 1886 he had taken office as Minister of Public Instruction; in 1889 he had become perpetual secretary of the Académie des Sciences; from 1895 to 1896 he had served his country as Minister for Foreign Affairs; and in 1900 he was elected to the Académie française. He died in 1907.

By that time his host in the little Rue Mazet restaurant had been dead nearly thirty years. Madame Magny died on 30 June 1877 at the age of forty-nine, and Magny himself breathed his last at four o'clock on the morning of 19 April 1879. The restaurateur was escorted to his last resting-place in the Cimetière Montparnasse two days later by a large crowd, and the graveside oration was pronounced by the chief pallbearer, Monsieur Bignon, President of the Union Syndicale et Mutuelle des Restaurateurs et Limonadiers du Département de la Seine. The family mourners were led by Paul-Victor-Modeste Magny, who as a little boy had once joined the so-called "dinner of atheists" in his father's restaurant, and who towards the end of the century, ironically enough, was to become a high official in the Ministry of Cults. In 1914 Paul Magny became Senator for the Seine; he died in 1925.

As for the Restaurant Magny, after its owner's death it passed into the hands, first of a Monsieur Bouland, then of a Monsieur Cuvenel. Even under Magny's personal management its fortunes

had begun to decline after the Siege of Paris, and matters were
not improved by Monsieur Cuvenel's obvious preference for
another establishment which he owned in the Auvergne. In
1894, to the accompaniment of a funeral fanfare of largely inaccurate articles in the press, it finally closed its doors.

Today the Rue Mazet is barely recognisable as the street in
which Modeste Magny plied his trade a hundred years ago. A
modish dress-shop has replaced the estaminet on the corner
of the Rue Saint-André-des-Arts, an ultra-modern university
restaurant fronts the streets where the Auberge du Cheval-
Blanc and the *Folies Dauphine* used to stand, and a commonplace
apartment building has occupied the site of the Restaurant Magny
since the end of the last century. But if nothing now remains of the
most famous literary restaurant in Paris, any lover of nineteenth-
century France who stands in the Rue Mazet late at night can still
hear in imagination Flaubert's guffaw, Turgenev's deep bass,
Sainte-Beuve's piping treble, and the angry, shouting, laughing
voices of the illustrious company which used to gather there for
dinner at Magny's.

Appendices

Appendices

NOTES

Chapter One

I have taken the liberty of presenting diners in this chapter who did not in fact begin attending the Magny Dinners until later. Thus Saint-Victor was first present on 31 January 1863, Turgenev on 28 February 1863, and Renan on 28 March 1863.

Chapter Two

Sainte-Beuve's letter to Veyne about the Magny Dinners is published in his *Correspondance Générale*, vol. XV, p. 331.

George Sand's first attendance at a Magny Dinner was in fact on this occasion, 12 February 1866, although she was an *habituée* of the restaurant. She described her impressions in her diary, in an entry reproduced in this book, and also wrote to her son Maurice: "I was welcomed with open arms. They have invited me to attend for three years. Today I decided to go *by myself*, which settled the question. I didn't want anybody to take me along" (Bibliothèque Historique de la Ville de Paris, Fonds Sand, G. 2070). Subsequently she appears to have attended five Magny Dinners in 1866, and one—on 25 March—the following year. A number of letters from George Sand to Magny or his wife are in Monsieur Raymond Oliver's Collection.

Again I have taken a slight liberty with the chronology of the Dinners by situating Paul Magny's attendance on 12 February 1866. He was in fact invited to make the number of diners up to fourteen on 17 August 1863. The letter to his mother quoted at the end of this chapter is dated Paris, Tuesday 18 August 1863, and is in Monsieur Raymond Oliver's Collection.

Chapter Three

The story of Bache and the Mayor of Hauvrincourt is told by Charles Monselet in *Mes souvenirs littéraires*.

Chapter Four

The execution described by Turgenev was that of Jean-Baptiste Troppmann, who was in fact guillotined on 21 January 1870 for the murder of an entire family at La Villette in September 1869. Cf. David Magarshack: *Turgenev's Literary Reminiscences* (London, 1958) for a long article on the execution.

Chapter Five

In the course of 1870, after the deaths of Sainte-Beuve and Jules de Goncourt, the Magny Dinners broke up, some of the *habitués* moving to Brébant's and the others continuing to dine together at Magny's, where I have situated this chapter.

Chapter Six

Magny's complaint about the quality of waiters is reported by René Héron de Villefosse in *Histoire et géographie gourmandes de Paris*, p. 218. The story of his encounter with Ferré during the Commune is told by Jules Troubat in *La Salle à manger de Sainte-Beuve*, p. 121. The recipe for *purée Magny* is given by an anonymous writer in *Naguère et Jadis*, November 1958. Both Flaubert and Goncourt were in Paris during the winter of 1872-3, but my dating of this dinner is arbitrary.

CULINARY APPENDIX

Of the four dishes created at the Restaurant Magny, the *château-briand* (or *chabrillan* as Magny would have called it) and the *tournedos Rossini* are universally known, while the recipe for the *purée Magny* has been given in this book. For readers interested in Magny's method of preparing the now classic *petites marmites*, I reproduce here the relevant passage from Pierre Andrieu's *Histoire du restaurant en France*:

It was in 1867 that Magny created the *petites marmites*, a dish which he served to his customers twice a week. Although he employed a chef and two cooks, he entrusted the task of preparing his *petites marmites* to nobody else. It was wonderful to see how carefully he prepared his little portions of beef and poultry according to quantity, for the *petites marmites* varied in capacity, holding anything from two to eight portions. Each portion was tied with a piece of string, and all were first placed together in a big earthenware stockpot—the mother stockpot—with the same number of pieces of oxtail, a piece of best rumpsteak, a chicken, and the requisite amount of water and rock salt.

Magny would cover the stockpot tightly and place it on the stove, leaving it to heat slowly until all the scum had risen to the surface. Then, with a magisterial air, he would remove all this scum with a skimmer at one stroke, gradually add a ladleful of water, and wait for a few more globules of scum to come to the top.

As soon as all the scum was removed, he would add a quantity of vegetables in a net bag, and the same quantity of leeks in little bundles, varying in size according to the size and number of the stockpots, add seasoning and leave to simmer on a low fire.

Meanwhile all the *petites marmites*—the little stockpots—were arranged in order of size on the stove, next to the big stockpot. Removing the lid of the latter, Magny would wipe the edge and carefully remove the bag of vegetables, which he would arrange on a large dish, and then the portions of beef and poultry, which he would place in the little stockpots after untying the string. The pieces of oxtail would follow, and also the vegetables, and all this would be covered with stock strained through a cloth. Then the *petites marmites* would be covered and allowed to simmer for another two hours.

When ready to serve, the stockpot would be taken to the table with some crusts of bread browned in the oven, and it was usually Magny himself who poured the soup on the *croûtons*.

GLOSSARY

ABOUT, Edmond (1828–85), a distinguished journalist and novelist, who was elected to the Académie française in 1884 but died before his reception. The *habitués* of the Magny Dinners regularly enjoyed his favourite liqueur, the so-called *mélange About*, which Sainte-Beuve used to mix for them.

AGOULT, Marie de Flavigny, Comtesse d' (1805–76), who wrote under the pseudonym of Daniel Stern, married the Comte d'Agoult in 1827 but left him for Liszt, to whom she bore three daughters.

ALLIX, Jules (1818–97), was a politican and inventor well known for his eccentric writings.

ARAGO, François (1786–1853), the astronomer and physicist, became director of the Paris Observatory in 1830, and was a member of the provisional government in 1848.

ARNOULD, Sophie (1740–1802), a singer at the Paris Opera, was noted for her beauty, her wit, and her amorous liaisons.

ASSELINE, Louis (1829–78), a journalist friend of the Goncourts.

AXENFELD, Auguste (1825–76), a Russian-born doctor who was an authority on nervous diseases.

BACHE, pseud. of Debruille, a famous comic actor at the Vaudeville and the Bouffes-Parisiens, who made his name as Jean Styx in Offenbach's *Orphée aux enfers*.

BALZAC, Honoré de (1799–1850), obtained his first literary success in 1829 with *Les Chouans*, and went on to write nearly a hundred novels and tales, most of them combined in his vast *Comédie humaine*. In 1832 he began a lengthy correspondence with a wealthy Polish countess, Madame Hanska, whom he married in 1850, a few months before his death.

BARBEY D'AUREVILLY, Jules-Amédée (1808–89), poet, novelist, critic and dandy, was a flamboyant, picturesque character known to his admirers as the *Connétable des Lettres*.

BÉRANGER, Pierre-Jean (1780–1857), probably France's greatest song-writer, whose popularity was due to his light-hearted, graceful, witty verse and a strange combination of republicanism and Bonapartism.

BERLIOZ, Louis Hector (1803–69), failed to win recognition in his own country for his Romantic compositions, and for many years supported himself and his wife, the Irish actress, Harriet Smithson, by writing musical criticism.

BERNARD, Claude (1813–78), studied medicine in Paris and was appointed in 1854 to the chair of General Physiology at the Collège de France. His *Introduction à l'étude de la médecine expérimentale* (1865) became a standard work, and was used by Zola to formulate his theory of the experimental novel.

BERNARDIN DE SAINT-PIERRE, Jacques-Henri (1737–1814), obtained fame and success with his picturesque *Études de la Nature* (containing *Paul et Virginie* (1787) in the fourth volume), which argued against atheism from the order and beauty of Nature.

BERTHELOT, Marcelin (1827–1907), was appointed in 1861 to a chair of Organic Chemistry at the Collège de France specially created in recognition of his original research in that field. He held this chair until his death, and published, among other works, a history of alchemy and a study of medieval chemistry. He also played an active part in public life after 1870, advising the Government of National Defence during the Siege of Paris, and serving as Minister of Public Instruction (1886–7) and Minister of Foreign Affairs (1895–6).

BISMARCK-SCHÖNHAUSEN, Otto Eduard Leopold, Prince von (1815–98), was the guiding spirit behind the Prussian defeat of Austria in 1866, the unification of Germany under Prussia, and the defeat of France in 1870–1. In 1871 he was created a prince and made Chancellor of the new German Empire, an office he resigned in 1890 in disapproval of the policy of Emperor Wilhelm II.

BITAUBÉ, Paul (1732–1808), a writer chiefly known for his translations of the *Odyssey* and the *Iliad*.

BONAPARTE, Jérôme (1784–1860), youngest brother of Napoleon I, was made King of Westphalia in 1807. After the fall of the Empire he lived for many years in Florence, but in 1848 was appointed Governor of the Invalides and was made a French marshal in 1850. His children by his second wife, Catherine of Württemberg, included Princess Mathilde and Prince Napoleon.

BONAPARTE, Louis (1778–1846), third brother of Napoleon I, was made King of Holland in 1806, but resigned the crown in 1810. He returned to Paris in 1814, settled in Florence in 1826, and died at Leghorn. In 1802 he married Hortense Eugénie Beauharnais, whose third son was the future Napoleon III.

BOSSUET, Jacques-Bénigne (1627–1704), France's greatest ecclesiastical orator, was appointed tutor to the Grand Dauphin in 1670, was elected to the Académie française in 1671, and was made Bishop of Meaux in 1681. He is chiefly famous for the educational works he wrote for the Dauphin, and his splendid funeral orations.

BOUILHET, Louis (1822–69), a poet and dramatist who lived in Rouen and was one of Flaubert's closest friends.

BRACQUEMOND, Félix (1833–1914), a famous engraver who was a friend of the Goncourts and took part in several of the early Impressionist exhibitions.

BRÉBANT, Paul, the brother-in-law of Modeste Magny, owned the Restaurant Brébant, on the Boulevard Poissonnière, which closed in 1892.

BURTY, Philippe (1830–90), an art critic and historian who, like the Goncourts, did much to introduce Japanese art to the French.

CALAMATTA, Madame Luigi, née Joséphine Raoul-Rochette, a religious painter whose only daughter, Lisa, married George Sand's son Maurice in 1862.

CAUS, Salomon de (1576–1626), a Huguenot engineer, born at Dieppe, who is said to have invented the steam engine.

CHABRILLAN, Lionel de Moreton, Comte de (1818–59), after a notorious liaison with the courtesan Céleste Mogador, married her in 1854 and took her to Australia, where he was French Consul-General in Melbourne, and where he died.

CHAMFORT, pseud. of Nicolas-Sébastien Roch (1741–94), dramatist, critic and wit, tried to commit suicide during the Terror and died shortly afterwards. The only work of his that is still read is his incisive *Maximes, caractères et anecdotes*, published after his death.

CHAMPFLEURY, pseud. of Jules Husson (1821–89), was an art historian, a literary theorist in *Le Réalisme* (1857), and a novelist whose *Les Aventures de Mademoiselle Mariette* (1853) presented a bleak, unsentimental picture of the Paris Bohemia he and Murger had both known. In later life he became Director of the State porcelain works at Sèvres.

CHAPUYS-MONTLAVILLE, Louis-Alceste, Baron de (1800–68), Prefect and Senator under the Second Empire.

CHARLES-EDMOND, pseud. of Charles-Edmond Chojecki (1822–99), was a Polish refugee who established himself as a journalist and playwright in Paris, where he became Librarian to the Senate in 1860.

CHARPENNE, Pierre (1810–93), a writer and art historian who was Curator of the Musée Calvet in Avignon.

CHATEAUBRIAND, François-René, Vicomte de (1768–1848), lived a life of adventure and contemplation straddling two centuries and two continents. After spending some time at the court of Louis XVI and visiting America, he returned to France on the fall of the monarchy, was wounded fighting with the army of the *émigrés*, and escaped to England, where he lived in poverty till 1800. Back in France, he won great fame with his monumental work of Christian apologetics, *Le Génie du Christianisme* (1802), and enduring popularity with *René*, the melancholy fragment of it published separately in 1805. After a lively political career including a period as French Ambassador in London, he retired into private life to write and re-write his autobiographical *Mémoires d'outre-tombe* (1849–50).

CHENNEVIÈRES, Philippe de (1820–99), a French art historian and a friend of the elder Goncourt.

CHOPIN, Frédéric (1810–49), born near Warsaw, came to Paris in 1831 and was introduced to George Sand by Liszt in 1836. Their liaison lasted for seven years, and part of it—the disastrous stay on Majorca—is described in Sand's *Un Hiver à Majorque* (1841).

CLAUDIN, Gustave (1823–96), a journalist and novelist best remembered for his recollections of boulevard life under Louis-Philippe and Napoleon III.

CLÉSINGER, Auguste (1814–1883), a sculptor who married George Sand's daughter, Solange, in 1847.

CLOTILDE, Princess (1843–1911), daughter of King Victor Emmanuel II, married Prince Napoleon in 1859.

COLET, Louise (1810–76), *née* Revoil, the wife of Hippolyte Colet (1808–51), a teacher at the Conservatoire, was less celebrated for her poetry and novels than for her prolonged liaison with the philosopher Victor Cousin and the love-affair with Flaubert which provided him with material for *Madame Bovary*.

CORNEILLE, Thomas (1625–1709), a talented dramatist, grammarian and editor who has always suffered from comparison with his elder brother, Pierre.

COUSIN, Victor (1792–1867), an eminent philosopher and brilliant lecturer who was elected to the Académie française in 1830, appointed Director of the École Normale in 1832, and made Minister of Public Instruction in 1840. He was for some time Louise Colet's lover.

DALLOZ, Paul (1829–87), editor of *Le Moniteur* during much of the Second Empire.

DAUDET, Alphonse (1840–97), born at Nîmes and brought up in Lyons, moved in 1857 to Paris, where from 1861 to 1865 he was private secretary to the Duc de Morny. He made his name with his sketches of Provençal life, *Lettres de mon moulin*, which were first published in *Le Figaro* in 1866, and went on to become a successful novelist.

DECAZES, Élie, Duc de (1780–1860), supported the Bourbon restoration, and after 1815 was the Minister of Louis XVIII, who made him a duke.

DELACROIX, Eugène (1798–1863), exhibited his first picture, *Dante et Virgile*, at the 1822 Salon, creating a sensation which was repeated by his later works. Apart from a visit to Morocco and Algeria, he spent most of his life in Paris.

DEMIDOFF, Anatole, Prince (1813–70), a wealthy Russian *boulevardier* who married Princess Mathilde in 1840 and was separated from her in 1846.

DENNERY, Adolphe Philippe (1811–99), a prolific writer of plays for the Paris boulevard theatres.

DESLIONS, Anna (d. 1873), a famous courtesan of the Second Empire and sometime neighbour of the Goncourts.

DILLON, William Patrick (?1812–57), a French diplomat of Irish ancestry who was *chargé d'affaires* at Port-au-Prince in Haiti in 1856.

DOUCET, Camille (1812–95), a dramatist who became Perpetual Secretary to the Académie française in 1876.

DROUET, Juliette (1806–83), met Victor Hugo when acting in his play *Lucrèce Borgia*. The resulting liaison lasted for the rest of their lives, giving rise to such poems as *Tristesse d'Olympio*.

DU CAMP, Maxime (1822–94), poet, journalist, novelist, and Academician, is now chiefly remembered for his friendship with Flaubert, with whom he travelled to the Middle East, but he left some remarkable *Souvenirs littéraires* (1882–83) and a valuable study of the workings of the French capital, *Paris, ses organes, ses fonctions et sa vie* (1875).

DU CAYLA, Zoé Talon, Comtesse (1784–1850), a lawyer's daughter who became Louis XVIII's favourite.

DUCROT, Auguste-Alexandre (1817–82), the French general chiefly responsible for the defence of Paris during the siege of 1870–1.

DUDEVANT, Casimir, Baron, in 1822 married Aurore Dupin (George Sand), who left him in 1831. He died in 1871.

DUMAS, Alexandre (Dumas *père*) (1802–70), became a secretary to the Duc d'Orléans (later Louis-Philippe) in 1822, and in 1829 made his name with the flamboyant historical drama *Henri III et sa cour*. He went on to write a number of successful Romantic dramas, including *Antony* (1831) and *La Tour de Nesle* (1832), before turning to novel-writing. Often working with collaborators, notably Auguste Maquet, he turned out a series of popular novels such as *Le Comte de Monte-Cristo* (1844–5), as well as travel books, a cookery book, a biography of Napoleon, and the 22 volumes of *Mes Mémoires* (1852–5) recounting the exuberant story of his life.

DUMAS, Alexandre (Dumas *fils*) (1824–95), the natural son of the above, made his name with the novel *La Dame aux camélias* (1848). He dramatised the novel in 1852, and went on to write some of the most successful plays of the Second Empire, most of them characterized by a strong moralising tendency. In contrast to his father, he was regarded as a pillar of respectability, but he lived with Princess Naryschkine for many years before marrying her secretly in 1864.

DUPANLOUP, Félix (1802–78), a famous prelate who became Vicar-General for Paris in 1838 and Bishop of Orléans in 1849. He was elected to the Académie française in 1854.

DUTACQ, Armand-Léon-Michel (1810–56), founded the newspaper *Le Siècle*.

DUVERGER, pseud. of Julie-Augustine Vaultrain de Saint-Urbain (1816–96), a well-known Second Empire actress and the mistress of Anatole Demidoff.

EUGÉNIE, Maria Eugenia de Guzman, Comtesse de Téba,

Empress (1826–1920), daughter of the Spanish Comte de Montijo, married Napoleon III in 1853, and after the fall of the Second Empire retired to England, losing her husband in 1873 and her only son, the Prince Imperial, in 1879.

FAVRE, Jules-Claude-Gabriel (1809–80), came to prominence in 1858, when he defended Orsini, and thereafter became one of the leaders of the republican opposition to Napoleon III. In September 1870 he was appointed Minister of Foreign Affairs, and in January 1871 negotiated the terms for the capitulation of Paris. He resigned his office in July 1871 and returned to the bar.

FEYDEAU, Ernest (1821–73), the author of *Fanny* (1858), a novel which Sainte-Beuve at first rated more highly than *Madame Bovary*, and the father of the now better remembered dramatist, Georges.

FIORENTINO, Pier Angelo (1809–64), an Italian music and literary critic, collaborated with Dumas *père* and translated Dante into French.

FIX, Delphine-Éléonore (1831–64), an actress at the Théâtre-Français.

FLAUBERT, Gustave (1821–80), born at Rouen, where his father was chief surgeon at the hospital, spent nearly all his life living with his mother (who died in 1872) at their home at Croisset, near his native city. His isolation was due partly to a natural timidity ill concealed by violent blustering, partly to devotion to literature, and partly to a mysterious illness, probably epilepsy, which struck him down as a young man. He had a stormy liaison with Louise Colet and sensual friendships with Madame Sabatier and Suzanne Lagier, but remained platonically devoted all his life to a Madame Schlésinger he had met as a schoolboy. He rarely left Croisset except to stay occasionally in Paris, to travel to the Middle East with Maxime Du Camp (1849–51), and to visit Tunisia in 1857 to collect material for his Carthaginian novel *Salammbô* (1862). Of his other works, *Madame Bovary* (1857) resulted in his being prosecuted for obscenity, *L'Éducation sentimentale* (1869) was misunderstood by the public and attacked by the critics, while *Trois Contes* (1877) was published only after the death of George Sand for whom it was written. Flaubert died before completing his comic novel, *Bouvard et Pécuchet* (1881).

FRANZ JOSEPH (1830–1916), Emperor of Austria, succeeded

Ferdinand I in 1848. Under his reign Austria lost Lombardy and Venetia to Sardinia in 1859 and 1866, and by the attack on Serbia in 1914 initiated the First World War.

FROEHNER, Wilhelm (1835–1925), a German archaeologist who became Assistant Keeper at the Louvre.

FULTON, Robert (1765–1815), an American engineer who invented torpedoes and was the first man to use steam successfully in navigation.

GARNIER, Charles (1825–98), became architect to the City of Paris in 1860 and was responsible for the design of the Opera.

GAUTIER, Théophile (1811–72), studied painting after leaving school, but like his friends Pétrus Borel and Gérard de Nerval soon committed himself to the cause of Romanticism in literature, and played a leading part in the so-called Battle of *Hernani* (1830). During the next decade he produced macabre poems, fantastic stories, autobiographical sketches, and the deliberately scandalous novel *Mademoiselle de Maupin* (1835). Later, despite the publication of a volume of poetry, *Émaux et Camées*, in 1852, he produced little else but travel sketches and a vast amount of literary, dramatic and artistic criticism. A kindly, well-loved figure—he was generally known as *le bon Théo*—he died of a heart disease probably exacerbated by his sufferings during the Siege of Paris.

GAVARNI, pseud. of Sulpice-Guillaume Chevalier (1804–66), became well known in the 1830s as a contributor of fashion plates and sketches of Parisian life to illustrate journals such as *Charivari*. After a traumatic visit to London in 1849, when he observed and recorded the living conditions of the poor, his work grew increasingly bitter and caricatural, and during his last years he became something of an eccentric recluse. The Magny Dinners were founded in an attempt to relieve his frequent fits of depression.

GENLIS, Félicité Ducrest de Saint-Aubin, Madame de (1746–1830), was a prolific writer of popular romances and educational treatises (she was governess to Louis-Philippe), but only her memoirs of eighteenth-century life are read today.

GIRARDIN, Madame Émile de, *née* Delphine Gay (1804–55), wrote poetry as a girl and was the idolised muse of the Romantic *cénacles*. In later years, under the pseudonym "Charles de Launay", she wrote a weekly gossip column in her husband's newspaper, *La Presse*.

GONCOURT, Edmond (1822–96) and Jules (1830–70), lived and wrote together in one of the closest and most remarkable partnerships in literary history. At first they produced studies in art history and social history, but in 1851 they published their first novel, *En 18..*, and began writing their famous memoirs of literary life, the *Journal des Goncourt*. Their fictional works, carefully documented studies of life in a variety of classes and professions, were not very successful, although *Germinie Lacerteux* (1864) influenced Zola and may be regarded as the first Naturalist novel. Jules died from syphilis in 1870, leaving his brother to write four more novels and found the Académie Goncourt to perpetuate their name.

GRAMONT-CADEROUSSE, Ludovic, Duc de (1833–65), a notorious rake and *viveur* of the Café Anglais set, who was the lover of the Duchesse de Persigny and Hortense Schneider.

GRASSOT, Paul-Louis-Auguste (1800–60), one of the most famous comic actors of the nineteenth century.

HALÉVY, Ludovic (1834–1908), collaborated for many years with Henri Meilhac in writing comedies and the libretti for Offenbach's operettas. He also wrote novels and memoirs of the Second Empire, when he was Secretary to the Legislative Body for several years.

HAREL, Charles-Jean (1790–1846), a sub-prefect under the Empire, was exiled after the Hundred Days but returned to Paris in 1820 to become a journalist and theatre manager. He staged many of the great Romantic dramas and was known as the "Napoleon of Managers".

HARRISSE, Henry (1830–1910), a New York lawyer, historian and bibliographer who became a devoted friend of George Sand and was occasionally invited to Magny's.

HASE, Karl Benedikt (1780–1864), a distinguished German Hellenist.

HAUSSMANN, Georges-Eugène (1809–91) became Prefect of the Seine in 1853, and then embarked on a vast transformation of Paris, demolishing old districts, building wide boulevards and laying out parks. He was made a Baron and a Senator, but the cost of building the new Paris made him increasingly unpopular, and he was dismissed in 1870.

HEINE, Heinrich (1797–1856), first attracted attention with his *Gedichte* in 1821, and established his reputation with *Reisebilder*

H

and *Das Buch der Lieder* in 1826–7. In 1830, excited by the July Revolution, he went to Paris, where he spent the rest of his life. From 1848 until his death he was confined to his bed with spinal paralysis.

HOPPE (d. 1855), a Dutch banker who became famous through his liaison with the actress Jenny Colon.

HOUSSAYE, Arsène (1815–96), was at one time Director of the Théâtre-Français, and also wrote poetry, novels and plays, but he is chiefly remembered for his *Confessions*, recollections of the period 1830–90.

HUGO, Adèle, *née* Adèle Foucher (1803–68), married Victor Hugo in 1822. Her love affair with Sainte-Beuve, whom she and her husband met in 1827, did much to poison relations between the two men. In 1863 she published *Victor Hugo raconté par un témoin de sa vie*, a work of fulsome admiration said to have been dictated by Hugo himself.

HUGO, Léopoldine (1824–43), Victor Hugo's eldest daughter, whose death in a boating accident with her husband on 4 September 1843 inspired the poet's famous elegy *À Villequier*.

HUGO, Victor-Marie (1802–85), began writing poetry at school and won a royal pension from Louis XVIII with his first collection of poems, *Odes et poésies diverses*, published in 1822, the year of his marriage to Adèle Foucher. Within a few years he had become the accepted leader of the Romantic movement in France, with verse such as *Les Feuilles d'Automne* (1831), novels such as *Notre-Dame de Paris* (1831), and plays such as the epoch-making *Hernani* (1830). However, after the failure of *Les Burgraves* (1843) and the death of his eldest daughter, he devoted himself increasingly to politics. After the *coup d'état* of 1851 he went into voluntary exile in Brussels, Jersey (1853) and Guernsey (1855), hurling anathema at Napoleon III in *Napoléon le Petit*, (1852) and *Les Châtiments* (1853). During his exile he wrote or began some of his finest works, including *Les Contemplations* (1856), *La Légende des Siècles* (1859–83), and *Les Misérables* (1862). In 1870 he returned to Paris with his wife, his family, and his ageing mistress Juliette Drouet, to spend the rest of his life as a revered patriarchal figure with no influence but immense prestige.

INGRES, Jean-Dominique-Auguste (1780–1867), studied under David, and worked for several years in Rome and Florence, where he painted some of his finest portraits. In 1826 he was appointed Professor of Fine Arts in Paris, and in 1834 succeeded Horace Vernet as Director of the French Academy in Rome. In 1841 he returned to Paris, where he spent the rest of his life.

JANIN, Jules-Gabriel (1804–74), wrote the weekly theatrical *feuilleton* for the *Journal des Débats* for over thirty years, and became known as the 'Prince of Critics'. He was elected to Sainte-Beuve's chair in the Académie française in 1870.

JUAREZ, Benito (1806–72), was elected President of Mexico for four years in 1861, and led the Mexican people in their resistance to the French occupation and the puppet Emperor Maximilian. He re-entered Mexico City in 1867 and was re-elected President then and in 1871.

KARR, Alphonse (1808–90), wrote a number of novels, earned many enemies with a series of satirical monthly pamphlets entitled *Les Guêpes*, and coined such epigrams as *Plus ça change, plus c'est la même chose*. He retired to Nice in 1855.

KOCK, Paul de (1794–1871), a prolific author of coarse, sentimental novels which were very popular in both England and France in the 1830s and 1840s.

LACROIX, Paul (1806–84), the scholar, editor and bibliographer often referred by to his pseudonym *le Bibliophile Jacob*.

LAGIER, Suzanne (1833–93), a well-known Second Empire actress and a friend of Flaubert.

LAMBALLE, Marie-Thérèse Louise de Savoie-Carignan, Princesse de (1749–92), was widowed at 18, became a close friend of Marie-Antoinette, and was killed in the September Massacres.

LAMENNAIS, Félicité-Robert de (1782–1854), became a priest at the age of 34, and the next year made his mark as a writer with the first volume of his *Essai sur l'indifférence*. With his subsequent writings advocating a form of Christian democracy, he influenced Hugo, Sainte-Beuve and George Sand, but after two Papal encyclicals condemning his ideas he broke with the Church in 1834.

LASALLE, Antoine-Charles-Louis, Comte de (1775–1809), served as a general in the Napoleonic Wars.

LASSAILLY, Charles (1806–43), a minor Romantic author and one of Balzac's collaborators, is said to have gone mad from unrequited love, and died in Doctor Blanche's nursing-home, aged 36.

LATOUCHE, Henri de, pseud. of Hyacinthe Labaud (1785–

1851), an influential writer of the Romantic period, who produced the first edition of André Chénier's works (1819), and from 1825 edited the literary review, *Le Mercure de France au XIXe siècle*.

LAURENT-JAN, pseud. of Laurent-Jean Lausanne (d. 1877), a Bohemian writer best known for his friendship with Balzac.

LE FLÔ, Adolphe-Emmanuel-Charles, General (1804–87), was Minister of War in the Government of National Defence, 1870–1.

LEMAÎTRE, Frédérick (1800–76), the greatest French actor of the Romantic period, for whom some of the most famous theatrical roles of the nineteenth century—such as Dumas's *Kean* and Hugo's *Ruy Blas*—were written.

L'ÉPINE, Ernest (1826–93), a journalist, playwright and humorous writer who was the Duc de Morny's secretary for several years.

LESPÈS, Léo, pseud. of Napoléon Lespès (1815–75), was well known during the Second Empire for his newspaper articles signed *Timothée Trimm*.

LEVALLOIS, Jules (1829–1903), Sainte-Beuve's secretary from 1855 to 1859, subsequently became a literary critic on his own account.

LIMAYRAC, Paulin (1817–68), literary critic on the *Revue des Deux Mondes* and *La Presse*.

LISZT, Franz (1811–86), frequented many of the leading writers in Paris during the period he spent with the Comtesse d'Agoult (1835–45). He later retired to Weimar to teach, compose, and direct operas and concerts, and died at Bayreuth, where he is buried.

LOUIS XVIII, Louis-Stanislas-Xavier (1755–1824), younger brother of Louis XVI, assumed his title in 1795 and returned to France in April 1814. On Napoleon's return from Elba he fled to Ghent, where he remained during the Hundred Days, being restored to the throne a second time after Waterloo.

LOUIS-PHILIPPE (1773–1850), succeeded his father, Philippe Égalité, as Duc d'Orléans in 1793, and became the constitutional monarch of France, or King of the French, after the July Revolution of 1830. Fleeing to England after the 1848 Revolution, he spent the last two years of his life as the Comte de Neuilly at Claremont in Surrey.

MAGNY, Charles-Paul (1884–1945), younger son of Paul-Victor-Modeste Magny, was made honorary Prefect of the Seine in 1945.

MAGNY, Louis-Paul (1883–1955), elder son of Paul-Victor-Modeste Magny, and like him a civil servant. With his brother Charles-Paul, he is the only Magny named on the family tombstone.

MAGNY, Modeste (1812–79), born at Montmort (Marne) on 14 November 1812, the son of Modeste Magny and Victoire-Adélaïde Michel, founded the Restaurant Magny at No. 3, Rue Contrescarpe-Dauphine, Paris, in 1842, and died at that address at 4 a.m. on 19 April 1879.

MAGNY, Madame Modeste, *née* Ernestine-Laure Brébant (1828–77), the daughter of François-Nicolas Brébant and Françoise-Antoinette Lalos, married Modeste Magny on 8 December 1846, and died on 30 June 1877.

MAGNY, Paul-Victor-Modeste (1854–1925), son of Modeste Magny, a civil servant for many years, became Senator of the Seine in 1914. He attended one of the Magny Dinners as a boy to make up the number of diners to fourteen.

MANCEAU, Alexandre (1816–65), an engraver who was George Sand's lover from 1850 until his death.

MARCHAL, Charles (1825–77), a painter friend of Dumas *fils* and George Sand, who, realising that he was going blind, committed suicide.

MASSENET, Jules-Émile-Frédéric (1842–1912), studied at the Paris Conservatoire where he returned as Professor of Composition in 1878. His works include the opera *Manon* (1884), based on the Abbé Prévost's *Manon Lescaut*.

MATHILDE, Princess (1820–1904), daughter of King Jérôme and niece of Napoleon I, married Anatole Demidoff in 1840 and was legally separated from him in 1846. During the reign of her cousin Napoleon III she gave help and patronage to writers such as Gautier, Flaubert, Sainte-Beuve and the Goncourts, whom she entertained in her Paris *salon* or at her country house at Saint-Gratien.

MAURY, Alfred (1817–92), medieval historian and Professor at the Collège de France, was appointed Librarian at the Tuileries in 1860.

MAXIMILIAN, Emperor of Mexico (1832–67), the younger brother of Franz Joseph I, accepted the crown of Mexico in 1864 from a Mexican assembly summoned by the French. Napoleon III withdrew his troops from Mexico, and despite

attempts by Maximilian's wife Charlotte, a daughter of Leopold I
of Belgium, to win support for her husband, he was captured by
Juarez's forces and shot in June 1867.

MENDÈS, Catulle (1841–1909), wrote many novels and successful plays, but is best remembered as a Parnassian poet. He married
Théophile Gautier's daughter, Judith, in 1866 and divorced her
in 1896.

MENKEN, Adah, *née* Adelaide McCord (1835–68), poetess,
actress and bareback rider, was born in Louisiana but made her
name in Europe in *Mazeppa* (1864). She became friendly with a
number of famous writers, including Charles Reade, Dickens
and Dumas *père*.

MÉRIMÉE, Prosper (1803–70), first made his mark as a writer
with the pseudo-Spanish *Théâtre de Clara Gazul* in 1825, but
produced his finest work between 1829 and 1850, in the stories
which constitute his chief claim to fame. From 1834, when he
was appointed Inspector General of Historical Monuments, he
worked to preserve the architectural heritage of France, and he
became a Senator during the Second Empire.

MEURICE, Paul (1820–95), novelist, dramatist and journalist,
sometime editor of *L'Événement* and *Le Rappel*, and Victor Hugo's
executor.

MICHELET, Jules (1798–1874), began publishing his monumental *Histoire de France* in 1833, breaking the chronological
sequence to write *La Révolution française* (1847–53). He was appointed to the Chair of History at the Collège de France in 1838,
but had to resign it when he refused to swear allegiance to the
Second Empire. He retired into private life to complete his
History and to write a number of lyrical works on the subject of
natural science.

MOLTKE, Helmuth, Count von (1800–91), studied at the Copen-
hagen military academy, but entered the Prussian army in 1822.
He was Chief of the General Staff in Berlin from 1858 to 1888,
during which period he reorganised the Prussian army and conducted the successful wars against Denmark in 1863–4, Austria
in 1866 and France in 1870–1.

MOMMSEN, Theodor (1817–1903), the leading Roman historian
of the nineteenth century, was Professor of Ancient History at
Berlin from 1858.

MORNY, Charles-Auguste-Louis-Joseph, Duc de (1811–65),

half-brother of Napoleon III, adopted by the Comte de Morny, planned the *coup d'état* of 1851, became Minister of the Interior, and was President of the Legislative Body from 1854 until his death.

MURGER, Henry (1822–61), won fame with his first and best work, *Scènes de la Vie de Bohème* (1848), which provided the story for Puccini's opera *La Bohème* (1896). Most of his later works treated the same subject of the down-at-heel existence of poor Parisian writers and artists, an existence with led to Murger's own premature death at the age of 38.

MUSSET, Alfred de (1810–57), published his first collection of poems in 1830 but wrote little of note before 1833, when he embarked on his famous, stormy liaison with George Sand. His finest works, including *Confession d'un enfant du siècle, Le Souvenir, Les Nuits* and most of his comedies and proverbs, were written after the final break with Sand in 1835.

NADAR, pseud. of Félix Tournachon (1820–1910), was one of the most picturesque figures in nineteenth-century Paris, author, balloonist, Bohemian, writer and photographer. He was one of the first advocates of heavier-than-air flight, a pioneer of aerial photography, and possibly the greatest of all portrait photographers.

NAPOLEON III, Charles-Louis-Napoléon Bonaparte (1808–73), the third son of King Louis of Holland and Queen Hortense, became Bonapartist pretender to the throne of France on the death of the Duc de Reichstadt in 1832. He made two unsuccessful attempts to overthrow Louis-Philippe, and in 1848 returned from London to France, where he was elected to the Constituent Assembly. In December 1848 he was elected Prince-President of the Second Republic, organised a *coup d'état* with his half-brother the Duc de Morny on 2 December 1851 to consolidate his power, and was proclaimed Emperor Napoleon III on 2 December 1852. His health declined during the 1860s, with the result that he pursued an erratic, vacillating policy both at home and abroad. Defeated and captured at Sedan in 1870, he was imprisoned in Germany for a while, then joined the Empress Eugénie and their only son the Prince Imperial in exile at Chislehurst in Kent, where he died.

NAPOLEON, Joseph-Charles-Paul, Prince (1822–91), son of King Jérôme, was banished from France in 1845, but returned in

1848. In 1859 he married Princess Clotilde, by whom he had two sons and a daughter. In 1870 he fled to England, but returned to France in 1872, only to be exiled in 1886 as a pretender to the throne, the Prince Imperial having been killed in 1879.

NARYSCHKINE, Nadejda, Princess (1826–95) *née* Knorring, the wife of Prince Alexander Naryschkine, became the mistress of Dumas *fils* in 1852 and married him after the Prince's death in 1864.

NEFFTZER, Auguste (1820–76), one of the leading journalists of the Second Empire, founded *Le Temps* in 1861 and remained its editor until 1871.

NERVAL, Gérard de, pseud. of Gérard Labrunie (1808–55), published a translation of *Faust* (1828) which Goethe praised, joined the *Jeunes-France* group led by Gautier and Borel, and during the following years wrote a considerable number of poems, stories, sketches and reviews. His best known works include the fantastic *Contes et facéties* (1853), the autobiographical tales *Les Filles du feu* (1854), and the hallucinatory collection of prose and poetry entitled *Le Rêve et la vie* (1855). In later years Nerval's mind was unbalanced, and his corpse was found hanging from a railing in the Rue de la Vieille Lanterne.

NODIER, Marie, the daughter of the novelist Charles Nodier, who as librarian of the Bibliothèque de l'Arsenal in Paris was host to the first of the Romantic *cénacles*.

OLLIVIER, Émile (1825–1913), a leading lawyer and politician during the Second Empire, was invited by Napoleon III to form a constitutional ministry in January 1870. He led France into war with Prussia, and was overthrown in August 1870.

ORSINI, Felice (1819–58), an Italian conspirator who on 14 January 1858 tried to assassinate Napoleon III near the Paris Opera. He and his associates killed ten people, and he was executed two months later.

OURLIAC, Édouard (1813–48), a minor novelist who after conversion became a writer for the *Univers*.

OZY, Alice, pseud. of Julie-Justine Pilloy (1820–93), an actress at the Variétés whose many lovers included the Duc d'Aumale, Gautier, Chassériau, Charles Hugo, Edmond About and Gustave Doré.

PATRU, Olivier (1604–81), an advocate elected to the Académie française in 1640 and recognised as an authority on style and the French language.

PEARL, Cora, pseud. of Eliza Emma Crouch (*c.* 1835–86), the daughter of a Plymouth music teacher, became one of the most celebrated courtesans of Second Empire Paris, whose lovers included the Duc de Morny and Prince Napoleon. She created a sensation on 26 January 1867 by appearing as Cupid in a revival of Offenbach's *Orphée aux Enfers*.

PERSIGNY, Duchesse de, *née* Églé-Napoléone-Albine Ney de la Moskowa, Ney's granddaughter, married Persigny, then Minister of the Interior, in 1852.

PHILIPPE, one of the leading restaurateurs of the nineteenth century, founded his restaurant in the Rue Montorgueil in 1804. His son took over the business in 1837 and sold it twenty years later to Pascal, the former chef of the Jockey Club. Magny was a pupil of Philippe *père*.

PLON-PLON, nickname of Prince Napoleon, q.v.

PORTAL, Antoine, Baron (1742–1832), appointed Professor of Medicine at the Collège de France in 1769, became chief physician to Louis XVIII, and founded the Académie royale de médecine in 1820.

PRADIER, James, pseud. of Jean-Jacques Pradier (1792–1852), a French sculptor noted for his statues of women, especially *The Three Graces* for which Juliette Drouet posed.

PROUDHON, Pierre-Joseph (1809–65), made his name with his first notable work, *Qu'est-ce que la propriété?*, which began with the dictum: "Property is theft." He became a deputy after the 1848 Revolution, but after a prison sentence he retired into private life. He had to flee to Brussels in 1858 and died three years after his return to Paris.

PYAT, Félix (1810–89), a politician and playwright who lived in exile in England during the Second Empire, but returned to Paris to take part in the Commune.

RATTAZZI, Madame, *née* Marie-Laetitia-Studolmine Wyse (1833–1902), granddaughter of Lucien Bonaparte, married Frédéric de Solms in 1849, and on his death married the Italian statesman Urbano Rattazzi (1808–73). Twice expelled from France by her cousin Napoleon III, she was notorious for her liaisons with writers such as Eugène Sue and Ponsard.

RÉCAMIER, Madame, *née* Jeanne-Françoise Bernard (1777–1849), married the French banker Récamier in 1793. A woman of great beauty, immortalised in the famous portraits by David and

Gérard, she held a *salon* after 1819 in her rooms at the Abbaye-aux-Bois, in Paris, where the leading personality was her sometime lover Chateaubriand. He remained a faithful visitor till his death in 1848, and she died ten months later.

RENAN, Ernest (1823–92) was destined for the priesthood and entered the seminary of Saint-Sulpice in Paris in 1843. However, he came to question the divine inspiration of the Bible, and left Saint-Sulpice in 1845 to become a schoolteacher and study at the École Normale. In the 1850s he published some remarkable essays on religious history and a history of the Semitic languages, and in 1860–1 he led a Government archaeological expedition to the Holy Land, during which his sister Henriette died. In 1862 he was appointed Professor of Hebrew at the Collège de France, but the chair was abolished in 1863 after the scandal caused by his *Vie de Jésus*, the first part of *Les Origines du Christianisme* (1863–83). In 1870 Renan was reinstated at the Collège de France, of which he became head in 1883, and in 1878 he was elected to the Académie française.

RICORD, Philippe (1800–89), chief surgeon at the Hôpital du Midi in Paris, was a specialist in the treatment of syphilis.

ROBIN, Charles (1821–85), a distinguished anatomist, was appointed Professor of Histology in Paris in 1862.

ROCHEFORT, Henri, pseud. of Victor-Henri, Vicomte de Rochefort-Luçay (1830–1913), in 1868 founded *La Lanterne*, a weekly which attacked Napoleon III and his Government. He had to flee to Belgium, but returned in 1869 on his election to the Chamber of Deputies, and founded the *Marseillaise*. In 1871 he sided with the Communards, was sentenced to life imprisonment, but returned to France in 1880 to found the *Intransigeant* and devote his energies to supporting Boulanger and attacking Dreyfus.

ROEDERER, Pierre-Louis, Comte (1754–1835), a professor of political economy, became a Senator in 1802, and later served King Joseph as Minister of Finance.

ROSSINI, Gioacchino Antonio (1792–1868), studied music and singing at Bologna and after his early successes settled in Paris, where he adapted his works to French taste and wrote his *Guillaume Tell* (1829). In 1836 he went back to Bologna, moving to Florence in 1847 and returning to Paris in 1855. He became a popular figure in the French capital, where he was highly regarded not only as a musician but also as a gastronome. It was at Magny's that he and the restaurateur invented the *tournedos Rossini*.

ROYER-COLLARD, Pierre-Paul (1763–1845), was appointed Professor of Philosophy in Paris in 1810, and in the following years turned the course of French philosophy away from materialism. Elected to the Académie française in 1827, he became President of the Chamber of Representatives the next year, and in 1830 presented the address which Charles X refused to hear.

SABATIER, Madame, or *La Présidente*, name given to Apollonie-Aglaé Savatier (1822–90), the mistress of the banker Hippolyte Mosselman, inspired some of Baudelaire's finest poems, served as the model for Clésinger's sensational *Femme piquée par un serpent*, and often entertained Flaubert, Gautier and other writers on Sunday evenings at her Rue Frochot flat.

SACY, Samuel Silvestre de (1801–79), a distinguished contributor to the *Journal des Débats*, became a member of the Académie française in 1855 and a Senator in 1867.

SAINTE-BEUVE, Charles-Augustin (1804–69), born at Boulogne-sur-Mer, became a critic on the *Globe* in 1824, and in 1827 a favourable review of Hugo's *Odes et Ballades* led to a brief friendship with the poet and an ill-starred liaison with Hugo's wife. Although he published two collections of verse, an autobiographical novel entitled *Volupté* (1834), and an edition of his love poems to Adèle Hugo for private circulation, he owed his reputation as the greatest critic of modern times to *Port-Royal* (1840–59), *Chateaubriand et son groupe littéraire* (1861), and the weekly articles which he contributed every Monday from 1849 to 1869 to either the *Constitutionnel*, the *Moniteur* or the *Temps*. He was one of the founders of the Magny Dinners, over which he usually presided, and which were sometimes referred to as the Sainte-Beuve Dinners. Appointed a Senator in 1865, he earned the displeasure of Napoleon III and Princess Mathilde by speaking courageously in favour of freedom of thought and speech.

SAINT-MARC GIRARDIN, pseud. of Marc Girardin (1801–73), a distinguished critic and contributor to the *Revue des Deux Mondes* and the *Journal des Débats*, was Professor of French Poetry at the Sorbonne for thirty years.

SAINT-VICTOR, Paul, Comte de (1825–81), son of the poet and historian Jacques de Saint-Victor, was a talented dramatic critic,

contributing notably to *La Presse*, and also wrote art criticism and
a study of Victor Hugo.

SALA, George Augustus (1828–95), a journalist and novelist who
was the *Daily Telegraph*'s special correspondent in the American
Civil War, in Italy with Garibaldi, and in France in 1870–1.

SAND, George, pseud. of Lucile-Aurore Dupin, Baronne
Dudevant (1804–76), brought up at her paternal grandmother's
country house at Nohant, married Baron Dudevant, a retired army
officer, in 1822, and bore him two children, Maurice and Solange,
but left him in 1831 to lead an independent life in Paris. Taking the
pseudonym George Sand (from the name of her sometime lover
Jules Sandeau), she won immediate fame with her Romantic
novel *Indiana* (1832), and went on to write a ceaseless succession
of novels, plays, and country romances, the most famous of
which were *Lélia* (1833), *La Mare au diable* (1846), *La Petite
Fadette* (1849) and *François le Champi* (1850). She had a number of
much publicised liaisons, notably with Musset and Chopin, but
after the 1848 Revolution she spent most of her time in the
country, where she became known as *la bonne dame de Nohant*,
wrote many novels and her autobiography, *Histoire de ma vie*
(1854–5), amused herself with a puppet theatre, doted over her
grandchildren, and entertained friends such as Flaubert and Dumas
fils. She was a regular visitor to Magny's from its foundation to
the time of her death, and a close friend of Magny and his wife.

SARCEY, Francisque (1827–99), was one of the leading dramatic
critics of the nineteenth century, contributing a weekly article of
theatre criticism to *Le Temps* for thirty-three years.

SARDOU, Victorien (1831–1908), a prolific writer of cleverly
constructed comedies and historical dramas in the Scribe tradition, wrote several plays for Sarah Bernhardt, including *Tosca*, the
melodrama used by Puccini for his opera.

SCHNEIDER, Hortense (1838–1920), the most famous comic-
opera singer of the Second Empire, was the star of nearly all
Offenbach's operettas, and also a notorious courtesan.

SCRIBE, Eugène (1791–1861), obtained such success with his
skilfully constructed vaudevilles and comedies that he set up a
theatrical factory and turned out over 300 plays written by himself or in collaboration.

SÉBASTIANI, Horace François de la Porta, Comte (1772–1851),
a Corsican who served Napoleon devotedly in many campaigns,

undertook missions to Turkey from 1802 to 1806, and was made a Marshal in 1840.

SECOND, Albéric (1817–87), an author, playwright and journalist, founded *Le Grand Journal* in 1863.

SELIM III (1761–1807), Sultan of Turkey, who succeeded his brother in 1789, carried out many reforms but was deposed by the Janissaries in 1807 and killed in prison.

TAINE, Hippolyte (1828–93), though a brilliant student at the École Normale, failed his examination for the title of *agrégé* in 1851 on account of his advanced opinions, but established his reputation as a scholar with his doctoral thesis on La Fontaine (1853). In 1864 he succeeded Viollet-le-Duc as Professor of Aesthetics at the École des Beaux-Arts, a post which he held until 1883. In his *Essais de critique et d'histoire* (1858), his *Nouveaux essais* (1865), his Introduction to the *Histoire de la littérature anglaise* (1863), and his *De l'intelligence* (1870), Taine expounded his famous theories of *la race, le milieu, et le moment* which Zola was to take as the basis for such novels as *Thérèse Raquin*.

THIERS, Louis-Adolphe (1797–1877), made his name with his 10-volume *Histoire de la Révolution française* (1823–27), founded the *National* with Carrel and Mignet in 1830, and embarked on a political career which lasted the rest of his life. Several times Foreign Minister and President of the Council under Louis-Philippe, he suffered an eclipse during the Second Empire, but became head of the provisional government after France's defeat by Prussia, made peace in 1871, and after suppressing the Commune was made President of the Republic. He resigned his office in 1873, giving place to Marshal MacMahon.

TOURBEY, Jeanne de, pseud. of Marie-Anne Detourbay (1837–1908), a celebrated Second Empire courtesan who entertained Flaubert and others at a literary *salon* which she revived after the Franco-Prussian War when she became the Comtesse de Loynes.

TROCHU, Louis-Jules (1815–96), became a general during the Crimean War, and in August 1870 was appointed Military Governor of Paris. Under the Republic he became President of the Government of National Defence. His conduct of the defence of the besieged capital was bitterly criticised, and he resigned the Governorship of Paris on 22 January 1871. He retired into private life in 1873 to publish his memoirs and various books in his own defence.

TROUBAT, Jules (1836–1914), Sainte-Beuve's secretary, who after his employer's death acted as his executor and published some engaging reminiscences of the great critic.

TURENNE, Henri de la Tour d'Auvergne, Vicomte de (1611–75), the brilliant soldier and strategist, was made Marshal-General of France in 1660 and was killed advancing victoriously into Germany.

TURGAN, Julien, a sometime medical student, became a prominent journalist, and after 1852 edited *Le Moniteur* with Paul Dalloz.

TURGENEV, Ivan Sergeitch (1818–83), spent one year in a Tsarist government office (1840–1), and then retired into private life. He made his name with *A Sportsman's Sketches* (1846), and his liberal views led to his seclusion on his family estate estate from 1852 till 1855. After this he lived chiefly in Baden-Baden and Paris, paying occasional visits to Russia and England. Over the years he became a well-known and well-loved figure in Paris, where he attended many Magny Dinners and became particularly friendly with Flaubert, and where he died in 1883.

VACQUERIE, Auguste (1819–95), a talented playwright, critic and essayist, was the brother of Charles Vacquerie, the husband of Victor Hugo's daughter Léopoldine.

VAQUEZ, Madame de, pseud. of Mademoiselle Devaquez (d. 1854), the daughter of a French thresher who pretended to be Spanish and was Sainte-Beuve's mistress during the last three years of her life.

VERHUELL, Carel Hendrick (1764–1845), a Dutch admiral who in 1805, as Navy Minister, led the delegation which offered the throne of Holland to Louis Bonaparte. It has often been suggested that he, and not King Louis, was the father of the future Napoleon III.

VEYNE, François-Auguste (1813–75), studied medicine with Claude Bernard, and was the friend and doctor of Gavarni and Sainte-Beuve, with whom he founded the Magny Dinners.

VIARDOT, Madame, née Pauline Garcia (1821–1910), daughter of the singer and composer Manuel Garcia and sister of La Malibran, married the journalist Louis Viardot. She became a celebrated mezzo-soprano singer and was Turgenev's mistress for many years.

VIGNY, Alfred, Comte de (1797–1863), began writing while serving in the royal bodyguard from 1815 to 1827. In 1826 he established his literary reputation with his *Poèmes antiques et modernes* and his historical novel *Cinq-Mars*, a reputation consolidated by the success of his best play, *Chatterton*, and his stories *Servitude et grandeur militaires* in 1835. In the same year he broke with his mistress, the actress Marie Dorval, and retired to his country home to nurse his invalid wife and write the poems published posthumously as *Les Destinées* (1864). He was elected to the Académie française in 1845.

VINOY, Joseph (1800–80), became a general in 1853 and on 22 January 1871 took Trochu's place as commander of the army in the besieged capital.

VIOLLET-LE-DUC, Eugène-Emmanuel (1814–79), the architect who became the foremost nineteenth-century restorer of ancient buildings, including the Sainte-Chapelle, Notre-Dame, Mont Saint-Michel and Pierrefonds.

WALEWSKI, Alexandre-Florian-Joseph Colonna, Comte (1810–68), the natural son of Napoleon I and Marie Laczynska, Comtesse Walewska, was Minister of Foreign Affairs from 1855 to 1860.

WILHELM I (1797–1888), seventh King of Prussia and First German Emperor, succeeded Friedrich-Wilhelm IV in 1861, and was proclaimed Emperor of Germany at Versailles on 18 January 1871.

WORTH, Charles Frederick (1825–95), was born in Lincolnshire, went to Paris in 1846, and became the leading dressmaker in France.

ZOLA, Émile (1840–1902), came to Paris from Aix-en-Provence in 1858 and published his first work, *Contes à Ninon*, in 1864. He gave an enthusiastic review to the Goncourt brothers' *Germinie Lacerteux*, and was welcomed by them as a disciple, but he was to incur the surviving brother's jealousy with the success of his *Rougon-Macquart* series of novels and his foundation of the so-called Naturalist school.

BIBLIOGRAPHY

The following is a selection of some of the works and articles consulted in the preparation of this book.

ALBALAT (Antoine): *Gustave Flaubert et ses Amis*. Paris, 1927.

ALLEM (Maurice): *La Vie quotidienne sous le Second Empire*. Paris, 1948.

ALMÉRAS (Henri d'): *La Vie parisienne pendant le Siège et sous la Commune*. Paris, n.d.

ANDRIEU (Pierre): *Histoire du restaurant en France*. Montpellier, 1955.

ANON.: *La Cuisinière assiégée, ou l'art de vivre en temps de siège par une femme de ménage*. Paris, 1871.

ANON.: "Le Restaurant Magny", *Naguère et Jadis*, Nov. 1958.

ARISTE (Paul d'): *La Vie et le Monde du Boulevard*. Paris, 1930.

ARSAC (Joanni d'): *Mémorial du siège de Paris*. Paris, 1871.

BALDICK (Robert): *The Life and Times of Frédérick Lemaître*. London, 1959.

—— *The Goncourts*, Cambridge, 1960.

—— *The First Bohemian: The Life of Henry Murger*. London, 1961.

—— *Pages from the Goncourt Journal* (ed. and trans.). London, 1962.

—— *The Siege of Paris*. London, 1964.

BANVILLE (Théodore de): *L'Ame de Paris: nouveaux souvenirs*. Paris, 1890.

BEAUREPAIRE (Edmond): "Paris qui s'en va. L'auberge du Cheval-Blanc et la Rue Mazet", *Le Magasin pittoresque*, 1907.

BERGERAT (Émile): *Théophile Gautier*. Paris, 1879.

BERTRAND (Georges): *Les Jours de Flaubert*. Paris, 1947.

BILLY (André): *Sainte-Beuve: sa vie et son temps*. Paris, 1952.

—— *Les Frères Goncourt*. Paris, 1954.

BODET (R.): *Toques blanches et habits noirs: l'hôtellerie et la restauration autrefois et aujourd'hui*. Paris, 1939.

BOLLÈME (Geneviève): *La Leçon de Flaubert*. Paris, 1964.

BOULENGER (Marcel): *La Païva*. Paris, 1930.

BRIFFAULT (Eugène): *Paris à table*. Paris, 1851.

BURY (J. P. T.): *France 1814–1940*. London, 1949.

CAIN (Georges): *Coins de Paris*. Paris, 1905.

CHAPMAN (J. M. and Brian): *The Life and Times of Baron Haussmann*. London, 1957.

CHATILLON-PLESSIS: *La Vie à table à la fin du XIXe siècle*. Paris, 1894.

CHAVETTE (Eugène): *Restaurateurs et restaurés*. Paris, 1867.

CLARETIE (Jules): *La Vie à Paris, 1881*. Paris, 1882.

—— *Souvenirs du dîner Bixio*. Paris, 1924.

CLAUDIN (Gustave): *Paris*. Paris, 1862.

—— *Mes souvenirs. Les Boulevards de 1840 à 1870*. Paris, 1884.

COMMANVILLE (Caroline): *Souvenirs sur Gustave Flaubert*, Paris, 1895.

CROUCH (E. E.): *Les Mémoires de Cora Pearl*. Paris, 1886.

DABOT (Henri): *Griffonnages d'un bourgeois du Quartier Latin*. Péronne, 1895.

—— *Souvenirs et impressions d'un bourgeois du Quartier Latin*. Péronne, 1899.

DANSETTE (Adrien): *Les Amours de Napoléon III*. Paris, 1938.

DELACROIX (Eugène): *Journal, 1823–1863*. Paris, 1893–95.

DELVAU (Alfred): *Histoire anecdotique des cafés et cabarets de Paris, 1862*.

—— *Les Lions du jour*. Paris, 1867.

—— *Les Plaisirs de Paris*. Paris, 1867.

DELZANT (Alidor): *Paul de Saint-Victor*. Paris, 1866.

DESCHARMES (R.) and DUMESNIL (R.): *Autour de Flaubert*, Paris, 1912.

DERYS (Gaston) and CURNONSKY: *Souvenirs de tables parisiennes*. Paris, 1933.

DU CAMP (Maxime): *Souvenirs littéraires*. Paris, 1882–3.

DUMESNIL (René): *En Marge de Flaubert*. Paris, 1928.

—— *Gustave Flaubert, l'homme et l'oeuvre*. Paris, 1932.

—— *Le Grand Amour de Flaubert*. Geneva, 1945.

—— *La Vocation de Flaubert*. Paris, 1961.

DURRY (Marie-Jeanne): *Flaubert et ses projets inédits*. Paris, 1950.

FLAUBERT (Gustave): *Correspondance entre George Sand et Gustave Flaubert*. Paris, 1904.

—— *Correspondance*. Paris, 1926–30.

—— *Lettres inédites à Tourguéneff*. Monaco, 1946.

FOSCA (François): *Edmond et Jules de Goncourt*. Paris, 1941.

FOUCHER (Paul): *Entre Cour et Jardin: Études et Souvenirs du Théâtre*. Paris, 1867.

FREJLICH (Hélène): *Flaubert d'après sa correspondance*. Paris, 1933.

—— *Les Amants de Mantes*. Paris, 1936.

GAUTIER (Théophile): *Tableaux de Siège: Paris, 1870–1871*. Paris, 1871.

—— *Histoire du Romantisme*. Paris, 1874.

GÉRARD-GAILLY: *Flaubert et les Fantômes de Trouville*, Paris, 1930.

—— *Les Véhémences de Louise Colet*. Paris, 1934.

—— *Le Grand Amour de Flaubert*. Paris, 1944.

GONCOURT (Edmond and Jules de): *Journal: Mémoires de la vie littéraire*. Paris, 1956–1959.

HALÉVY (Ludovic): *Carnets*. Paris, 1935.

HALPÉRINE-KAMINSKY (E.): *Ivan Tourguéneff d'après sa correspondance avec ses amis français*. Paris, 1901.

HÉNARD (Robert): "L'Auberge du Cheval-Blanc et la Rue Mazet à Paris", *Le Magasin pittoresque*, 1898.

HÉRON DE VILLEFOSSE (René): *Histoire et géographie gourmandes de Paris*. Paris, 1956.

HOLDEN (W. H.): *The Pearl from Plymouth: Eliza Emma Crouch, alias Cora Pearl*. London, 1950.

HOUSSAYE (Arsène): *Confessions. Souvenirs d'un demi-siècle (1830–90)*. Paris, 1891.

HUGO (Victor): *Choses vues*. Paris, 1913.

JOANNE (Adolphe): *Le Guide parisien*. Paris, 1863.

—— *Paris illustré*. Paris, 1863.

JOLLIVET (Gaston): *Souvenirs de la vie de plaisir sous le Second Empire*. Paris, 1927.

—— *Souvenirs d'un Parisien*. Paris, 1928.

KRACAUER (S.): *Offenbach and the Paris of his time*. London, 1937.

LA VARENDE: *Flaubert par lui-même*. Paris, 1958.

LEPAGE (A.): *Les Cafés politiques et littéraires de Paris*. Paris, 1874.

—— *Les Dîners artistiques et littéraires de Paris*. Paris, 1884.

LOLIÉE (Frédéric): *Les Femmes du Second Empire. La Fête impériale*. Paris, 1907.

—— *La Païva*. Paris, 1920.

MAGARSHACK (David): *Turgenev*. London, 1954.
—— *Turgenev's Literary Reminiscences*. (Trans.) London, 1958.
MAUPASSANT (Guy de): "Flaubert dans sa vie intime", *Nouvelle Revue*, Jan. 1881.
—— *Pierre et Jean*, Paris, 1888.
MAUROIS (André): *Lélia, ou la Vie de George Sand*. Paris, 1952.
—— *Olympio, ou la Vie de Victor Hugo*. Paris, 1954.
—— *Les Trois Dumas*. Paris, 1956.
—— *Prométhée, ou la Vie de Balzac*. Paris, 1965.
MIRECOURT (Eugène de): *Lola Montès*. Paris, 1870.
MONSELET (Charles): *Mes souvenirs littéraires*. Paris, 1888.
NICOLSON (Harold): *Sainte-Beuve*. London, 1957.
OXFORD GRADUATE (Henry William Gegg Markheim): *Inside Paris during the Siege*. London and New York, 1871.
RENAN (Ernest): *Oeuvres complètes*. Paris, 1947–1961.
RICHARDSON (Joanna): *Théophile Gautier*. London, 1958.
—— *The Courtesans*. London, 1967.
—— *Princess Mathilde*. London, 1969.
ROUFF (Marcel) and CASEVITZ (Thérèse): *La Vie de fête sous le Second Empire: Hortense Schneider*. Paris, 1931.
SAINTE-BEUVE (Charles-Augustin): *Souvenirs et indiscrétions. Le dîner du Vendredi saint*. Paris, 1872.
—— *Correspondance générale*. Ed. Jean Bonnerot. Paris, 1935–.
SAND (George): *Correspondance*. Paris, 1884.
SCHAEPDRYVER (K. de): *Hippolyte Taine: essai sur l'unité de sa pensée*. Paris, 1938.
SPENCER (Philip): *Flaubert*, London, 1952.
STARKIE (Enid): *Baudelaire*. London, 1957.
—— *Flaubert. The Making of the Master*, London, 1967.
STEEGMULLER (Francis): *Flaubert and Madame Bovary*. London, 1947.
SUFFEL (Jacques): *Gustave Flaubert*. Paris, 1958.
TAINE (Hippolyte): *Essais de critique et d'histoire*. Paris, 1858.
—— *Nouveaux essais de critique et d'histoire*. Paris, 1865.
—— *Voyage en Italie*. Paris, 1866.
—— *Notes sur Paris: vie et opinions de Frédéric-Thomas Graindorge*. Paris, 1867.
—— *De l'Intelligence*. Paris, 1870.
—— *Notes sur l'Angleterre*. Paris, 1871.
—— *H. Taine, sa vie et sa correspondance*. Paris, 1903–1907.

THIBAUDET (Albert): *Gustave Flaubert*. Paris, 1935.

TILD (Jean): *Théophile Gautier et ses amis*. Paris, 1951.

TROUBAT (Jules): *Souvenirs du dernier secrétaire de Sainte-Beuve*. Paris, 1891.

—— *La Salle à manger de Sainte-Beuve*. Paris, 1910.

VANDAM (A. D.): *My Paris Notebook (1855–93)*. London, 1894.

—— *Undercurrents of the Second Empire*. London, 1897.

VICAIRE (Georges): *Bibliographie gastronomique*. Paris, 1890.

VITU (Auguste): *Paris*. Paris, n.d.

WISSANT (Georges de): *Le Paris d'autrefois: cafés et cabarets*. Paris, 1928.

YARMOLINSKY (Avrahom): *Turgenev: the man, his art, and his age*. London, 1926.

ZED: *Le Demi-monde sous le Second Empire*. Paris, 1892.

Index

INDEX

N.B.—Persons and subjects discussed are listed alphabetically under the respective diners.